Organizational Behaviour in Health Care Series

Series Editor: **Annabelle L. Mark** *Middlesex University Business School, UK*

A series of biennial volumes, published in co-operation with the Society for Studies in Organising Healthcare (SHOC). Each volume is comprised of specially selected papers taken from the biennial conferences held by SHOC and presents a cohesive and focused insight into issues within the field of organisational behaviour in healthcare.

The Society's goals are:

- the promotion of excellence and encouragement of advancement in the organisation of healthcare through research, education and service to the community;
- to support and encourage the advancement through collaboration and when appropriate representative discussions and advice to governments and other communities at both political and administrative levels nationally and internationally;
- to develop and disseminate theory and practice in organising healthcare through the provision of conferences, seminars and associated publications both nationally and internationally;
- to comment on national needs and encourage international co-operation in the development and practice of organising for healthcare;
- to enhance the organisation of healthcare through the recognition and celebration of outstanding contributions; and
- in pursuit of the above to bring together such people and resources as are needed to create sustain and develop the society to achieve its purpose.

Titles include:

Annabelle Mark and Sue Dopson
ORGANISATIONAL BEHAVIOUR IN HEALTH CARE

Lynn Ashburner
ORGANISATIONAL BEHAVIOUR AND ORGANISATION STUDIES IN
HEALTH CARE

Sue Dopson and Annabelle Mark
LEADING HEALTH CARE ORGANIZATIONS

Ann L. Casebeer, Alexandra Harrison and Annabelle Mark
INNOVATIONS IN HEALTH CARE

Lorna McKee, Ewan Ferlie and Paula Hyde
ORGANIZING AND REORGANIZING

Jeffrey Braithwaite, Paula Hyde and Catherine Pope
CULTURE AND CLIMATE IN HEALTH CARE ORGANIZATIONS

Helen Dickinson and Russell Mannion
THE REFORM OF HEALTH CARE

Mary A. Keating, Aoife McDermott and Kathleen Montgomery
PATIENT-CENTRED HEALTH CARE

Susanne Boch Waldorff, Anne Reff Pedersen, Louise Fitzgerald and Ewan Ferlie
MANAGING CHANGE
From Health Policy to Practice

Organizational Behaviour in Health Care Series
Series Standing Order ISBN 978–0–230–34270–5
(*outside North America only*)

You can receive future titles in this series as they are published by placing a standing order. Please contact your bookseller or, in case of difficulty, write to us at the address below with your name and address, the title of the series and the ISBN quoted above.

Customer Services Department, Macmillan Distribution Ltd, Houndmills, Basingstoke, Hampshire RG21 6XS, England

Managing Change
From Health Policy to Practice

Edited by

Susanne Boch Waldorff
Copenhagen Business School, Denmark

Anne Reff Pedersen
Copenhagen Business School, Denmark

Louise Fitzgerald
University of Oxford, UK

Ewan Ferlie
King's College London, UK

First published 2015 by
PALGRAVE MACMILLAN

Palgrave Macmillan in the UK is an imprint of Macmillan Publishers Limited, registered in England, company number 785998, of Houndmills, Basingstoke, Hampshire RG21 6XS.

Palgrave Macmillan in the US is a division of St Martin's Press LLC, 175 Fifth Avenue, New York, NY 10010.

Palgrave Macmillan is the global academic imprint of the above companies and has companies and representatives throughout the world.

Palgrave® and Macmillan® are registered trademarks in the United States, the United Kingdom, Europe and other countries.

ISBN 978–1–137–51815–6

This book is printed on paper suitable for recycling and made from fully managed and sustained forest sources. Logging, pulping and manufacturing processes are expected to conform to the environmental regulations of the country of origin.

A catalogue record for this book is available from the British Library.

Library of Congress Cataloging-in-Publication Data
Managing change (Boch Waldorff)
    Managing change : from health policy to practice / [edited by] Susanne Boch Waldorff, Anne Reff Pedersen, Louise Fitzgerald, Ewan Ferlie.
        p. ; cm. — (Organizational behaviour in health care)
    The book draws upon the presentations and discussions at the 9th International Organisational Behaviour in Healthcare Conference (OBHC), which took place in Copenhagen in April 2014, hosted by Copenhagen Business School. The conference theme was "When health policy meets every day practices".
    ISBN 978–1–137–51815–6
    I. Boch Waldorff, Susanne, 1964–, editor. II. Reff Pedersen, Anne, 1970–, editor. III. Fitzgerald, Louise, 1945–, editor. IV. Ferlie, Ewan, 1956–, editor. V. Title. VI. Series: Organizational behaviour in health care series. [DNLM: 1. Health Policy. 2. Health Services Administration. 3. Organizational Innovation. 4. Professional Role. WA 525]
    RA971
    362.1068—dc23   2015020284

Contents

List of Tables and Figures   vii

Preface and Acknowledgements   viii

Notes on Contributors   x

Introduction   1
Susanne Boch Waldorff, Anne Reff Pedersen, Louise Fitzgerald and
    Ewan Ferlie

Part I   Designing Change Processes

1   The Ideas and Implementation of Public Health Policies:
    The Norwegian Case   9
    Charlotte Kiland, Gro Kvåle and Dag Olaf Torjesen

2   The Path from Policy to Practice: Resilience of Everyday
    Work in Acute Settings   26
    Robyn Clay-Williams, Julie K. Johnson, Deborah Debono
        and Jeffrey Braithwaite

3   Dealing with the Challenges of Healthcare Reform:
    American Hospital Systems Strive to Improve Access and
    Value through Retail Clinics   39
    Amer Kaissi

4   Institutional Logics and Micro-processes in Organizations:
    A Multi-actor Perspective on Sickness Absence
    Management in Three Dutch Hospitals   55
    Nicolette van Gestel, Daniel Nyberg and Emmie Vossen

Part II   The Role of Professions in Change Processes

5   The Persistence of Professional Boundaries in Healthcare:
    A Re-examination Using a Theory of Foundational Values   73
    Kathleen Montgomery, Wendy Lipworth and Louise Fitzgerald

6   Medical Doctors and Health System Improvement:
    Synthesis Results and Propositions for Further Research   88
    Jean-Louis Denis and G. Ross Baker

7   The Role of the Quality Coordinator: Articulation Work
in Quality Development   104
Marie Henriette Madsen

8   The Role of Outside Consultants in Shaping Hospital
Organizational Change   121
Amit Nigam, Esther Sackett and Brian Golden

Part III   Leadership and Organizational Change

9   NHS Managers: From Administrators to Entrepreneurs?   139
Mark Exworthy, Fraser Macfarlane and Micky Willmott

10   Opportunity Does Matter: Supporting
Doctors-in-Management in Hospitals   155
Marco Sartirana

11   A New Approach to Hybrid Leadership Development   170
Charlotte Croft

**Part IV   Change Programmes: Content and
Performance**

12   Scotland 'Bold and Brave'? Conditions for Creating a
Coherent National Healthcare Quality Strategy   189
*Aoife M. McDermott, David R. Steel, Lorna McKee, Lauren
Hamel and Patrick C. Flood*

13   The Social Spaces of Accountability in Hybridized
Healthcare Organizations   206
Aris Komporozos-Athanasiou and Mark Thompson

14   Culture Shock and the NHS Diaspora: Coping with
Cultural Difference in Public–Private Partnerships   222
Justin Waring and Amanda Crompton

15   Organizational Healthcare Innovation Performed by
Contextual Sense Making   238
Anne Reff Pedersen

Index   254

Tables and Figures

Tables

3.1 Summary of author's research on hospital-related retail
    clinics   45
3.2 List of interviewees, 2013   46
4.1 A shift from welfare to activation in sickness absence
    policies   59
4.2 Summary of the data set   61
4.3 Supporting the logic of activation   62
4.4 Reinforcing professional boundaries   64
4.5 Strategies of 'laissez faire', leading to a disconnection of
    practices   66
5.1 Healthcare-related F-values, A-values and P-values at the
    macrosocietal and meso (professional) levels   80
8.1 Data structure   124

Figures

3.1 Conceptual model   46
7.1 Illustration of the care pathway   111
10.1 Hospital clinical directorates   160
12.1 The emergence and evolution of Scotland's approach to
    quality (1983–2013)   192
12.2 Contextual factors influencing the development of
    Scotland's quality agenda   200
13.1 A tri-dimensional framework of perceived, lived and
    conceived organizational space   208
13.2 Tri-dimensional indicators for a more sensitive
    framework for accountability within devolved
    organizations   217
13.3 Tensions between dimensions of organizational space   218

Preface and Acknowledgements

This book is the result of the 9th Biennial Conference in the Organizational Behaviour in Healthcare (OBHC) conference series, which was held in Copenhagen Business School in April 2014.

The title of the conference was 'When health policy meets everyday practices', and the aim of the conference was to explore what happens when macro and top-down health policies – with ambitions for radical reform – meet the micro-work of day-to-day work practices, often strongly embedded in local healthcare practices. The conference was a great success with over 100 attendees coming from many different countries: Denmark, Sweden, Norway, the United Kingdom, Ireland, Germany, the Netherlands, Belgium, Italy, the United States, Canada and Australia. In this book, we have selected a strong collection of chapters from the wider conference papers, all grouped around the specific theme of 'Managing change – from policy to practice'. All chapters address the main question of how organizational change takes place in local work settings in healthcare, which thereby forms the core of this book.

The conference series is organized by the Society for Studies in Organizing Healthcare (SHOC), which is a learned society and a member of the UK Academy of Social Sciences. SHOC sets up a scientific committee to plan for and oversee each OBHC conference, including our local academic partners. We would like to thank all SHOC members for their active involvement in the conference. We are now very much looking forward to the 10th OBHC conference to be held at Cardiff and hosted by Cardiff University Business School in April 2016, titled 'Attaining, sustaining and spreading improvement: Art or science?'.

As editors, we would like to acknowledge the various people whose contributions were most helpful in making this book possible. We would like first of all to thank all our contributors for submitting and then revising their chapters, following a process of editorial peer review. Nor would it have been possible without the participation of all the interviewees. Liz Barlow, our Commissioning Editor at Palgrave Macmillan, has been a tireless support of the book and of the wider series which has now built up a sustained and impressive list of editions. Nanna Helene Jensen at Copenhagen Business School has provided invaluable administrative support, keeping the editors to time and task through her meticulous chapter spreadsheet! We would also like to acknowledge the extensive contribution of Professor Annabelle Mark, who was the original general editor of the series and who has now stepped down. We would also like to thank the CBS Public–Private Platform at Copenhagen Business School and Department of Organization for their support of the conference and the book.

Notes on Contributors

Editors

Susanne Boch Waldorff is an Associate Professor at the Department of Organization, Copenhagen Business School, Denmark, where she is also the Director of the Center for Health Management. She has published research on the organizational perspectives of the public sector, including the translation of policy into organizational practices, the complexity of governance approaches, reforms and professions, and collaborative innovation. Before her academic position, she worked for the Danish government.

Anne Reff Pedersen is an Associate Professor at the Department of Organization, Copenhagen Business School. Her research field is organizational studies with a particular interest in organization theory, ethnography, narratives, time and the public policy field of healthcare. She has published articles in *Organization, American Review of Public Administration, M@n@gement and Management Learning* and has also published several books about organizational change, public managers and management through the patient. She currently works in a research project about healthcare innovation with a special interest on change practices and narratives.

Louise Fitzgerald is Visiting Professor of Organizational Change at Saïd Business School, University of Oxford, and Emeritus Professor at De Montfort University, UK. Previously, she held management posts in the private sector and academic university posts, for example at Warwick University. Her research has focused on the implementation of organizational change in complex and public organizations, innovation diffusion and the nature of professional work. Her recent research explored issues of knowledge mobilization by managers in healthcare. She has published books and has contributed in journals such as *Human Relations, Academy of Management Journal, Leadership Quarterly* and *Social Science and Medicine*.

Ewan Ferlie is Professor of Public Services Management at King's College London. His publication interests are in the field of organizational change and restructuring in the public services, including healthcare. He is currently Honorary Chair of the Society for the Study of Organizing in Healthcare (SHOC), a learned society affiliated to the UK Academy of Social Sciences.

Contributors

G. Ross Baker is a full Professor at the Institute of Health Policy, Management and Evaluation, University of Toronto, Canada, where he teaches and carries out research on patient safety, quality improvement strategies and leadership and organizational change. He led a study of effective governance practices in improving quality and patient safety in 2009. He was a member of the National Steering Committee on Patient Safety, whose report in 2002 led to the creation of the Canadian Patient Safety Institute. He co-chaired a working group on methods and measures for patient safety for the World Health Organization (2006–2010) and chaired the Advisory Committee on Research and Evaluation for the Canadian Patient Safety Institute (2005–2010).

Jeffrey Braithwaite is Foundation Director of the Australian Institute of Health Innovation, Director of the Centre for Healthcare Resilience and Implementation Science and Professor of Health Systems Research, Faculty of Medicine and Health Sciences, Macquarie University, Australia. He has a PhD in Organisational Behaviour from the University of New South Wales, Sydney, Australia. His research examines the changing nature of health systems, patient safety, standards and accreditation, leadership and management, the structure and culture of organizations and their network characteristics, attracting funding of more than AUD\$59 million. He has conducted a great deal of work over two decades on clinical and organizational performance, health systems improvement and patient safety.

Robyn Clay-Williams is a Research Fellow at Macquarie University, Australia. She is a former military engineer and test pilot. Her doctoral work investigated the efficacy of aviation-style Crew Resource Management training in improving patient safety, by evaluating attitude and behavioural changes in multidisciplinary teams resulting from implementation of a teamwork intervention in the Australian healthcare field. She has since expanded her research to include safety and resilience in complex systems and human factors in healthcare. Specific areas of interest are resilience engineering, mathematical modelling of systems and behaviour, and usability test and evaluation of medical devices and IT systems.

Charlotte Croft is a postdoctoral Research Fellow at Warwick Business School. Her research interests include organizational behaviour in public sector organizations, leadership and issues of identity in professionalized settings. Her work has been published in several high-ranking peer-reviewed journals. Prior to moving into academia, she was a registered nurse in the United Kingdom, specializing in critical care.

Amanda Crompton joined Nottingham University Business School as Lecturer in Public Services Management in September 2013. She is a sociologist with a special interest in applying social theory to real-world policy development and delivery. Following completion of her doctorate (University of Nottingham, 2005), she worked at a number of leading policy research centres including the Centre for Research in Social Policy (Loughborough University) and the International Centre for Governance and Public Management (University of Warwick).

Deborah Debono is a postdoctoral Research Fellow at the Centre for Healthcare Resilience and Implementation Science, Australian Institute of Health Innovation, Macquarie University, NSW, Australia. Her academic qualifications, coupled with nursing experience, provide her with research expertise, as well as a first-hand understanding of clinical settings. Her research interests are quality improvement, patient safety and the influence of context, culture, technology and social relationships on clinicians' practice. Her doctoral research focused specifically on the role of workarounds in the delivery of healthcare.

Jean-Louis Denis is a full Professor and holds the Canada research chair on governance and transformation of healthcare organizations and systems at the École Nationale d'Administration Publique (ÉNAP). He is a researcher at the Institut de recherche en santé publique de l'Université de Montréal and a visiting professor at the Department of Management, Faculty of Social Science, King's College London. He is a member of the Royal Society of Canada, fellow of the Canadian Academy of Health Sciences and was chair of the advisory board of CIHR's Institute of Health Services and Policy Research (2009–2012), founding academic coordinator of the FORCES/EXTRA training programme (2003–2007) and principal investigator of a CIHR team grant on health system reconfiguration (2008–2013).

Mark Exworthy is Professor of Health Policy and Management at the University of Birmingham, UK. His research interests fall under three themes: (1) governance and implementation relating to policies to tackle health inequalities and other social 'problems'; (2) professionals and managerialism in healthcare organizations (especially relating to management of clinical performance); (3) decentralization in healthcare organizations. His research has been funded by the ESRC, NHS (Department of Health and NIHR), Joseph Rowntree Foundation, NHS Confederation and the Commonwealth Fund of New York.

Patrick C. Flood is Professor of Organisational Behaviour at Dublin City University. He is a fellow of the Academy of Social Sciences and the Royal Society of Arts. He received his PhD from LSE and is a former British Council FCO and Fulbright Scholar. He has worked at London Business School, University of Maryland, Australian Graduate School of Management and the University of Limerick. His books include *Change Lessons from the CEO* and *Persuasive Leadership* (2010 and 2013). He has published some 50 articles in journals such as the *Strategic Management Journal, Human Relations* and *Human Resource Management*.

Brian Golden holds a PhD from Kellogg School, Northwestern University and is Vice-Dean, Professional Programs, and the Sandra Rotman Chaired Professor in Health Sector Strategy at the Rotman School of Management, University of Toronto. He is Executive Director of The Collaborative for Health Sector Strategy, a policy, research and leadership development institute funded by the Ontario Ministry of Health. Among his published work are articles in *The Canadian Medical Association Journal, The Strategic Management Journal, Healthcare Quarterly, Healthcare Papers, The Annals of Pharmacotherapy, Management Science, Clinical Oncology, Health Policy* and *The Harvard Business Review*.

Lauren Hamel is an Assistant Professor in the Department of Oncology in the Wayne State University School of Medicine and the Karmanos Cancer Institute in Detroit, Michigan, USA. She is a communication scientist with expertise in human communication processes and organizational behaviour. Her research programme is focused on studying healthcare from two levels: the interpersonal communicative level and the organizational system level. Her overall goal is to improve communication and organizational processes in an effort to enhance the quality and efficiency of the delivery of cancer care. Her work is currently supported by funding from the National Institutes of Health and the National Cancer Institute.

Julie K. Johnson is a Professor at the Department of Surgery and Center for Healthcare Studies at Northwestern University, USA. Her career interests involve building a series of collaborative relationships to improve the quality and safety of healthcare through teaching, research and clinical improvement. She has a Master's in Public Health from the University of North Carolina and a PhD in Evaluative Clinical Sciences from Dartmouth College in Hanover, New Hampshire. Since completing her PhD, she has focused her research on activities related to quality and safety of patient care and qualitative evaluation of clinical micro-systems.

Amer Kaissi joined Trinity University in 2003 after receiving his PhD in Health Services Administration, Research and Policy from the University of Minnesota. Prior to that, he earned a Master of Public Health in Hospital Administration from the American University of Beirut, Lebanon. His research interests include convenient care, retail clinics, leadership, strategic planning, and quality of care and patient safety. He has published extensively on these topics in various administrative and clinical peer-reviewed journals. He has authored *Flipping Healthcare through Retail Clinics and Other Convenient Care Models* (2014), a resource on new delivery models.

Charlotte Kiland is a PhD student in Organization Theory and Management at the Department of Administration and Organization Theory, University of Bergen, Norway. She is currently an Assistant Professor at the Department of Public health, Sport and Nutrition, University of Agder, Norway. She has participated in research projects on government agency reform, inter-municipal co-operation and the management of health and welfare organizations. She has published articles on organizational change and management and inter-municipal co-operation.

Aris Komporozos-Athanasiou is Postdoctoral Research Associate in Social Science at King's College London School of Medicine, where he also co-leads the course 'Engaging publics in health research: theory, politics and practices'. He has a Bachelor's in Economics and a Master's in Organization Studies and Public Policy from the universities of Warwick and Cambridge. His work is eclectic and draws on the sociology of organizations, social theory as applied to public policy and ethnographic methodologies. He has published in major social science journals such as *Organization Studies* and *Public Administration* and in media outlets such as the *Guardian*.

Gro Kvåle is Associate Professor of Organization Theory and Management at the Department of Political Science and Management, University of Agder, Kristiansand, Norway. She has participated in national research projects on school reforms and on the management of health and welfare organizations. Furthermore, she has published books and articles on school management, on co-operation in and between health organizations and on organizational identity and reputation.

Wendy Lipworth is a Senior Research Fellow at the Centre for Values, Ethics and the Law in Medicine, University of Sydney, Australia. She is a medically trained bioethicist and qualitative researcher. Her research focuses on the ethics of health technology innovation. She is currently a National Health and Medical Research Council (NHMRC) Career Development Fellow and Lead Chief Investigator on grants focused on (1) funding high-cost cancer medicines and (2) managing conflict of interest in biomedicine. Methodologically, her work is best described as empirical bioethics in which empirical research into the values of all key stakeholders is used in conjunction with theoretical analysis in order to address real-world problems.

Fraser Macfarlane is a retired academic. He worked as a Senior Lecturer at the University of Surrey where he was programme leader for the MSc in Health Care Management. His research interests included talent management, diffusion of innovation and leadership skills within the public sector. His PhD looked at the organisational development of primary care within the UK with a particular focus on GPs' research activity. Prior to working in academia, he was a partner in a management consultancy specialising in providing human resource support to the NHS. He has an MBA from the London Business School. Before working as management consultant, he trained as a biochemist studying at Kings College London. He is a Fellow of the Chartered Institute of Personnel and Development.

Marie Henriette Madsen is a PhD student at the Department of Organization, Copenhagen Business School. Her research interest is especially related to the new conditions for the work, management and

xvi *Notes on Contributors*

organization of healthcare, given the many recent initiatives of quality and safety improvement. Since 2005, she has been employed at KORA, the Danish Institute for Local and Regional Government Research (former Danish Institute for Health Services Research), performing analysis of the Danish healthcare sector.

Aoife M. McDermott is Senior Lecturer in Human Resource Management at Cardiff Business School, where she coordinates the Cardiff Health Organization and Policy Studies group (CHOPS). Her research explores the role of people and change management in supporting service delivery and improvement. She is particularly interested in professional and public sector research contexts.

Lorna McKee is Professor of Management and Programme Director of the Delivery of Care Programme within the Heath Services Research Unit, University of Aberdeen, UK. Her current research interests include healthcare management and the management of change and innovation.

Kathleen Montgomery is a Professor at the Graduate Division and Emerita Professor of Organizations and Management at the University of California, Riverside. She has been a visiting scholar at Oxford University, Stanford and UCLA and is a long-time honorary associate of the Centre for Values, Ethics, and the Law in Medicine at the University of Sydney. She received her PhD in Sociology from New York University, where she began her research on the medical profession and relationships between professionals and their environment. Her current research continues this stream, now focusing on issues of trust, integrity and behavioural norms.

Amit Nigam is Senior Lecturer in Management at the Cass Business School. He received his PhD in a joint programme in Management and Sociology from Northwestern University and completed a post-doctoral fellowship at the Rotman School of Management at the University of Toronto. His primary research interests include organizational change, institutional change and the role of professions and occupations in change processes. His research has been published in a mix of management, medical sociology and health services journals including *Organization Science, Academy of Management Review, Organization Studies, Social Science & Medicine* and *Medical Care Research & Review*.

Daniel Nyberg is Professor of Management at Newcastle Business School, Australia, and an honorary professor at the University of Sydney. His research investigates how global and societal phenomena are translated into local organizational realities.

Esther Sackett is a PhD student in Management and Organizations at the Fuqua School of Business, Duke University, USA. She has a BA in Anthropology from Ithaca College and an MPA in Health Policy and Management from the Wagner School of Public Service, NYU. Prior to her doctoral studies, she worked in the healthcare industry for several years, developing, managing and evaluating interdisciplinary programmes in hospital settings. As a doctoral student, her research utilizes mixed-method approaches to investigate how individuals and teams manage the attentional demands that accompany complex work.

Marco Sartirana is a PhD student at Utrecht University, the Netherlands, with a research project on the organizational antecedents of doctors' involvement in management. He is interested in research topics at the intersection of organization studies and healthcare management, including medical management hybrids, HRM, organizational design, clinical pathways and clinical networks. He is also a research fellow at the Centre for Research on Health and Social Care Management (CeRGAS) at Bocconi University, Italy, and teaches HRM and organizational design in healthcare at SDA Bocconi School of Management. He has published articles and book chapters in international and Italian journals in the fields of healthcare management and public administration.

David R. Steel is a Research Fellow at the University of Aberdeen, UK. He has worked for 25 years in NHS management and was Chief Executive of NHS Quality Improvement Scotland from its creation in 2003 until his retirement in 2009. He chaired the Prioritisation Panel of the National Institute for Health Research Health Services and Delivery Research Programme until 2014. In 2008, he was awarded an OBE for services to healthcare.

Mark Thompson is Senior Lecturer in Information Systems at Cambridge Judge Business School and Strategy Director of Methods Group. His interests include the implications of process-based and affective ontologies for the study and practice of organizing, with a special focus on the public sector. He has undertaken a range of teaching and public policy roles and has published in journals such as *Journal of Public Administration, Research and Theory, Organization Science, Academy of Management Review* and *Human Relations*.

Dag Olaf Torjesen is Associate Professor of Health Management and Public Policy at the Department of Political Science and Management at the University of Agder, Kristiansand, Norway. His research and teaching are related to organization, governance and management in health and welfare organizations. He heads a Master's programme in Health Management at the University of Agder. At the moment his research is related to the research project 'The global financial crisis and the public sector in the Nordic countries'.

Nicolette van Gestel is Professor of New Modes of Governance in Social Security and Employment Services at Tilburg University, the Netherlands. Her research interests include public sector reform and its effects on organizations and professionals. She has published many books, chapters and articles in *Public Administration, Public Money & Management, Organization Studies* and *Personnel Review*, among others. She is co-chair of the EGOS Standing Working Group 'Organizing the Public Sector: Public Governance and Management' and a Crown Member of the Social and Economic Council (SER) of the Dutch government.

Emmie Vossen is a PhD candidate at Radboud University, Institute for Management Research, Nijmegen, the Netherlands. She has a disciplinary background in psychology and business administration from Radboud University, Nijmegen, and Tilburg University, the Netherlands. Her research investigates the ways in which employers in the Netherlands and Denmark translate national activation policies into local practices of sickness absence management.

Justin Waring studied Sociology and Social Policy at the University of Liverpool and then Healthcare Policy and Management at the University of Birmingham. After working at Aston University, he completed his doctorate at the University of Nottingham on 'The social construction and control of medical errors'. Following postdoctoral research at the University of Manchester, he was appointed Lecturer in Medical Sociology (2005–8) and then Associate Professor in Public Management (2009–11) at the University of Nottingham. After a short spell with Warwick University (2011–12), where he was Professor of Public Management, he is now Professor of Organisational Sociology at Nottingham University Business School.

Micky Willmott is a Research Associate in the School of Social and Community Medicine, University of Bristol, UK. She has experience of working at a local and national level in public health, health services and policy research in the United Kingdom and the United States. She has a particular interest in health policy analysis, and her recent research includes investigating the role of non-governmental organizations in local policy making in the United Kingdom and the experiences of Directors of Public Health in influencing decision-making in local government in England.

Introduction

Susanne Boch Waldorff, Anne Reff Pedersen, Louise Fitzgerald and Ewan Ferlie

This book is about managing change in healthcare settings. The book draws upon the presentations and discussions at the 9th International Organisational Behaviour in Healthcare Conference (OBHC), which took place in Copenhagen in April 2014, hosted by Copenhagen Business School. The conference theme was 'When health policy meets every day practices'. The conference was international, receiving papers from scholars in countries worldwide, including Denmark, Sweden, Norway, the United Kingdom, Ireland, Germany, the Netherlands, Belgium, Italy, the United States, Canada and Australia. To date, Palgrave Macmillan has published eight editions in a series linked to the OBHC conferences organized by the Society for Studies in Organising Healthcare (SHOC).

From the Copenhagen OBHC conference, a shared theme emerged as to how to understand the complex and often bumpy processes of implementing healthcare reforms, policies and programmes into healthcare practices. These processes entail various aspects of managing change such as the design of change processes, the translation of new managerial concepts into a local context, the interaction and sense making among organizational actors, and the management and measurement of performance. These processes may evoke not only engaged collaboration but also resistance from the field.

The main contribution of this book is twofold: first, to explore organizational change in healthcare as influenced by contemporary policy and management concepts and, second, it aims to present and apply theoretical perspectives, which can create new insights into implementation processes and the hard work of managing change.

This book consists of 15 chapters examining the management of change in a range of healthcare settings. The chapters demonstrate academic rigour, theoretical contributions and international perspectives.

The chapters are divided into four subthemes. Each theme deals with critical issues, models, theories and frameworks (both theoretical and empirical) that expound understandings of managing change and the processes, practices and behaviours supporting its attainment. Theme 1 contributes to understanding the challenge of designing organizational change processes; theme 2 to understanding the role of professions in change processes; theme 3 to understanding the development of leadership competences necessary for creating organizational change; and theme 4 to understand change programmes' content and outcomes.

Before presenting the chapters, we will explain the three contributions which the book offers across the chapters.

First, we would like to share our observation that healthcare reforms and change processes all over the world have become more and more dedicated to implementing particular managerial concepts. These concepts are promoted as the solutions to current problems in healthcare and societal challenges. Many of these reforms and change processes have performance-oriented goals, but little is said about the detailed design of the implementation process. This vagueness could cause frustrations in the local contexts, but it could also trigger different contextualized implementation processes and local adaption. The chapters in this book illustrate that some change processes are designed as traditional top-down processes, perhaps with the support from external consultants, whereas others are designed as cross-collaborative ways of organizing.

Second, we see that most of the new change concepts are developed to support and strengthen the role of leaders (widely defined) in healthcare organizations. Particularly, two types of actors are positioned as crucial for creating desired organizational change: healthcare professionals and clinical leaders. Thus, we have dedicated two sub-themes in this book which examine the role of healthcare professionals and clinical leaders in change processes. The book chapters reveal that these actors have particular strong values and beliefs which can influence which meanings and practices become possible in the local context and how new ideas are translated into local work practices. If healthcare professionals and clinical leaders refuse to participate in local change processes, then change becomes very difficult. We find it very interesting that many change processes evolve around the development of these leaders and professionals, their skills and opening up access to the leadership discipline. Yet, we do not want to signal that we think that the roles of patients, policymakers and other actors in healthcare should be neglected. On the contrary, their involvement is critical. Thus, the book also includes chapters providing insights into the roles of other actors such as external consultants in change processes.

Finally, the book offers an analytic contribution to understanding and exploring change in healthcare. Insights from organizational theory and behaviour theory conceptualize organizational change as continuous change processes involving interaction, sense making and local adaption and innovation among loosely coupled actors. This breaks with the common definition of change promoted in many change programmes as rational and planned episodic change which is effected in a defined short period of time. Thus, many of the chapters in this book apply organization and behavioural theory to explore change processes which are seen as complex interaction processes. This also reveals how local and institutionalized values and logics can influence change processes. Thereby, the book challenges existing, and much conventional, healthcare management research, which understands change as taking the form of designed, strategic and rational processes, which can be readily managed in order to create improvements. Several chapters explore the messy work and the complexity of organizing change processes in healthcare.

Designing change processes

Part I of this book looks at how change processes in the healthcare sector are designed in order to create changes in practices. The empirical cases are drawn from different national contexts; each identifying specific challenges in a change process and emphasizing the importance of local interpretation of the initiative. In Chapter 1, 'The Ideas and Implementation of Public Health Policies: The Norwegian Case', Charlotte Kiland, Gro Kvåle and Dag Olaf Torjesen explore how implementation of new health legislation in Norway is designed to accommodate a shift in healthcare from treatment to illness prevention. The authors show how the inconsistence in policy ideas and goals may function as a catalyst for local adaption. This point about local discretion is also investigated in Chapter 2, 'The Path from Policy to Practice and the Resilience of Everyday Work in Acute Settings', by Robyn Clay-Williams, Julie Johnson, Deborah Debono and Jeffrey Braithwaite. The authors explore an Australian setting and argue that the prerequisite for successful implementation is dialogue between medical staff and managers, and room for local adaption of policy. In Chapter 3, 'Dealing with the Challenges of Healthcare Reform: American Hospital Systems Strive to Improve Access and Value through Retail Clinics', the author Amer Kaissi explores how the innovation of retail clinics has contributed to the implementation of a healthcare reform in American Hospitals. The clinics were not part of the initial implementation design, but they positioned themselves as central and became important drivers in the implementation. Finally, in Chapter 4, 'Institutional Logics and Micro-processes in Organizations: A Multi-actor Perspective on Sickness Absence Management in Three Dutch Hospitals', the authors Nicolette van Gestel, Daniel Nyberg and Emmie Vossen investigate the implementation of sickness absence management in three Dutch hospitals. The authors discuss how different interpretations of an activation logic enabled a reinforcement of professional boundaries and a disconnection of relevant organizational practices. Thus, despite a robust local intention and support for change, the particular process resulted in the maintenance of established practices.

The role of professions in change processes

The second sub-theme, that is Part II of this book, emphasizes the importance of analysing the role of professionals as they have a major impact on change processes in healthcare. The chapters build on different cases from the United States, Canada, England and Denmark; in sum, an international picture can be drawn on the current devolvement of the role of professions in healthcare. Chapter 5, 'The Persistence of Professional Boundaries in Healthcare: A Re-examination of a Theory of Foundational Values', by Kathleen Montgomery, Wendy Lipworth and Louise Fitzgerald, studies the role of the medical professions; the authors investigate the boundaries of the medical professionals in contrast to other professions. This chapter demonstrates how the medical professions have foundational values like surviving and flourishing and how these values have an impact on their relation with other professions and contribute to a strong domination of the medical profession. Yet, professionals might also become engaged in shaping changes. In Chapter 6, 'Medical Doctors and Health System Improvement: Synthesis Results and Propositions for Further Research', Jean Louis Denis and G Ross Baker investigate the role of leadership of physicians. In the chapter, they present the challenges and possibilities in making transformative change and discuss how leadership of physicians is a multifaceted process containing both institutional and contextual conditions. Chapters 7 and 8 challenge the dominant role of physicians in healthcare. In Chapter 7, 'The Role of the Quality Coordinator: Articulation Work in Quality Development', by Marie Henriette Madsen, she discusses the emergence of a new healthcare profession and the quality coordinators, and lists the possibilities of this new profession, as well as how they can negotiate in new ways among the traditional healthcare professions. Chapter 8, by Amit Nigam, Esther Sackett and Brian Golden, 'The Role of Outside Consultants in Shaping Hospital Organizational Change', also deals with a partly new development in healthcare, how change processes become the responsibility of external consultants, and how these external actors have a capacity to make change as they do not represent the internal hospital culture. Together the four chapters in Part II both demonstrate the constant power of the medical profession in healthcare in relation to their foundational values and engagement in clinical leadership and introduce new professions and actors, who potentially challenge the role of the physicians, but not in a traditional sense; external consultants and quality coordinator will never become the new dominants of healthcare profession, but by their existence and their work, they put emphasis on the role of organizing and change. The manner in which both external and internal expectations about healthcare professions are rising also becomes change agents and takes responsibility for change processes.

Leadership and organizational change

The third sub-theme, Part III of this book, examines the nature of the leadership role in healthcare and how such roles may be best supported. The chapters draw on research from Italy and the United Kingdom. Chapter 9, entitled 'NHS Managers: From Administrators to Entrepreneurs?', by Mark Exworthy, Fraser Macfarlane and Micky Willmott, directly addresses the conference theme by reviewing the policy variations over time in the United Kingdom and demonstrating how managers face the challenges from competing pressures of public sector bureaucracy and new public management entrepreneurialism. In particular, the authors review the rise of 'entrepreneurialism'. In Chapter 10, 'Opportunity Does Matter: Supporting Doctors-in-Management in Hospitals', by Marco Sartirana, the author explores the role of clinical hybrid managers within the Italian healthcare system. The author demonstrates how clinical directors' managerial behaviour is influenced not only by the motivation and ability but also by the opportunities and support afforded to them by their organization. The final chapter in Part III of this book, Chapter 11, titled 'A New Approach to Hybrid Leadership Development', picks up on the theme of the support and training required for leadership. This chapter by Charlotte Croft explores the appropriate forms of leadership training for strategic leaders, drawing on novel data from leadership training for nurses. The chapter illustrates the benefits of leadership development which prioritizes understanding of the organizational and wider policy context over a focus on skills competency. The chapter also underlines the 'darker' side of this approach, which may be used as a process of normative control.

Change programmes: Content and performance

It seems a common condition across all healthcare systems that new organizational and managerial change programmes are introduced, often with the aim of reducing costs and increasing quality. The chapters in this section will explore different change programmes and initiatives in healthcare organizations and explore their sometimes perverse or unanticipated outcomes. The concrete change programmes and initiatives analysed include the design of quality and safety programmes at the national level (taking the specific case of Scotland) (see Chapter 12, 'Scotland "Bold and Brave"? Conditions for Creating a Coherent National Healthcare Quality Strategy', by Aoife M. McDermott, David R. Steel, Lorna McKee, Lauren Hamel and Patrick C. Flood), the relationship between co-production, public and patient involvement programmes and formal accountability regimes that find modes of experiential knowledge difficult to measure (see Chapter 13, 'The Social Spaces of Accountability in Hybridized Healthcare Organizations', by Aris Komporozos-Athanasiou and Mark Thompson), and the exploration of major cultural differences apparent in a growing number of public–private partnership programmes (see Chapter 14, 'Culture Shock and the NHS Diaspora: Coping with Cultural Difference in Public–Private Partnerships', by Justin Waring and Amanda Crompton). Chapter 15, 'Organizational Healthcare Innovation as a Change Programme Performed by Contextual Sense Making', by Anne Reff Pedersen, explores the process of a diffusion of an innovation in Danish healthcare settings, stressing that the local meanings that healthcare professionals accord to such an innovation must be taken fully into account: it adopts a micro-level and sense-making perspective. The chapters point to the relevance of developing appropriate theoretical frameworks and also empirical indicators as an important condition for assessing the nature and impact of such organizational change.

Part I
Designing Change Processes

1
The Ideas and Implementation of Public Health Policies: The Norwegian Case

Charlotte Kiland, Gro Kvåle and Dag Olaf Torjesen

Introduction

In Denmark, Norway and Sweden, the municipal and regional administrative levels are in charge of implementing public health policies and measures on behalf of the state. In fact, both in Denmark (Waldorff, 2010; Vrangbæk and Sørensen, 2013) and in Norway (Report to the Storting no. 47, 2008–2009; Rommetveit et al., 2014; Torjesen and Vabo, 2014), recent reforms have emphasized the role of the municipalities in carrying out public health policies. In this chapter, we investigate the challenges of managing organizational change processes, in order to create changes in practices within the field of public health in the case of Norway. We study the relationship between changes in national policies and legislation and implementation at the municipal level. Our main question concerns how national public health policies are put into local practice. To answer this, we need to (1) investigate which ideas about the government of public health are articulated in national policies, (2) study how these policies are received and acted upon locally and (3) explain local choices regarding public health practices. Furthermore, in this chapter we present a theoretical framework focusing on major ideas on public health management and on the relation between ideas and practice in a neo-institutional perspective. This is followed by a brief presentation of the material and methods, as well as an explanation on how the empirical data are analysed. Then the analysis of the empirical data is presented, concluding the chapter with a discussion.

From ideas to implementation of public health policy

Broadly speaking, it is possible to distinguish between two different ideas of the management of public health: one that can be labelled 'collectivist–integration' and the other 'individual–empowerment'. A *collectivist–integration* idea of public health entails that health is seen as a common good that should be distributed in an equal way. Poor health is a product of the structures of society. It is taken for granted that public health is a political responsibility. Governing public health is about regulative policies and formal structures at the system level. This policy corresponds with the World Health Organization (WHO) strategy 'Health 2020' (WHO, 2012), which emphasizes the interdependencies between social non-medical conditions and health status in the population and that health is a political issue as much as a scientific matter. This recognition leads to a whole-of-society and a 'health-in-all-policies' (HiAP) paradigm. A multi-sectoral approach is therefore crucial for promoting better health (Raphael, 2009; Jacab, 2011). With regard to management, this corresponds with the whole-of-government (WoG) approach (Christensen and Lægreid, 2007), focusing on coordination and integration between sectors and organizational units. These ideas are also anchored in the normative features of the Nordic welfare state, emphasizing equality, solidarity, redistribution and security for all (Esping-Andersen, 1990; Fosse, 2011). We would expect this idea of public health to dominate in a Nordic type of welfare state like Norway, and consequently that public health issues should be integrated within and across policy areas and organizational units.

However, the Nordic welfare system has changed towards neo-liberal values like efficiency, freedom, empowerment and self-responsibility (Mik-Meyer and Villadsen, 2007; Magnussen et al., 2009). Within the *individual–empowerment* idea, health is a product of choice, public health is the aggregate of individual choice and policy is about influencing health-related behaviour in more or less subtle ways. By the use of the concept *empowerment*, responsibility and control are moved from the state to the citizens (Andersen, 2003). The argument is that the empowered individual becomes responsible by taking healthy choices, obtaining self-control and accepting the fact that the health sector has limited resources. The state can be characterized as the 'good shepherd' or a 'pastoral state' (Dean, 2010: 91), and the government assumes that it is in a position to (re)define what is 'for the citizen's own good' and to lead them to the appropriate 'pasture'. With this idea about public health, improvement is achieved by encouraging, persuading and training the citizens to a healthy lifestyle. Manifestations of this idea would be regulative and educational measures directed at the individual. How are these ideas articulated in the Norwegian public health policy, and how are they handled by the municipalities? One approach to understanding the relationship between ideas and practices is a neo-institutional perspective. Inspired by Meyer and Rowan (1977), Scott and Meyer (1994) and Scott (2013), we regard ideas about the management of public health as rationalized myths or cultural rules that puts an institutionalized pressure on organizations seeking legitimacy. However, the rationalized myths may not comprise an efficient solution for the organization, in terms of facing demands originating from the technical environments (Meyer and Rowan, 1977). In addition, competing and internally inconsistent rational myths can exist simultaneously. The theoretical argument is that organizations decouple their practices from their formal structure to solve problems of such institutionalized pressure and conflicting demands. Thus, organizations adopt new structures without necessarily implementing the related practices. In Nils Brunsson's (2003) conceptualization, the conflicting demands and expectations result in a decoupling of *talk, decisions and action.* If this is the case regarding national policy ideas about public health, we will expect the organizational handling on the local level to result in decoupling of policy from actual local practice.

A related approach to understanding the relationship between ideas and practice is to recognize the ambiguities of change processes: change in practice occurs, but not necessarily as planned (Czarniawska and Sêvon, 1996; Brunsson, 2003). Røvik (2014) introduces 'the translation doctrine' in implementation studies, that is, the process in which an idea is made meaningful and useful by the associations of the actors involved, within the context where it is adopted (Latour, 1986; Czarniawska and Sevôn, 1996). As a result of the active process of interpretation, it could be claimed that implementation *never* occurs as a copy of the original decision or that outcomes are universal across different locations (ibid.). On the contrary, ideas will *always* be modified across time and space. However, according to Røvik (2007) *both* reproduction and modification of the original idea might be the outcome, depending on pragmatic local considerations and decisions regarding meaningful and useful practices. The more abstract, differentiated, ambiguous, but also embedded, the ideas or policies are, the more likely they are to be open to interpretation and change (ibid.). The more concrete, simple and disembedded they are, the easier they are to reproduce in a literal sense (Røvik, 2007). In accordance with this approach, we

would expect that different ideas and policies are subject to translation processes resulting in modification or reproduction of the ideas in
practice.

To summarize our theoretical framework, we have elaborated on
two different *ideas* or rationalized myths concerning the management
of public health: *the collectivist–integration*   idea and the *individual–
empowerment* idea. Further, we use the framework of the 'translation
doctrine' to analyse how these ideas are interpreted and developed into
a local *practice* in the field of public health, with possible outcomes like
decoupling, modification and reproduction.

Material and methods

The empirical material in this chapter relies on primary data in the form
of interviews and survey data[1] and on secondary data in the form of
national policy documents. We have conducted 16 in-depth one-on-one
interviews with key individuals, at the national, regional and municipal levels. At the national level, we interviewed two senior advisors in
the Norwegian Directorate of Health, in January 2013. We have also
interviewed four public health coordinators from the two counties in
the southern part of Norway, and at the local level six municipal doctors and four local public health coordinators from six municipalities
in the same region were interviewed. These interviews were conducted
between February and June 2013.

The national policy documents include three government white
papers on public health launched between 2002 and 2013: the Coordination Reform, Planning and Building Act and Public Health Act. The
empirical material is also based on secondary data, particularly recent
research reports from the Norwegian Institute for Urban and Regional
Research (NIBR).

Methodically, qualitative content analysis of documents is used to
obtain the dominating ideas within the national public health policy and the public health field. The interviews from the national level
(The Norwegian Directorate of Health) are used to deepen and discuss the content in the documents. Data from the interviews with key
informants, from the regional and local level, are analysed to obtain
subjective but typical experiences and reactions. The qualitative data
are triangulated with the survey data to strengthen the validity and
reliability of our interpretations.

To investigate how the ideas about public health are articulated in
Norwegian public health policies, we have focused on definitions of

problems, goals, legal requirements, financial incentives, guidelines, recommendations, organizational concepts and so on, articulated by central authorities. To understand the practical implications, we looked for the practices, that is, routines, procedures, organizational arrangements, services and so on, chosen by local actors regarding the policy.

The national public health agenda

The collectivist–integrative idea in public health policies

In 2002, the Norwegian government introduced a 'national public health chain' (Report to the Storting no. 16, 2002–2003), a partnership model based on vertical and horizontal integration. The ambition was to establish vertical partnerships between the national, regional and local levels combined with horizontal partnerships between the public sector, the voluntary sector and other relevant bodies. At the regional level, the counties played an important role in contributing to this partnership model until 2010, as they coordinated and distributed state funding within the public health field (Report to the Storting no. 12, 2006–2007). By 2007, the vertical integration was strengthened, as all counties had established partnerships with relevant national bodies and with 59% of the municipalities (The Norwegian Directorate of Health, 2011). The stimulation funding for cooperation became a part of the municipal funding framework in 2010. This led to a breach in the national public health chain organized as a partnership model. However, the partnership model materialized in a new organizational design through the Coordination Reform that was introduced in 2009 to strengthen cooperation between the hospital sector and primary care. One of the instruments put forward by the national authorities in obtaining the goal of the Coordination Reform is organizing through multi-sectoral coordinating and cooperative bodies and positions, for example the Regional Cooperation Committees with participants from hospitals/health enterprises, municipalities and other actors. Public health issues are supposed to be a major concern for these committees (Torjesen and Vabo, 2014). Coordination and integration of actors at different levels and from different sectors of society clearly is in line with the collectivist–integration idea in the governance of public health.

Another manifestation of the collectivist–integrative idea is a national educational programme called 'Health in Planning', initiated in 2005 by the Norwegian Directorate of Health in collaboration with the Norwegian Association of Municipalities. The programme focuses on increasing the knowledge of planning and planning processes at the municipal and regional levels. The project includes continuing education programmes, teaching national policies and legislation connecting planning processes and public health. Methodologies are developed to realize public health goals by including them in the overall, social or land-use planning. Organization and cooperation, political anchoring, competence building and the distribution of information are also included as measures in this context.

The revised Planning and Building Act from 2008 is greatly inspired by the collectivist–integrative idea concerning public health. The act embedded public health issues and strategies in a cross-sectoral community perspective on preventive public health based on regional and local planning to increase social sustainability in health. Municipal master plans were seen as vital tools for defining future challenges and municipal priorities in all political areas in order to promote public health (Amdam and Veggeland, 2011: 37; Aarsæther et al., 2012: 76). With the introduction of the Public Health Act in 2012, the overall planning approach to public health was strengthened through the principle of 'health in all policies' (Public Health Act, 2012; Grimm et al., 2013). This is a WoG policy (Christensen and Lægreid, 2007) focusing on integration of public health issues within and across policy areas and organizational units. To sum up our findings so far, the public health chain, the 'health-in-planning' programme, the Planning and Building Act, the Public Health Act and the Coordination Reform are examples of the introduction of regulative policies and structures at the system level, underlining the collectivist–integration idea in public health.

The individual–empowerment idea in public health policies

The Coordination Reform also put the individual's responsibility within the public health field on the agenda, in addition to the approaches in line with the collectivistic–integration idea, as described in the previous section. The Coordination Reform reinforced the development and use of so-called learning-and-mastery centres in specialist healthcare (The Norwegian Directorate of Health, 2013). The aim is to improve the quality of 'learning-and-mastery' services in the specialist health services and in the municipal health and care services. Patients are guided and supported to handle their own health conditions to regain control over their lives and the resources that affect them, that is, self-medication, self-monitoring, nutrition guidance and the ability to handle pain.

Report on Public Health (Report to the Storting no. 34, 2012–2013) also emphasizes the individual–empowerment idea. In the Report's introductory chapter, one of the principles for the public health policy is as follows:

> Each of us has a considerable responsibility for our own health and empowerment of our own life…The society is responsible for organising and preparing for equal opportunities, for giving people opportunities to exploit their own resources and for the possibility to use the freedom of choice.
>
> (ibid.: 8)

The Report also states that

> [i]t is a social responsibility to influence health related choices by informing, adding knowledge and influencing attitudes.
>
> (ibid.: 13)

These principles, clearly inspired by the individual–empowerment idea, are materialized in specific organizational units called 'healthy-lifestyle' centres, initiated by the Norwegian Directorate of Health. It is not mandatory by law to establish a 'healthy-lifestyle' centre, but it is strongly recommended for the municipalities to make use of this *new health and care service* (The Norwegian Directorate of Health, 2013). These organizational arrangements are presented as municipal resource centres for guidance and follow-up for people who are in need of help to change their health behaviour. The 'healthy-lifestyle centre' concept is based upon quite detailed and explicit national guidelines (ibid.). For example, the guideline concerns who the target groups should be (people with problems regarding physical activity, nutrition and tobacco), what services and activities should be offered (individual consultations, standardized courses on nutritional guidance and 'walking classes'), what approaches and methods should be used in dealing with individual users (the 'healthy-lifestyle dialogue') and so on. The patients are identified by their general practitioner (GP), other health personnel or the social welfare services, who can issue a so-called healthy-lifestyle prescription, a standardized 12-week individually designed counselling and activity programme. Besides these requirements, the municipalities are free to develop other services and to organize the centres, for example inter-municipal collaborations (ibid.).

The 'healthy-lifestyle-centre' concept is thus clearly an expression of public health governance by the 'pastoral state' (Dean, 2010). The citizens are guided on an individual basis towards healthy choices and behaviour. It is also a detailed recipe for municipalities to follow, in order to facilitate the implementation of this policy and the diffusion of this particular organizational practice.

A mix of ideas: Contradictory, complementary or ambiguous public health policy?

To summarize the empirical findings regarding national policies on public health, two major ideas seem to exist side by side. One favours social and physical planning and coordination between agencies and authorities as the path to improve and manage the health of people. This is expressed through the Public Health Act and Planning and Building Act, which emphasizes a multi-sectoral health approach to all municipal planning and policies. To ensure the implementation of this policy, a national education programme has been carried out. The Coordination Reform also underlines the importance of a WoG approach through a more integrated cooperation between the hospital sector and the municipalities and a stronger focus on prevention and health promotion. The other idea emphasizes individuals' behaviour and responsibility, expressed in the Report on Public Health and in the Coordination Reform. The idea materializes in the 'learning-and-mastery' centres in the hospitals and the local 'healthy-lifestyle' centres. In other words, different ideas are mixed between and within the primary policy documents that govern the public health field in Norway. The Coordination Reform and the Public Health Act go in both directions. The Report on Public health characterizes public health as a balancing act. The implications of the mixed ideas and policies could be that they both contradict and complement each other.

An advisor in the Norwegian Directorate of Health describes the national public health policy as follows:

> While the resources are directed towards the 'right', concentrating on individual health behaviour and habits, the political rhetoric goes to the 'left', focussing on structural mechanisms, public health and planning, the importance of the local community.

This implies a decoupling between *decisions*, on the one hand, and *talk*, on the other, creating an ambiguous public health policy. Another advisor in the Norwegian Directorate of Health puts it bluntly:

> The whole concept of public health is problematic, and the whole reform isn't exactly clear.

Thus, it makes it interesting to study how these parallel ideas and different policies about public health are received and put into practice at the local level. What sense do they make, what activities do they instigate and what organizational structures are set up?

Practice: Local perception and action

The multiple meanings and approaches to public health are also present in the local practice. How the concept of 'public health' is perceived locally could be illustrated by one of the public health advisors at the county level, who says,

> The concept of public health has almost become a buzz-word, and is almost unmanageable because it comprises so many things which are both a strength and a weakness, and people can get a bit disillusioned because it's so difficult to concretize.

A municipal public health coordinator comments on the ambiguity in the national policy ideas:

> The national level tells us to focus on a new public health strategy involving overall municipal planning, requiring local and regional analysis of public health challenges in the municipality or within our region. But what kind of projects do they fund? We need more financial support and guidance to develop more sophisticated data to be able to produce some useful analysis for the planning strategy, but instead money goes to the 'healthy-lifestyle' centres, despite our local challenges and needs.

Another public health coordinator recognizes the 'health in all policies' approach but expresses confusion and lack of knowledge and thus implies difficulties in implementing this principle:

> The biggest challenge is to maintain what is required by law, to know what works and to understand exactly what it is that influences public health in every sector, to focus on social inequity, which goes far beyond eating healthy food.

These statements point out not only the popularity of the concept but also the diversity and possible ambiguity of national policy, and how this confuses and challenges the local level. One of the chief municipal doctors[2] says,

> Many of my colleagues freak out when they hear the word 'public health'...

He presumably implies that ambiguous goals, expectations and tasks create frustration among those responsible for carrying them out. How this can be handled is explained by a municipal doctor:

> Most municipal doctors probably do what we do; 'park' public health with some coordinator... I believe most municipal doctors think that the public health coordinator should take care of it, and I can give some advice or something.

This implies that the municipal doctors hesitate to have anything to do with this area.

According to the 2012 Public Health Act, chief municipal doctors and public health coordinators are expected to be driving forces within the multi-sectoral public health work in the municipalities. However, Grimm et al. (2013: 231) show that 50% of the municipalities involve chief municipal doctors and public health coordinators only to a modest or medium degree in planning processes. This implies that it is hard for them to get a central role in the formulation of local public health policies or the integration of health into all policies. Two of the municipal doctors describe the situation:

> If I should describe how much of my time I spend on public health and preventive work in my position as municipal doctor... I would say approximately 20–25%.

> I work in a 30% position as municipal doctor and the time I spend on public health-related issues is close to none, it is the community nurse who takes care of the public health work, you should talk to her.

These stories are corroborated by a countrywide survey conducted in 2014, where the position as public health coordinator is on average reported to be 34% of a full position (Karlsen, 2014). This shows that the room to coordinate is limited, and it indicates that it is not a prioritized task.

Public health is still often organized within the health sector (Helgesen and Hofstad, 2012). In 2014, 37% of Norwegian municipalities organized public health within a health and care services unit, 24.5% have made it the Chief Municipal Executive's responsibility and 4.5% have located public health within the municipality's planning unit (Karlsen, 2014). The remainder is a mixture of various affiliations ranging from culture and education to technical services (ibid.). Quite a few of the interviewees prefer an organizational solution which locates the responsibility for public health within the municipal planning unit or closer to the top administrative level, in order to broaden the perspective and achieve results. A public health coordinator explains that:

> public health is organised within the health and care department, but we are about to reorganise and move this area to the city and society unit within the technical services department, and we have a cross-sectoral forum for public health led by the chief municipal doctor... but ideally it would have been beneficial to move the coordinating function to the level of Chief Municipal Executive.

Traditional specialization and fragmentation between sectors and services are experienced as real barriers to cooperation and integration. Nationally, approximately 60% of the public health coordinators have a health-related profession and education (Helgesen and Hofstad, 2012: 84; Karlsen, 2014). The rest is a 'motley crew' consisting of engineers, teachers and people with a background in culture or sports. This shows that the local practice in the field of public health still is dominated by health professionals and closely connected to the municipal healthcare sector. This makes it difficult both to anchor it into the general municipal organization and to implement the cross-sectoral principle of 'health in all policies' (Helgesen and Hofstad, 2012: 75).

Our interviewees report that to some extent public health has been integrated into the municipal master plans as required by law. It is linked to various local policy areas like technical services, culture, sports and education. But, what is written into the municipal master plans is one thing; it is another thing to follow it up by actual prioritizing. This is expressed by one of the municipal doctors who points out that:

> the word public health is mentioned more frequently in our plans, but the resources have not changed significantly.

A survey conducted in 2011 (Helgesen and Hofstad, 2012) investigated those public health topics that were included into the municipal master plans and sectoral plans. The survey data show that topics that could be related to the collective–integrative idea, for example living conditions, social and physical environment and multi-sectoral cooperation, are included in the municipal plans (ibid.). A follow-up study executed in 2014 (Helgesen et al., 2014) conveyed that the local practice is characterized by activities mainly focusing on health behaviour, lifestyle and lifestyle habits (ibid.: 114–119), activities anchored in the individual–empowerment idea. This indicates a decoupling (Meyer and Rowan, 1977) between what the municipalities incorporate as their public health strategies in the plans and what they actually implement into the local practice.

The number of 'healthy-lifestyle' centres, even if they are *not* mandatory by law, has increased from 42 in 2008 to 212 (of 428 municipalities) in 2014.[3] More than 50% of these centres have less than one full-time position, with varied competence and knowledge (Helgesen et al., 2014). The centres are often organized in public–private partnerships or as inter-municipal cooperations. Sports clubs and other voluntary associations can be involved, as can privately be owned commercial actors in the development and rendering of services, for example individual guidance and group-based activities directed at changing lifestyle habits regarding nutrition, physical training and smoking. Helgesen et al. (2014: 117) find that what municipalities see as the most important public health mannerism for adults is to prevent obesity and inactivity through referrals to the 'healthy-lifestyle' centres.

A summary of the empirical data on the local reception and practice reflects that the national public health policy is perceived as unclear and ambiguous, consequently challenging and difficult for implementing all aspects. Trying to make sense of it creates confusion and frustration, hesitation and inaction in the day-to-day coordination. The collectivist–integration idea has to some extent been integrated into municipal planning and local organizational structures, for example the positions of public health coordinators as well as various cooperative units. However, these coordinating and cooperative instruments do not seem to have got a prominent organizational location. This might lead to an isolation of both the public health coordinators and the public health policy. They are still mostly organized within the healthcare sector and only infrequently moved over to a planning unit or to top-level management, which would indicate priority to coordination and the 'health in all policies' principle. At the same time, 'healthy-lifestyle' centres are becoming more and more popular. An increasing number of municipalities have implemented them, and more are in the process of being established. In other words, the individual–empowerment idea appears to dominate when it comes to the actual local practice.

Discussion

In spite of efforts at carrying out both these ideas, the municipalities do not succeed in *combining* the policies. Instead, they are decoupled, and the individual–empowerment idea seems to dominate in practice. How can this be explained?

Firstly, the collectivist–integration idea presupposes a WoG approach in accordance with the recommendations from the WHO (Jacab, 2012; WHO, 2012). However, this approach is known to entail problems and challenges (Sarapuu et al., 2014). It can be a time-consuming and resource-demanding effort to get professionals in front-line services in municipalities, counties and civic organizations to work together, and it can take a long time before reform effects appear (Christensen and Lægreid, 2007). Previous research on the multi-sectoral WoG approach in the Norwegian public health field concludes that it is difficult to establish a new understanding and conception that health problems should be handled through joint-up action and inter-sectoral planning instead of isolating the responsibility within the municipal healthcare sector (Grimm et al., 2013). Fosse (2012: 202) refers to many of the same integrative implementation problems related to fulfil the 'health in all policies' idea in the collectivist–integrative approach, that is, insufficient anchoring in the sectors involved, cooperation and coordination problems, a lack of common concepts across sectors, insufficient competence and resources. Axelsson and Axelsson (2006) emphasize that inter-sectoral, multidisciplinary teams tend to be fragile and volatile organizations that require a lot of support and attention. Our data suggest that such committed leadership is lacking when it comes to the organization of local public health. In sum, the difficulties in reproducing a successful multi-sectoral organizing and management of public health stand in the way and slow down the implementation of the collectivist–empowerment idea.

Secondly, the tendency to revert to the individual–empowerment approach could be understood in the light of some of the characteristics of the concept of 'healthy-lifestyle' centres. It appears to be a solution that is easy to adopt (Røvik, 2007). It is relatively simple and concrete, with more or less standardized, manual-based instructions of how it should be designed, implemented and run. These organizations demand neither much skilled planning nor complex structures and coordination to operate effective services and programmes for individual users. The competence and technologies required to develop and render these kinds of services are tied to professions, not persons, and are as such general and widespread. They are thus easy to reproduce in a new context (Røvik, 2007). At the same time, the concept is flexible enough to be able to adapt to local conditions, needs and opportunities for health promotion, for example in terms of adding (ibid.) services and activities to the concept. In other words, the simplicity, explicitness, disembeddedness and the elasticity of the 'healthy-lifestyle' centres make them easy to reproduce and thus to implement the individual–empowerment idea.

Conclusion

Our empirical material clearly shows that two different ideas exist in the field of public health policy. On the one hand, there is the collective–integration idea, which is concerned with social inequality in health, underlining the need for overall municipal planning strategies and cross-sectoral cooperation. On the other hand, there is the individual–empowerment idea, which is concerned with individual health and personal empowerment strategies as the appropriate solution. The national public health policy tries to combine these ideas, but both national and local actors find the policies put forward in the various laws and steering documents unclear, ambiguous and confusing. Even though these ideas potentially could be regarded as complementary, they seem to produce a tension into the national policy and thereby pose a real challenge to local action and implementation.

Notes

1. Thanks to Associate Professor Tor-Ivar Karlsen at the University of Agder for contributing with survey data from his ongoing project 'Working Conditions and Organizational Affiliations among Public Health Coordinators'.
2. The municipal doctor (*Norwegian: kommunelege*) is responsible for medical quality in municipal health services.
3. http://www.helsedirektoratet.no/folkehelse/frisklivssentraler/Sider/default.aspx.

References

Aarsæther, Nils, Falleth, Eva, Nyseth, Toril and Kristiansen, Ronny (eds.) (2012) *Utfordringer for norsk planlegging. Kunnskap, bærekraft, demokrati.* Oslo: Cappelen Damm.
Amdam, Jørgen and Veggeland, Noralv (2011) *Teorier om samfunnsstyring og planlegging.* Oslo: The University Press.
Andersen, Nils Åkerstrøm (2003) *Borgerens kontraktliggørelse.* Copenhagen: Hans Reitzel forlag.

Axelsson, Runo and Axelsson, Susanna B. (2006) 'Integration and collaboration in public health – a conceptual framework', *International Journal of Health Planning and Management,* 21: 75–88.

Brunsson, Nils (2003) 'Organized hypocrisy', in Barbara Czarniawska and Guje Sêvon (eds.), *The Northern Lights – Organization Theory in Scandinavia.* Oslo: Abstrakt forlag.

Christensen, Tom and Lægreid, Per (2007) 'The whole-of-government approach to public sector reform', *Public Administration Review,* 6: 1059–1066.

Czarniawska, Barbara and Sevôn, Guje (1996) 'Introduction', in B. Czarniawska and G. Sevôn (eds.), *Translating Organizational Change.* Berlin: Walter de Gruyter.

Dean, Mitchell (2010) *Governmentality. Power and Rule in Modern Society,* 2nd edition. London: Sage Publications.

Esping-Andersen, Gösta (1990) *The Three Worlds of Welfare Capitalism.* Princeton: Princeton University Press.

Fosse, Elisabeth (2011) 'Different welfare states – different policies? An analysis of the substance of national health promotion policies in three European countries', *International Journal of Health Services,* 2: 255–272.

Fosse, Elisabeth (2012) 'Norwegian experiences', in Dennis Raphael (ed.), *Tackling Health Inequalities. Lessons from International Experiences.* Toronto: Canadian Scholars' Press.

Grimm, Marie J., Helgesen, Marit K. and Fosse, Elisabeth (2013) 'Reducing social inequities in health in Norway: concerted action at state and local levels?' *Health Policy,* 113: 228–235.

Helgesen, Marit K. and Hofstad, Hege (2012) *Regionalt og lokalt folkehelsearbeid. Ressurser, organisering og koordinering. En baseline undersøkelse.* NIBR Rapport nr. 13. Oslo: Norsk Institutt for By og Regionforskning.

Helgesen, Marit K., Hofstad, Hege, Risan, Lars, Stang, Ingun, Rønningen, Grethe E., Lorentzen, Cathrine and Goth, Ursula S. (2014) *Folkehelse og forebygging. Målgrupper og strategier i kommuner og fylkeskommuner.* NIBR-report no. 3. Oslo: Norwegian Institute for Urban and Regional Research.

Jacab, Zsuzsanna (2011) 'Embarking on developing the New European Health Policy – Health 2020', *Journal of Public Health,* 21(1): 130–132.

Karlsen, Tor I. (2014) *Arbeids- og organisasjonsforhold blant folkehelsekoordinatorer.* Unpublished manuscript, University of Agder.

Latour, Bruno (1986) 'The powers of association', in John Law (ed.), *Power, Action and Belief.* London: Routledge and Kegan Paul.

Magnussen, Jon, Vrangbæk, Karsten and Saltman, Richard B. (2009) 'Introduction: the Nordic model of health care', in Jon Magnussen, Karsten Vrangbæk and Richard B. Saltman (eds.), *Nordic Health Care Systems. Recent Reforms and Current Policy Challenges. European Observatory on Health Systems and Policies Series.* Maidenhead: Open University Press, pp. 3–20.

Meyer, John W. and Rowan, Brian (1977) 'Institutionalized organizations: formal structure as myth and ceremony', *American Journal of Sociology,* 83: 340–363.

Mik-Meyer, Nanna and Villadsen, Kasper (2007) *Magtens former. Sociologiske perspektiver på statens møde med borgeren.* Copenhagen: Hans Reitzel forlag.

Nasjonalt nettverk for implementering av samhandlingsreformen (2014) *Statusrapport for samhandlingsreformen, November, 2014.* Available from: http://fylkesmannen.no/Documents/Dokument%20FMST/Helse%20og%20omsorg/

Samhandlingsreformen/Nasjonalt%20nettverk%20-%20statusrapport/
Nasjonalt%20nettverk%20Statusrapport%20171214.pdf

The Norwegian Directorate for Health (2011) *Partnerskap som arbeidsform i regionalt folkehelsearbeid – med oversikt over fylkeskommuners organisering av folkehelsearbeidet*, IS-1935. Available from: https://helsedirektoratet.no/publikasjoner/partnerskap-som-arbeidsform-i-regionalt-folkehelsearbeid-med-oversikt-over-fylkeskommuners-organisering-av-folkehelsearbeidet

The Norwegian Directorate for Health (2013) *Veileder for kommunale frisklivssentraler – Etablering og organisering*, (revidert utgave). Available from: https://helsedirektoratet.no/Lists/Publikasjoner/Attachments/53/IS-1896-Frisklivsveileder.pdf

Plan and Building Act. Available from: https://lovdata.no/dokument/NL/lov/2008-06-27-71

Public Health Act. Available from: https://lovdata.no/dokument/NL/lov/2011-06-24-29

Raphael, Dennis (ed.) (2009) *Social Determinants of Health: Canadian Perspectives*, 2nd edition. Toronto, ON: Canadian Scholars' Press.

Report to the Storting no. 16 (2002–2003) *Prescriptions for a Healthier Norway*. Oslo: Norwegian Ministry of Health.

Report to the Storting no. 12 (2006–2007) *Regional Advantages – Regional Future*. Oslo: Norwegian Ministry of Local and Regional Government.

Report to the Storting no. 47 (2008–2009) *The Coordination Reform*. Oslo: Norwegian Ministry of Health and Care Services.

Report to the Storting no. 34 (2012–2013) *The Public Health Report. Good Health – Common Responsibility*. Oslo: Norwegian Ministry of Health and Care Services.

Rommetveit, Hilmar, Opedal, Ståle, Stigen, Inger Marie and Vrangbæk, Karsten (2014) *Hvordan har vi det idag, da? Flernivåstyring og samhandling i norsk helsepolitikk*. Bergen: Fagbokforlaget.

Røvik, Kjell A. (2007) *Trender og translasjoner. Ideer som former det 21. århundrets organisasjon*. Oslo: The University Press.

Røvik, Kjell A. (2014) 'Translasjon – en alternativ doktrine for implementering', in Kjell A. Røvik (ed.), *Reformideer i norsk skole. Spredning, oversettelse og impelmentering*. Oslo: Universitetsforlaget, pp. 403–418.

Sarapuu, Külli, Lægreid, Per, Randma-Liiv, Tiina and Rykkja, Lise H. (2014) 'Lessons learned and policy implications', in Per Lægreid, Külli Sarapuu, Lise H. Rykkja and Tiina Randma-Liiv (eds.), *Organizing for Coordination in the Public Sector. Practices and Lessons from 12 European Countries*. Basingstoke: Palgrave Macmillan, pp. 263–277.

Scott, W. Richard (2013) *Institutions and Organizations. Ideas, Interests and Identities*, 4th edition. Los Angeles, CA: Sage.

Scott, W. Richard and Meyer, John W. (ed.) (1994) *Institutional Environments and Organizations: Structural Complexity and Individualism*. Thousand Oaks, CA: Sage.

Torjesen, Dag O. and Vabo, Signy I. (2014) 'Samhandlingsreformen – virkemidler for koordinering', in Mia Vabø and Signy I. Vabo (eds.), *Velferdens organisering*. Oslo: Universitetsforlaget.

Vrangbæk, Karsten and Sørensen, Lærke M. (2013) 'Does municipal co-financing reduce hospitalisation rates in Denmark?' *Scandinavian Journal of Public Health*, 41(6): 616–622.

Waldorff, Susanne B. (2010) 'Et nytt sundhedscenter – men for hvem', in Peter Kjær and Anne R. Pedersen (eds.), *Ledelse gennem patienten.* Copenhagen: Handelshøjskolens forlag.

World Health Organization (2012) *Implementing Health 2020: 2012–2014.* Available from: https://euro.sharefile.com/download.aspx?id=s73db1a792664325a

2

The Path from Policy to Practice: Resilience of Everyday Work in Acute Settings

Robyn Clay-Williams, Julie K. Johnson, Deborah Debono and Jeffrey Braithwaite

Implementation of policy in terms of detailed rigid protocols and procedures is perennially at odds with how everyday work is enacted in healthcare. This is especially evident when the needs of patients cannot be met by following guidance as written and can manifest as disconnects and misunderstandings between policymakers and clinicians. Healthcare is a complex adaptive system that does not lend itself to linear processes and 'one-size-fits-all' solutions, or standardization. This chapter provides a critique of policy implementation processes and presents an alternate perspective of policy implementation translated in terms of intent rather than inflexible directives. Several examples from acute care settings are provided to illustrate this perspective. Allowing for flexible interpretation of policy to meet the needs of patient care can result in a more resilient – and potentially safer – healthcare system.

Policy and practice in a complex adaptive system

Policy is a statement of intent, and this intent is normally given effect by translating it into protocols and procedures to be used within organizations. Development of policies and subordinate guidance is meant to give effect to above-down workplace decisions and provide a degree of standardization and predictability of outcomes. Safety is another aim – often, a by-product – of policy implementation.

A commonly held theory of policy enactment is that it cascades through the organizational layers down to the coalface, such that behaviours on the ground are enabled or constrained by policy effect. A closer look suggests this is an idealized perspective rather than a convincing depiction of the world. Consider: if we look at a typical hospital through multiple lenses (Bolman and Deal, 2008), we may see a complex political milieu with murky and deceptive cultural displays instead of an orderly layered arrangement. There is not one clear organizational structure but a dual hierarchy (Rizzo et al., 1970). One hierarchy represents the non-clinical business aspects of running the organization, and most hospitals produce an improbably neat wiring diagram showing functional relationships between departments such as administration and finance, human resources, logistics, governance and information technology. The other hierarchy is the clinical system, consisting of doctors, nurses and allied health professionals working in clinical pecking orders, in departments structured in terms of organ, disease, acuity level or patient population. Instrumental thinkers assume in such a system that policy developed at peak organizational level is interpreted and implemented as intended at departmental level and distributed from the business hierarchy where the executives reside to health professionals at the bedside, via the clinical and information systems (Braithwaite et al., 2009). Substantial compliance is assumed.

Structural diagrams provide a rationalized, aggregated and completely misleading view of how hospital systems and their components interact and of how policy is enacted in the workplace. In reality, healthcare is a complex adaptive system, with capacity to self-organize and learn, and hospitals consist of a bewildering range of interacting agents and processes (Zimmerman et al., 1998; Braithwaite et al., 2013a). A functioning clinical unit has both clinical and business aims, and to maintain itself as a functioning unit it must (1) do the work, (2) meet the needs of both its staff and the patients for whom it provides care (Nelson et al., 2011) and (3) create a sustainable culture which is purposeful enough to succeed under varying conditions (Braithwaite et al., 2009). Even when a unit is sufficiently purposeful, politics, subcultures, multiple agendas, power plays and sociological complexity are rife. On the tortuous path from policy to practice, processes and protocols emanating from policy directives can be transformed, distorted, re-interpreted, ignored, resisted, miscommunicated or worked around to such a degree that there is little relationship between the original intent and the eventual action.

Analysing the gap

One gateway for analysing the gap between policy and practice is through Argyris's distinction between 'theory espoused' versus 'theory in use' (Argyris and Schon, 1974; Argyris, 2010). Clinicians typically believe that they are acting in a way consistent with the organization's vague but oft-repeated vision to provide safe and effective patient care, but in fact they are discharging their professionally anchored obligations. They deliver care to patients minute by minute, hour by hour, day by day, mostly safely, and with high levels of expertise, because that is their professional and moral duty. As a consequence largely of workload, task fragmentation, work pace and social or other pressures, they are not routinely following the institutional protocols that were designed to achieve that vision (Hunt et al., 2012; Runciman et al., 2012). They have recourse more to their own mindlines (their own theory in use) for care delivery than formalized guidelines (the organization's espoused theory) (Gabbay and May, 2004). The continuing everyday accomplishment of successful patient care by staff on the front line using workarounds or modified procedures can thus mask the fact that policy is not necessarily being followed.

Some examples of the policy–practice disconnect

We provide some examples of nurses' use of workarounds to illustrate the central point, drawn from Debono (Debono, 2014) as part of an ethnographic study of in situ behaviours in acute settings in Australia. Workarounds are practices that may differ from organizationally prescribed or intended procedures that are employed to circumvent a perceived or actual hindrance to achieving a goal (Debono et al., 2013, Alter, 2014). The goal in the described scenarios was safe patient care. Workarounds highlight how clinicians navigate tensions between the implementation of policy and technology as intended and the demands of delivering care in real time (Koppel et al., 2008; Debono and Braithwaite, 2015) and as such provide a useful lens with which to examine the policy–practice disconnect.

The first example, captured in an interview with a senior registered nurse, describes a potential threat to patient safety should nurses always follow medication orders. While the Five Rights of medication administration (5 Rs) may have been correct (Right medication, Right dose, Right route, Right time, Right patient), administering the medication as ordered posed an aspiration risk for some patients even when mixed with thickened fluids. Having identified a potential threat to patient safety, formal solutions to quality and safety concerns developed by those disconnected from the delivery of care can be slow to be designed or delivered, ineffective, time consuming and poorly aligned with current workflow. The second example exposes emergence of a policy–practice disconnect when technology designed to enforce policy does not support it in practice. These examples elucidate the perceived powerlessness of front-line nurses in the development and introduction of policies and guidelines that purport to directly influence their clinical practice. In both scenarios, workarounds were employed until an acceptable solution was available.

Example 1

Many elderly patients on medical wards have difficulty swallowing. To protect their airway and minimize the risk of aspiration and subsequent pneumonia, these patients are restricted to 'thickened fluids'. Elderly patients are often ordered medication to ensure bowel regularity (aperient). A popular and consistently prescribed aperient medication, available as a powder, is mixed with fluid and administered as a drink. However, the medication inactivates the thickening agent, making the reconstituted medication thin. This presents an aspiration risk for those patients who, because of their swallowing difficulties, are ordered thickened fluids.

A nurse in Debono's (2014) example explains that, given the potential risk to those patients with compromised swallowing and the propensity of some nurses to follow medication orders without questioning, she has agitated for safety measures to be introduced in relation to the medication. Two solutions have been offered by hospital managers to alleviate this safety concern. The first solution involves thickening agent and equipment not yet available. A second solution, which is to implement instructions contained in a document borrowed from another hospital detailing a specific method to prepare the medication, underscores the perceived disconnect between those who prepare guidelines and those who have to implement them:

> we're trying to medicate the patient, feed the patient, bathe the patient, observe the patient, write notes on the patient. It's got to be a quick and simple solution, if not we'll just go [a different brand], that's the option... Well they did produce some document; they got some document from another hospital saying 'this is how you make it up'. I was like, 'Have you actually done it?' None of them had, none of them of course because they don't do meds.... but they came and said here's the policy, follow that and I went 'Have you actually done this?' [they responded] 'No, why would I?' I said 'That's exactly right, why are you making decisions about what nurses do?'

Unable to find a simple or acceptable solution to the problem, the nurse works around the problem by introducing a blanket rule that the medication is banned on the ward for all patients (even those who can tolerate thin fluids). This workaround reduces the risk of patients with compromised swallowing inadvertently being administered thin fluids. In essence, the nurse has created a workaround because she needs a practical solution to the problem (Debono, 2014).

Example 2

Information technology (IT) has been implemented to support safe patient care. IT may enforce existing policy and be accompanied by new guidelines and policies that direct how it should be used in practice. Like many policies, technology designed away from the clinical coalface may be unable to adjust to the constantly shifting priorities and demands or accommodate failures in the system when delivering care. Clinicians use workarounds to manage a mismatch between technology and associated policies and actual workflow (Varpio et al., 2006; McAlearney et al., 2007; Koppel et al., 2008; Rack et al., 2012).

We describe nurses' use of workarounds with electronic medication management systems as an exemplar of policy–technology–practice disconnect. Increasingly, electronic medication records (EMRs) are replacing paper medication records (PMRs). Medication administration policy dictates that the EMR must be taken to the patient bedside to enable the patient identification information (PII) on the EMR to be checked against the PII on a patient's identification band (ID band). Once checked, policy further dictates that the medication be signed off as administered in the EMR only after it has been administered. In reality, sometimes 'IT black spots', causing loss of EMR connectivity, prohibit a responsive EMR being taken to the bedside. There is no practical way to comply with the guidelines as written. Nurses work around the barrier created by the 'IT black spots' by leaving the EMR outside the patient's room, signing off the medication before actually administering it and transcribing PII on paper or memorizing it from the EMR to check against the patient ID band (Koppel et al., 2008; Debono, 2014).

Because the workarounds in our nursing examples do not result in adverse events (to the contrary, they are acting to prevent patient harm), these deviations from policy are unlikely to come to the attention of management. This also means that these types of problems are unlikely to be addressed. Unaware that there are problems that are being solved constantly by front-line staff, organizations are unable to address and improve them (Tucker et al., 2002; Tucker and Edmondson, 2003). Indeed, organizations are thought to be at risk of being brittle where there is a disconnect between how managers believe work is done and how tasks are actually accomplished at the coalface (Dekker, 2006; Dekker, 2011). It is easy to see in such circumstances how new policy is developed based on a false understanding of how care is actually maintained and how over time policy can diverge markedly from practice. As we saw in the examples, however, strong insistence on policy compliance is unlikely to hold the key to better patient care. If the nurses in our examples did not deviate in practical, sensible and innovative ways from policy as prescribed, standards of care might be compromised.

Processes for improving care may have lessons for policy into practice

Theory drawn from patient safety may hold some clues in how to proceed. Traditional approaches to patient safety involve reducing the number of things that go wrong, or the instances of variation from rules or procedures, or mitigating the level of harm that occurs. This thinking, known as 'Safety-I', is grounded in the idea that things that go wrong are caused by different processes to things that go right. This approach results in an organization where resources dedicated to safety are in competition with resources needed to conduct core business. However, in everyday activities, positive outcomes are the norm rather than the exception. Things that go right happen all the time and are therefore readily ignored or forgotten – they are nothing out of the ordinary. Safety-I thinking can lead to effective solutions in situations where processes are linear and modes of failures are repetitive or predictable. Complex adaptive systems such as healthcare, however, are intractable. Rigid processes and stringent application of policy directives can be problematic in healthcare due to the variability, complexity and need for flexibility in diagnosing and treating patients and can often – as we have seen – encourage workarounds and violations of policy directives.

In a complex adaptive system, safety and performance are likely to be greater if we encourage organizational resilience (Hollnagel et al., 2011). Resilience is 'the intrinsic ability of a system to adjust its functioning prior to, during, or following changes and disturbances, so that it can sustain required operations under both expected and unexpected conditions' (Hollnagel et al., 2011: xxxvi). Resilient systems will likely succeed under varying conditions. Resilience is the opposite of brittleness, which tends to be a characteristic of systems with overly prescriptive mandates and tightly coupled elements such as in inflexible chains of command. A resilient organization will be tolerant to variation between policy and practice, and clinicians will have some degrees of freedom to alter practice to meet the intent of the policy, whereas a system that is brittle will only tolerate relatively rigid compliance with policy directives (Hollnagel et al., 2013).

First story, second story

We can look at any adverse system event in terms of a 'two stories' perspective (Cook et al., 1998). The 'first story', in linear thinking mode, goes as follows: something has gone wrong, find out what happened, attribute actions to people, uncover the root causes and fix the system so this doesn't happen again (Cook, 2013). For example, after investigation and root cause analysis of an adverse event leading to a death in a large Australian hospital, it was decided that reinforcing compliance with protocols was the most promising solution to prevent future occurrences. However, when implementing this solution, governance staff discovered that multiple and conflicting protocols were potentially applicable to the situation and that determining the correct protocol to follow in the situation investigated, within the time required to safely treat the patient, would have been almost impossible (Johnson, 2013). The hospital is now investigating a multipronged approach to safety, where insistence on compliance with protocols is supported by alternate methods of best practice. This brings us to the 'second story'. This departs from first story accounts by pointing out that on inspection things are far more complex than first thought. This view says that there are multiple interacting variables where guidance as to course of action may be conflicting and there may be no identifiable 'root cause' to an adverse event. Indeed, typically there are many interacting, cross-cutting, deceptive and ambiguous determinants and pseudo-determinants of events in organizational settings.

A better solution may be to uncover areas where things went right and strengthen the system so that more things are done well instead of striving to stamp out harm. This alternative approach is known as 'Safety-II' (Hollnagel et al., 2013). In this logic, people may need to adhere to the *intent* of the policy and not its specific rules, thereby allowing – and even promoting – flexibility as to how that intent is enacted. To illustrate, we present a brief outline, drawn from a case study of implementation of a new rounding policy in an acute general medical ward.

Lessons from a case study: A new rounding policy and protocol

As part of a ward restructuring process, a large regional hospital in Australia recently made a policy decision to introduce a highly structured inpatient ward round at approximately the same time each day. The bedside round is coordinated by an early-career doctor, and conducted with input from the patient, family, nursing staff, allied health professionals including pharmacists and other doctors (ranging from junior, to mid-career, to senior medical practitioner). Although not a new idea, but more of a return to a previous era of hospital care, multidisciplinary rounds on general medicine units have seen a resurgence as clinical teams work to improve quality and safety of patient care (O'Leary et al., 2010, 2011a, 2011b). One manifestation of this concept has emerged from ward redesign at Emory Healthcare in Atlanta by the name of Structured Interdisciplinary Bedside Rounds (SIBR), which includes a structured ward round conducted in combination with an actively managed unit-based team, accompanied by joint nursing–medical leadership, explicit team values and the provision of regular performance feedback to the unit (Pain et al., 2012). While SIBR was designed as a rigid protocol where members of the rounding team are required, under strict time limits, to deliver reports about patient condition and treatment using predefined criteria, the *intent* of the redesigned round was to increase interdisciplinary communication and collaboration and thereby improve team functioning, patient care and staff satisfaction. Thus, it turns out that it is not rigid in its application, but a flexible solution to the challenging problem of improving teamwork in a clinical microsystem (Mohr and Batalden, 2002; Mohr et al., 2004).

If we look at the redesign of ward rounds as an example, we can learn several lessons from the process for implementation of a protocol that is aligned with clinical work processes. First, it must be *adaptive*, with managers partnering with clinicians throughout the implementation process with dedicated lead-in time to the new care model. For example, leaders of a multi-institutional redesign effort can conduct site visits to see how the redesign works in practice and hospital leaders can work with clinicians on the ward to be explicit about the assumptions and values that are driving the change. Second, clinician engagement is required in planning the implementation so that there is greater understanding of workflow and priorities in the unit. To be successful, each member of an interdisciplinary team needs to understand how other members of the team conduct their business: what are the tasks that nurses need to accomplish in the morning prior to the ward rounds? What are the pharmacist's responsibilities to other units in the hospital? How do requests for blood draws and lab results by a certain time affect the rest of hospital? Until this level of understanding occurs, it is infeasible to implement the policy at the ward level.

In addition to spending more time consulting with staff who are directly participating in the policy implementation, early consultation with other hospital departments that interface with the unit may avoid potential difficulties. Radiology, pathology and the emergency department processes can directly impact on the restructured unit as they are primary sources of patients and data to support care. Inclusion of these departments in planning, and creating more opportunities for their bottom-up involvement and input, may help both implementation and ongoing operation of the unit to run more smoothly.

In contradistinction, we often see executives attempting to implement a protocol instrumentally, without informing clinicians of the intent behind the changes. While there are generally excellent organizational reasons for clinical redesign, including consolidation of resources and better distribution of experienced staff, without adequate clinician engagement the disconnect between the executives and the coalface can be exacerbated, especially if clinicians misinterpret the directives as financially driven, excessively controlling or micromanaging. Further, there can be a disconnection between how some executives see the engagement process and how it is viewed at the front line. The time required by front-line staff to accept and prepare for change is often longer than anticipated by organizational executives. Greater preparation time would help some staff to better acclimatize to the changes. There is variation in how people adapt to change, and those who perceive change as a threat or disruption may take longer to adapt.

Discussion

If we want to implement policy in a way that is compatible with how everyday activities are conducted and in terms of Safety-II thinking, we need an accommodative process, which must recognize local cultural characteristics (Stetler et al., 2011). The importance of culture in the healthcare workplace is often discussed, but the full implications of the impact of culture when making changes are frequently underestimated

(Braithwaite et al., 2009). It is often the small things that define a culture, which can ultimately make a big difference to job satisfaction and teamwork. Our case study of redesigned ward rounds demonstrates how changing processes of care can involve new inter-professional ways of working that disrupts older stovepiped clinical cultures and relationships (Braithwaite et al., 2013b). Development of a new culture takes time (Braithwaite et al., 2005) and can lag organizational structural changes by months or even years (Clay-Williams, 2013). In addition, modern hospital systems often perpetuate the old culture, for example a system where clinical staff rotate every 10 to 12 weeks as is common in medicine. The systems that have been carefully constructed have the potential to disrupt or slow down development of the new culture.

Distributed leadership is a critical theme in supporting a culture of flexible resilience that is required in implementing protocols (Ingebrigtsen et al., 2014). There is a need for buy-in from executives, doctors and senior nursing and allied health professionals – all staff working at the front lines of patient care. Engagement and consultation, both prior to and during implementation of a policy, are essential (Edmondson et al., 2001).

It was also important in our ward rounding case example for leaders to foster teamwork, including explicit efforts to establish a vision for the newly constituted unit, to clarify project and unit values and goals and to place considerable emphasis on clear and open communication – formal and informal communication at multiple levels, using a variety of media. Leaders who focus on the benefits of any proposed new model of care are likely to be more successful in fostering changes than others. Engagement and ongoing consultation, supported by effective communication, also help in minimizing the differences between how work is conducted and how work is envisioned by executives and policymakers.

Conclusion

We began with the proposition that the application of policy is best seen in complex rather than linear terms and argued that resilient care is more likely when policy is expressed as broad guidance rather than when it is overdetermined by authorities beyond the clinical coalface. Our examples of nurse workarounds emerging from policy–practice disconnects and the use of adaptive thinking in a new model for inpatient ward rounds highlight this thesis. Hospitals are full of smart, well-trained and motivated people who can interpret guidance, implement solutions and deliver care that to a considerable extent is high quality and safe for patients. We illustrated this in two examples and a case study.

It is the role of leaders to provide encouragement, engagement and responsibility to improve patient care and to maintain strong connections with front-line clinicians to facilitate as smooth a path as possible between policy and practice in everyday activities. And it is the role of clinicians at the coalface to appreciate the broad intent of the policy landscape and adjust their practices to carry out that broad intent rather than to slavishly follow policies to the letter.

References

Alter, S. (2014) 'Theory of workarounds', *Communications of the Association for Information Systems*, 34: 1041–1066.

Argyris, C. (2010) *Organizational Traps: Leadership, Culture, Organizational Design*. Oxford, UK: Oxford University Press.

Argyris, C. and Schon, D. A. (1974) *Theory in Practice: Increasing Professional Effectiveness*. San Francisco: Jossey-Bass.

Bolman, L. G. and Deal, T. E. (2008) *Reframing Organizations: Artistry, Choice, and Leadership*, 4th edition. San Francisco: Jossey-Bass Publishing.

Braithwaite, J., Westbrook, M. T., Iedema, R., Mallock, N. A., Forsyth, R. and Zhang, K. (2005) 'A tale of two hospitals: assessing cultural landscapes and compositions', *Social Science & Medicine*, 60: 1149–1162.

Braithwaite, J., Hyde, P. and Pope, C. (2009) *Culture and Climate in Health Care Organisations*. UK: Palgrave Macmillan.

Braithwaite, J., Clay-Williams, R., Nugus, P. and Plumb, J. (2013a) 'Health care as a complex adaptive system', in E. Hollnagel, J. Braithwaite and R. Wears (eds.), *Resilient Health Care*. Surrey, UK: Ashgate Publishing Limited.

Braithwaite, J., Westbrook, M. T., Nugus, P. I., Greenfield, D. R., Travaglia, J. F., Runciman, W. B., Foxwell, A. R., Boyce, R., Devinney, T. M. and Westbrook, J. (2013b) 'Continuing differences between health professions' attitudes: the saga of accomplishing systems-wide interprofessionalism', *International Journal for Quality in Health Care*, 25(1): 1–8.

Clay-Williams, R. (2013) 'Restructuring and the resilient organisation: implications for health care', in E. Hollnagel, J. Braithwaite and R. Wears (eds.), *Resilient Health Care*. Surrey, UK: Ashgate Publishing Limited.

Cook, R. (2013) 'Resilience, the second story, and progress on patient safety', in E. Hollnagel, J. Braithwaite and R. Wears (eds.), *Resilient Health Care*. Surrey, UK: Ashgate Publishing Limited.

Cook, R., Woods, D. D. and Miller, C. (1998) *A tale of two stories: contrasting views of patient safety*, Report from a workshop on assembling the scientific basis for progress on patient safety. Chicago: National Patient Safety Foundation.

Debono, D. (2014) Engaging with electronic medication management systems in everyday practice: how is it done? Unpublished PhD field notes. University of New South Wales, Sydney, NSW, Australia.

Debono, D. and Braithwaite, J. (2015) 'Workarounds in nursing practice in acute care: a case of a health care arms race?' in R. Wears, E. Hollnagel and

J. Braithwaite (eds.), *The Resilience of Everyday Clinical Work*. Surrey, UK: Ashgate Publishing Limited.

Debono, D., Greenfield, D., Travaglia, J., Long, J., Black, D., Johnson, J. and Braithwaite, J. (2013) 'Nurses' workarounds in acute healthcare settings: a scoping review', *BMC Health Services Research*, 13: 175.

Dekker, S. (2006) 'Resilience engineering: chronicling the emergence of confused consensus', in E. Hollnagel, D. D. Woods and N. Leveson (eds.), *Resilience Engineering: Concepts and Precepts*. Surrey, UK: Ashgate Publishing Limited.

Dekker, S. (2011) *Drift into Failure*. Surrey, UK: Ashgate Publishing Limited.

Edmondson, A. C., Bohmer, R. M. and Pisano, G. P. (2001) 'Disrupted routines: team learning and new technology implementation in hospitals', *Administrative Science Quarterly*, 46: 685–716.

Gabbay, J. and May, A. L. (2004) 'Evidence based guidelines or collectively constructed "mindlines?" Ethnographic study of knowledge management in primary care', *British Medical Journal*, 329: 1013.

Hollnagel, E., Braithwaite, J. and Wears, R. (2013) *Resilient Health Care*. Surrey, UK: Ashgate Publishing Limited.

Hollnagel, E., Pariès, J., Woods, D. D. and Wreathall, J. (2011) *Resilience Engineering in Practice: A Guidebook*. Surrey, UK: Ashgate Publishing Limited.

Hunt, T., Ramanathan, S. A., Hannaford, N. A., Hibbert, P. D., Braithwaite, J., Coiera, E., Day, R. O., Westbrook, J. I. and Runciman, W. B. (2012) 'CareTrack Australia – assessing the appropriateness of adult healthcare: protocol for a retrospective medical record review', *BMJ Open*, 2: e000665.

Ingebrigtsen, T., Georgiou, A., Clay-Williams, R., Magrabi, F., Hordern, A., Prgomet, M., Li, J., Westbrook, J. and Braithwaite, J. (2014) 'The impact of clinical leadership on health information technology adoption: systematic review', *International Journal of Medical Informatics*, 83: 393–405.

Johnson, A. (2013) The right medical leader for the time. *2013 Royal Australian College of Medical Administrators (RACMA) Conference, 4–6 September, Gold Coast, Australia.*

Koppel, R., Wetterneck, T., Telles, J. and Karsh, B. T. (2008) 'Workarounds to barcode medication administration systems: their occurrences, causes, and threats to patient safety', *Journal of the American Medical Informatics Association*, 15: 408–423.

McAlearney, A., Vrontos, J. J., Schneider, P., Curran, C., Czerwinski, B. and Pedersen, C. (2007) 'Strategic work-arounds to accommodate new technology: the case of smart pumps in hospital care', *Journal of Patient Safety*, 3: 75–81.

Mohr, J. J. and Batalden, P. B. (2002) 'Improving safety on the front lines: the role of clinical microsystems', *Quality and Safety in Health Care*, 11: 45–50.

Mohr, J. J., Batalden, P. and Barach, P. B. (2004) 'Integrating patient safety into the clinical microsystem', *Quality and Safety in Health Care*, 13: ii34–ii38.

Nelson, E. C., Batalden, P. B., Godfrey, M. M. and Lazar, J. S. (2011) *Value by Design: Developing Clinical Microsystems to Achieve Organizational Excellence*. San Francisco: Jossey-Bass.

O'Leary, K. J., Buck, R., Fligiel, H. M., Haviley, C., Slade, M. E., Landler, M. P., Kulkarni, N., Hinami, K., Lee, J. and Cohen, S. E. (2010) 'Structured interdisciplinary rounds in a medical teaching unit: improving patient safety', *Archives of Internal Medicine*, 171: 678.

O'Leary, K. J., Haviley, C., Slade, M. E., Shah, H. M., Lee, J. and Williams, M. V. (2011a) 'Improving teamwork: impact of structured interdisciplinary rounds on a hospitalist unit', *Journal of Hospital Medicine,* 6: 88–93.

O'Leary, K. J., Ritter, C. D., Wheeler, H., Szekendi, M. K., Brinton, T. S. and Williams, M. V. (2011b) 'Teamwork on inpatient medical units: assessing attitudes and barriers', *Quality and Safety in Health Care,* 19: 117–121.

Pain, C., Odetoyinbo, D., Castle, B., Methvin, A., Vazquez, J. and Burleson, M. (2012) 'Accountable care unit on a medical ward in a teaching hospital: a new care model designed to improve patient and hospital outcomes [abstract]', *Journal of Hospital Medicine,* 7: 191.

Rack, L., Dudjak, L. and Wolf, G. (2012) 'Study of nurse workarounds in a hospital using bar code medication administration system', *Journal of Nursing Care Quality,* 7: 232–239.

Rizzo, J. R., House, R. J. and Lirtzman, S. I. (1970) 'Role conflict and ambiguity in complex organizations', *Administrative Science Quarterly,* 25(2): 150–163.

Runciman, W. B., Hunt, T. D., Hannaford, N. A., Hibbert, P. D., Westbrook, J. I., Coiera, E., Day, R. O., Hindmarsh, D. M., McGlynn, E. A. and Braithwaite, J. (2012) 'CareTrack: assessing the appropriateness of healthcare delivery in Australia', *Medical Journal of Australia,* 197: 100–105.

Stetler, C. B., Damschroder, L. J., Helfrich, C. D. and Hagedorn, H. J. (2011) 'A guide for applying a revised version of the PARIHS framework for implementation', *Implementation Science,* 6: 99.

Tucker, A. and Edmonson, A. (2003) 'Why hospitals don't learn from failures: organizational and psychological dynamics that inhibit system change', *California Management Review,* 45: 55–72.

Tucker, A., Edmonson, A. and Spear, S. (2002) 'When problem solving prevents organizational learning', *Journal of Organizational Change Management,* 15: 122–137.

Varpio, L., Schryer, C., Lehoux, P. and Lingard, L. (2006) 'Working off the record: physicians' and nurses' transformations of electronic patient record-based patient information', *Academic Medicine,* 81: S35–S39.

Zimmerman, B., Lindberg, C. and Plsek, P. E. (1998) *Edgeware: Insights from Complexity Science for Health Care Leaders.* Irving, TX: US Veterans Health Administration.

3
Dealing with the Challenges of Healthcare Reform: American Hospital Systems Strive to Improve Access and Value through Retail Clinics

Amer Kaissi

Introduction

The passage of new legislation in a certain healthcare system can spark significant change processes in healthcare organizations, where local interpretations, sense making and inherent challenges affect what specific change practices are implemented. The Patient Protection and Affordable Care Act (PPACA), signed by President Barrack Obama on March 23, 2010, is the most significant piece of legislation in the history of American healthcare. Never before has a healthcare-related policy been so fiercely debated, widely beloved and vehemently opposed. The provisions of the act aim to expand coverage, control healthcare costs and improve the healthcare delivery system and therefore have many substantial implications on the way hospital systems provide healthcare services and the way they get paid for those services.

Prior to the passage of PPACA, many hospital systems struggled to provide services for an increasingly large population of uninsured and underinsured patients that could not afford to pay for their care. At the same time, the public and private reimbursement systems favoured these hospitals by paying them for the quantity of services they provided (fee-for-service) without any real concern for quality of care. This situation created interesting strategic and operational dynamics in which many health systems used revenue from payments by privately and publicly insured patients to subsidize some of the uncompensated

39

care that they provided for uninsured patients. In addition, the short-age of primary care physicians (PCPs) and the lack of care alternatives created a real access problem for millions of patients as they faced over-whelmed physician offices and overcrowded emergency rooms (ERs). With the passage of PPACA, many of these dynamics are starting to shift, and while some problems are being fixed, others are left unresolved, and new difficulties are starting to surface.

To deal with the new healthcare landscape, hospital systems have been designing new strategies and changing their day-to-day orga-nizational practices. One of these most recent trends has been the development of hospital-related retail clinics, which are small clinics located in retail and general merchandise stores. In this chapter, we draw heavily upon the results of our previous and current research on retail clinics as well as synthesize the literature in order to examine how the retail clinic strategy fits with hospital system response to PPACA and assess the drivers, interpretations and resisters within hospital systems operating retail clinics. We first review the major provisions of PPACA as it relates to hospital systems and describe retail clinics. We use disruptive innovation theory and constructive destruction theory as two theoreti-cal lenses to help us better evaluate hospital-related retail clinics as a new phenomenon in healthcare. Then, we discuss the strategic and opera-tional challenges that are faced by hospital systems as they engage in this new strategy. We conclude by examining some future implications.

PPACA provisions affecting hospital systems

The Patient Protection and Affordable Care Act (PPACA, also known as Healthcare Reform or Obama-Care in the United States) was passed in 2010. Of the hundreds of the provisions contained in the act, many will directly or indirectly affect hospital systems. The major aspect of the act includes a variety of provisions that aim to address the insurance cover-age gap. These include the individual mandate, the employer mandate, Medicaid expansion, health insurance exchanges and coverage of young adults. The individual mandate requires all citizens and legal residents to have qualifying health coverage or pay a tax penalty of the greater of $695 per year up to a maximum of three times that amount ($2,085) per family or 2.5% of household income (PPACA, 2013). The employer man-date requires employers with 50 or more full-time employees to offer coverage for their employees or pay a premium tax credit fee of $2,000 per full-time employee, excluding the first 30 employees from the assess-ment (PPACA, 2013). In addition, the act calls for all states to expand

Medicaid, the public programme for the poor. The expansion applies to all individuals under age 65 (children, pregnant women, parents and adults without dependent children) with incomes up to 133% of the Federal Poverty Level (FPL). The American Health Benefit Exchanges and Small Business Health Options Program (SHOP) exchanges allow individuals and small businesses with up to 100 employees to purchase health insurance coverage in a newly created healthcare marketplace, in which prices and benefits are easily explained and compared. And lastly, young adults under age 26 are now allowed to be covered under their parents' existing health insurance plan (PPACA, 2013).

As a result of these various provisions, it is expected than an additional 32 million Americans will have insurance coverage by the year 2019 and that the number of underinsured could decrease by 70% (Schoen et al., 2011). This will have major implications on all providers of healthcare services, especially hospital systems and their physicians. As individuals find themselves with coverage or with more adequate coverage, demand for primary care, emergency and specialty services will exponentially increase. However, the supply of physicians, in general, and of PCPs, in particular, is not likely to meet those expected demands. It is well documented that a shortage of about 46,000 PCPs will be observed in the United States by the year 2025 (Bodenheimer and Pham, 2010).

In addition to the general provisions discussed above, PPACA includes several sections relating directly to hospitals and other providers. To help reduce costs and improve quality of care, two new payment systems will be implemented within the next few years: value-based purchasing and bundled payments. These systems will aim to tie public (and private) reimbursement to performance, a clear contrast to previous fee-for-service systems that paid hospitals for the quantity of services delivered. Under value-based purchasing, hospitals will be reimbursed for reporting and meeting specific standards related to efficiency, patient satisfaction and clinical quality metrics (Centres for Medicare and Medicaid, 2013). Under bundled payments, providers will receive a single payment for an episode of care, beginning three days before admission to the hospital and ending 30 days after the patient is discharged. Hospitals and physicians, who previously received separate payments for each service and procedure, will now share one 'capitated' payment, regardless of patient utilization (Centres for Medicare and Medicaid, 2013). Therefore, greater accountability and financial risk will be required by providers, who will see their role shifting from treating individual patients in hospitals or physician offices to managing 'population health' through integrated programmes that allow the system to oversee, and be financially responsible for, a patient's entire continuum of care. As a result, several hospital systems have engaged in new organizational structures referred to as Patient-Centered Medical Homes (PCMHs) and Accountable Care Organizations (ACOs) (American Hospital Association, 2010).

In summary, PPACA creates unique challenges for American hospital systems: an unprecedented increase in demand for primary care and specialty services without a real increase in PCP supply and a new reimbursement system that will reward efficiency and performance, penalize waste and incentivize access, care coordination and population health.

Retail clinics

To respond to the challenges discussed above, hospital systems have experimented with a variety of new strategies and practices as well as with diversification of services to include care provided in new settings such as retail clinics. In this section, we describe the retail clinic trend as a disruptive innovation that was first introduced by non-hospital organizations.

Retail clinics are walk-in clinics located in grocery stores, drugstores and general merchandise retailers. In the United States, these clinics have surfaced in popular stores that are visited by customers several times per week, such as CVS, Walgreens, Target and so on. They offer a limited scope of diagnostic and treatment services for common medical conditions as well as preventative and wellness services (Fottler and Malvey, 2010). Studies show that 90% of retail clinic visits are for simple conditions and services (Mehrotra et al., 2008). Care is delivered by a non-physician provider such as a nurse practitioner or physician assistant, and many clinics have up-front menu-style pricing, a feature that is unparalleled in the American healthcare system (Lin, 2008). The clinics operate on a walk-in basis, with no need for appointments and very short wait times, and are open on evenings and weekends when most PCP offices are closed. They charge an average of $85 per visit and accept all types of insurance plans.

Although innovative, retail clinics can no longer be considered a new model of healthcare delivery as they have been in existence since 2000 and currently number 1,868 clinics nationwide (Merchant Medicine, 2015). Several concerns have been raised about retail clinics' potential for increasing costs, compromising patient safety and quality of care, encouraging over-prescription of antibiotics and reducing delivery of preventive care. However, evidence from recent research suggests that these concerns have been unfounded (Mehrotra et al., 2009; Rohrer et al., 2009; Wilson et al., 2010; Weinick et al., 2010; Jacoby et al., 2011; Rohrer et al., 2012).

Disruptive innovation theory

It is important to note that in the early stages of retail clinic development, retailers and investor-owned companies were driving the growth, while hospital systems were watching from the sidelines. In fact, the retail clinic trend represents a classical example of a disruptive innovation that was introduced by new organizations to replace existing services offered by established organizations such as hospitals and their associated physician offices. Disruptive innovations are a well-known concept that has been coined by Harvard Business School professor Clayton Christensen. They represent powerful changes in which a larger population of less-skilled providers can provide care in more convenient, less expensive settings that historically was provided only by expensive specialists in centralized, inconvenient locations (Christensen, 1997).

When introduced to a market, the performance of a product or service gradually improves over time. There are two types of trajectories of performance improvement: sustaining innovations and disruptive innovations. Sustaining innovations, as the label suggests, sustain the existing trajectory of performance improvement. These are products and services of the highest quality that are sold to the best and most sophisticated customers at higher profits. However, while sustaining innovations meet the demands of these customers, they almost always overshoot their needs and their ability to absorb it. When that happens, the potential for disruptive innovations emerges, and before long, the majority of the market will prefer the disruptive innovation and the sustaining one will fail or cease to exist (Huang and Christensen, 2008). Disruptive innovations have been slow to come in healthcare, especially before the year 2000. The main reason is the strong resistance that has come from hospitals and physician associations that see the alternatives as a threat to their livelihood (Christensen et al., 2000).

Creative destruction theory

Another theoretical lens that can help better understand the emergence of retail clinics is the theory of creative destruction, coined by Austrian economist Joseph Schumpeter (Schumpeter, 1942). Creative destruction refers to the constant product/service and process innovation mechanism by which new production units and new ways to deliver services replace outdated ones. This innovation is characterized by countless decisions to create and destroy production arrangements and service delivery models. Schumpeter noted that:

> [t]his process of Creative Destruction is the essential fact about capitalism. [...] The fundamental impulse that sets and keeps the capitalist engine in motion comes from the new consumers' goods, the new methods of production or transportation, the new markets, the new forms of industrial organization that capitalist enterprise creates. (p. 83)

In this sense, innovators and entrepreneurs introduce new products and services in order to generate profits. New models, new goods and new services compete with existing ones in the marketplace, taking customers by offering lower prices, better performance, new features, faster service or more convenient locations. Paradoxically, this pursuit of self-interest by innovators starts the progress that benefits everyone in the marketplace. Existing companies survive by streamlining production with newer and better tools that make employees more productive, whereas those that no longer deliver what consumers want at competitive prices lose customers and eventually wither and die. Resources are shifted from declining sectors to more valuable uses as workers, inputs and financial capital seek their highest returns. The emergence of retail clinics represents an intriguing example of gradual creative destruction in primary healthcare delivery. The entrepreneurs, retailers and venture capitalists that first introduced the model were driven by profit maximization motives. However, by introducing an innovation that provides services that are cheaper, faster, more convenient and as effective as services provided in PCP offices, they generated a greater good for healthcare consumers. Some hospital systems saw the potential for improved delivery and revenue generation and made strategic decisions to streamline their existing services and integrate them with retail clinics.

Hospital system strategies and practices

Hospital systems are quickly seeking to take advantage of the retail clinic model by expanding their continuum of care and controlling referrals to their own physicians, ERs and the hospitals. Building on their recognizable community brand, they have started to compete head-to-head with the major for-profit retail clinic operators. Given that a significant number of patients are worried about staff qualifications and misdiagnoses in the retail clinic setting (Leppel, 2010), hospital systems seem to be in an excellent position to ensure quality and patient safety (Lin, 2008).

Some of the most prestigious hospital systems in the United States such as the Mayo Clinic, Geisinger Health System, Sutter Health and Intermountain Healthcare directly own retail clinics, while others such as the Cleveland Clinic, HCA, Oshner and Allina Health affiliate with retail clinic operators (Fenn, 2008; Lin, 2008; Newbold and O'Neil, 2008; Pollert et al., 2008; Fottler and Malvey, 2010; Kaissi, 2010a).

Table 3.1 summarizes our previous and current research on hospital-related retail clinics. In 2009, prior to the passage of PPACA, we conducted a first wave of eight in-depth interviews with executives in hospital systems that have a relationship with retail clinics. We have reported the results of that work in two papers (Kaissi, 2010a, 2010b). In 2011, with PPACA just signed into law, Merchant Medicine, a consulting company that we are partnered with, conducted a survey of 20 executives from health systems operating retail clinics. The findings were reported in two other papers (Kaissi and Charland, 2013a, 2013b). Lastly, early in 2013, we conducted another wave of interviews with hospital executives with retail clinic relationships, as well as retail clinic executives, retail clinic researchers and other experts in the convenient care and retail clinic field (Kaissi, 2014) (see Table 3.2). Through professional relationships of the study author, we approached these individuals and set up the interviews. The interviews were done by phone between January and March of 2013, and lasted

Table 3.1   Summary of author's research on hospital-related retail clinics

Nature of research	Year conducted	Publications
Qualitative: Interviews with 8 health system executives	2009	Kaissi (2010a) Kaissi (2010b)
Quantitative: Survey of 20 health system executives	2011	Kaissi and Charland (2013a) Kaissi and Charland (2013b)
Qualitative: Interviews with 6 health system executives and retail clinic experts	2013	Kaissi (2014)

Source: Author's own.

Table 3.2   List of interviewees, 2013

Interviewees
1: Expert/retail clinic researcher
2: Health system executive, overseeing 'convenient care' division
3: Health system executive, with retail clinic affiliation
4: Health system executive, with owned retail clinics
5: Expert in retail clinics
6: Executive at retail clinic chain with health system relationships

Source: Author's own.

between 45 and 90 minutes, using structured open-ended questions (Appendix A).

In the following subsections, we draw on the above-mentioned research to analyse hospital systems response by uncovering the strategic drivers, models and challenges (Figure 3.1).

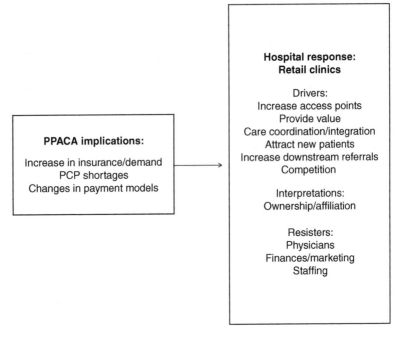

Figure 3.1   Conceptual model
Notes: PPACA – Patient Protection and Affordable Care Act; PCP – primary care physicians.
Source: Author's own.

Strategic drivers

A minority of hospital systems were already involved with retail clinics prior to the passage of PPACA. In 2009, there were 25 health systems nationwide operating retail clinics (Kaissi, 2010a). However, the legislation created new forces that changed the strategic priorities of these systems and forced many other systems to join the trend. Currently, 76 hospital systems operate a retail clinic (Merchant Medicine, 2013). Our research, dating back to 2009, allows us to assess the strategic drivers that were in play before the passage of PPACA, and to understand how these drivers have changed, as implications of PPACA were analysed by existing and new hospital systems that operate retail clinics.

The general reasons that drove general retail clinic growth were overcrowding in hospital ERs, a growing PCP shortage, reduced patient access to care due to increased insurance costs and growing consumer demands for convenience, reliability and affordability (Lin, 2008; Fottler and Malvey, 2010). Our analyses revealed an additional number of strategic drivers that were considered by hospital systems deciding to operate retail clinics prior to the PPACA (Kaissi, 2010a):

- Increasing market share through enhanced referrals to physician offices and hospitals
- Growing closer to consumers and to the community
- Experimenting with non-traditional ways of delivering healthcare
- Branding the health system
- Beating the competition to be the market leader
- Providing a 'release valve' for overcrowded ERs and PCP offices

Our subsequent quantitative research involving 20 hospital systems that own retail clinics confirms that they were overall satisfied with the performance of the clinics in relation to these strategic priorities: 79% of the hospital executive respondents indicated that their organizations were strongly satisfied/satisfied with improved access, 69% were strongly satisfied/satisfied with increased referrals, 74% were strongly satisfied/satisfied with defence against competitors and 79% were strongly satisfied/satisfied with increased brand exposure (Kaissi and Charland, 2013a).

As previously discussed, PPACA will require hospitals to take on substantial financial risks for population health management (Dunn, 2011). Interestingly, hospital systems were already starting to think about the implications of the impending reforms before it passed. For example, one respondent from our 2009 interviews noted that:

> reform will have a positive effect. There are incentives to provide greater access. Retail clinics are part of the reimbursement formula. There is a push for more use of non-traditional providers. New evidence shows that retail clinics provide better value for the dollar, and reform will focus on value.
>
> (Kaissi, 2010b)

The reform becomes much more pronounced and articulated in our recent interviews conducted in early 2013. An executive operating a newly created 'convenient care' division stated:

> PPACA has positioned convenience care very well as a concept in an organization, especially for integrated care and bundled payments. You need to have a breadth of services to meet patients when and where they need them. Especially important for patients who don't have an affiliation with a health system, they want flexibility. So you have to create access points on the patients' terms.
>
> (Kaissi, 2014)

Another hospital executive with partnership relationships with retail clinics stated that systems have 'a need for a network of access points that meet three goals: provide stream of business into the health system, manage care effectively – right care at the right time in the right place, and position the system for clinical integration and managing population health' (Kaissi, 2014). In summary, hospitals systems have geared up for increased demand by offering low-cost, high-value touch points that are compatible with new payment and reimbursement realities.

Strategic models/interpretations

Hospital systems have historically acted as large bureaucratic entities that focus on traditional care provided within the four walls of the hospital or physician office. Their involvement in retail clinics represents an entrepreneurial and innovative strategic move that has been rarely witnessed before. Our research has shown that the two common models of operations between hospital systems and retail clinics include a partnership/affiliation between the retail chain and the hospital system, or full ownership of the retail clinic by the hospital system.

Under a partnership, the retail chain owns and operates the clinics and makes decisions about the location of the clinics and the hiring of the clinicians, while the hospital system provides physician supervision, marketing and support for referrals. With ownership, the hospital system owns the clinics, decides on the location of the clinics, employs the clinicians and pays rent to the retail chain for the space provided (Kaissi, 2010a).

Three main management structures are typically used by hospital systems to run owned retail clinics: management by the hospital system medical group (40%); management by the hospital system outpatient services group (35%); and management by a group within hospital system administration (25%) (Kaissi and Charland, 2013b). Experts suggest that while the partnership model represents the least amount of risk for the hospital system, the ownership model has the greatest potential for achieving integration goals and better positioning the organization for PPACA (Pollack et al., 2010).

Resisters/challenges

Early adopters of retail clinics among hospital systems entered into this strategy with the assumption that it is a straightforward business model that will generate significant revenues and lucrative downstream referrals at a relatively low cost. However, they soon realized that many significant operational, financial and promotional resisters exist. Our 2009 research suggested that physician resistance and scepticism topped the list of challenges (Kaissi, 2010a). Several physician groups have raised serious concerns about retail clinics (Paddock, 2007). These concerns relate to the potential for fragmentation of care, especially for patients with special healthcare needs and chronic conditions, and to the possibility of compromised quality and patient safety, particularly when patients present with serious conditions that may be beyond the scope of practice of nurse practitioners and physician assistants. Not surprisingly, physicians felt threatened by the competition presented by retail clinics, as these tend to attract their easy-to-treat patients and leave them with the most complex patients.

Moreover, many of the retail clinics were facing serious financial struggles, which led to clinic closures in some markets. One medical director of a clinic explained: 'The margin of profitability is very narrow, if you are seeing 25–30 patients per day then you need to hire a second clinician, which is very expensive. No one is going to make a lot of money from this business' (Kaissi, 2010a). A related concern has to do with marketing and the difficulty to change public perceptions. While the number of retail clinics had grown exponentially by 2009, many people still did not understand what these clinics do and what services they offer, while others were very sceptical about their quality of care (Leppel, 2010).

In addition, staffing, recruitment and retention of mid-level providers proved problematic for some systems. The non-challenging and limited nature of the services provided made it hard to keep the providers motivated and engaged. In order to deal with this issue, some systems had their retail clinic nurse practitioners work one or two days per week at a family clinic in order to keep them challenged and satisfied (Pollert et al., 2008).

Subsequent research conducted in 2011 showed that many of these issues were still relevant among hospital system owners of retail clinics (Kaissi and Charland, 2013a). Executives from these systems indicated moderate-to-low levels of satisfaction with physician support and backing (47%). Moreover, 63% indicated they were dissatisfied/strongly dissatisfied with profitability of the clinics, 53% were dissatisfied/strongly dissatisfied with patient volumes and 42% were dissatisfied/strongly dissatisfied with response to marketing initiatives. Additional analyses revealed that only 5 out of 20 hospital systems had their retail clinics operating at financial breakeven (Kaissi and Charland, 2013b).

More recent interviews offer mixed results. An executive at a retail clinic chain with relationships with hospital systems offered this explanation:

> Consumers are accepting of the concept [of retail clinics], payers have been contracting with retail clinics, and retailers want the clinics. And physician resistance has dissipated. The basic value proposition of quality, convenience and affordability is very attractive to consumers and payers. But the business model is still challenging. You have to process a lot of patients at a relatively low margin. So how do you turn it into a sustainable business? We are providing value; there is no question about that. But the question is how to create a sustainable, efficient model?
>
> (Kaissi, 2014)

In addition, staffing remains an important issue. As competition for nurse practitioners and physician assistants continue to intensify, their salaries continue to climb. One executive of a health system that owns clinics summarized:

The major challenge is finding an adequate number of mid-level providers. There is a lag in supply, and an increase in the number of clinics hiring them. Also, the challenge is also to keep them, as many of them want broader scope of practice and are trained to do so much more.

(Kaissi, 2014)

Tracking downstream referrals and revenues also continue to worry hospital system executives. An executive in a hospital system partnering with retail clinics recently warned:

One area that we haven't managed well with retail clinics is hard-wiring of downstream referrals. We have provided them with our physician referral line, but what we need is to go ahead and schedule the appointment with our physician while the patient is still at the clinic, and track that patient down, call them a day before the visit, and if they don't show up to the visit and call them to follow-up and reschedule. We need better capturing of downstream business to quantify the benefits and return on investment. Just co-branding is not sustainable.

(Kaissi, 2014)

This represents a serious issue for many cost-conscious health executives who have to continuously justify the investment in retail clinics by showing potential increased referrals and profits.

Conclusion

Our findings suggest that specific strategic drivers related to the PPACA, such as the need to improve access points and to provide a continuum of care that directs patients away from expensive delivery settings, have impacted hospital systems' decisions to operate retail clinics. The change processes and models implemented in response to these drivers include affiliation with existing retail clinic chains or building and ownership of new retail clinics. Several challenges such as opposition from physicians, financial and staffing concerns, and unrealized downstream referrals have slowed down or impeded some of these practices. Retail clinics can be described as a disruptive innovation and as an example of creative destruction in primary healthcare delivery. However, according to disruptive innovation theory, incumbent organizations with sustaining innovations are driven out by new organizations with disruptive innovations and tend to disappear and cease to exist. Retail clinics as a disruptive innovation seem to follow a slightly different path. While they were originally introduced by new organizations such as retailers and investor-owned companies, hospitals have joined the trend and got involved in the disruptive innovation, partly in order to better position themselves for the PPACA.

Given the recency of the policy change (PPACA) and its gradual implementation in the last four years and expected continued implementation over the next few years, much remains to be seen about how hospital systems will continue to address the trend. While the majority of health systems believe that the trend is here to stay and that they will continue their retail clinics strategies, others don't share this view and are still unsure if this is a viable long-term plan (Kaissi, 2010b; Kaissi and Charland, 2013a). Furthermore, hospital systems are getting involved in additional convenient care strategies that provide services in nontraditional settings such as urgent care centres and online healthcare services. Future research should continue to investigate the implications of these trends on cost, quality and access in American hospital systems and within the context of healthcare reform.

Appendix A: Questions for 2013 interviews

1. When did your organization start getting involved in retail clinics and other convenient care models?
2. How many retail clinics and other convenient care models do you have?
3. What are some the major challenges faced by your retail clinics and other convenient care models?
4. What do you do to insure quality of care?
5. What are your expectation/forecasts for growth for your clinic(s)? For the field itself?
6. What do you think the implications of the Affordable Care Act will be on your organization? On the field?
7. What do you think the implications of the PCP shortage will be on your organization? On the field?

References

American Hospital Association (2010) *Committee on Research. AHA Research Synthesis Report: Accountable Care Organization.* Chicago: American Hospital Association.

Bodenheimer, T. and Pham, H. H. (2010) 'Primary care: current problems and proposed solutions', *Health Affairs*, 29: 799–805.

Centres for Medicare and Medicaid (2013) [Online] Available from: http://www.cms.gov/Medicare/Quality-Initiatives-Patient-Assessment-Instruments/hospital-value-based-purchasing/index.html?redirect=/Hospital-Value-Based-Purchasing/ [Accessed November 23rd, 2014].

Christensen, C. (1997) *The Innovator's Dilemma: When New Technologies Cause Great Firms to Fail*. Boston: Harvard Business School Press.

Christensen, C., Bohmer, R. and Kenagy, J. (2000). 'Will disruptive innovations cure health care?' *Harvard Business Review*, September–October; 78(5): 102–12, 199.

Dunn, L. (2011) 'From treating the sick to managing community health: hospitals' new role in managing population health', *Becker's Hospital Review*. [Online] Available from: http://www.beckershospitalreview.com/hospital-management-administration/from-treating-the-sick-to-managing-community-health-hospitals-new-role-in-managing-population-health.html [Accessed November 11th, 2013].

Fenn, S. (2008) 'Integrating retail clinics into the hospital system', *Frontiers of Health Services Management*, 24(3): 33–36.

Fottler, M. and Malvey, D. (2010) *The Retail Revolution in Health Care*. Santa Barbara: Praeger.

Huang, J. and Christensen, C. M. (2008) 'Disruptive innovation in health care delivery: a framework for business-model innovation', *Health Affairs*, 27(5): 1329–1335.

Jacoby, R., Crawford, A. G., Chaudhari, P. and Goldfarb, N. I. (2011) 'Quality of care for 2 common paediatric conditions treated by convenient care providers', *American Journal of Medical Quality*, 26(1): 53–58.

Kaissi, A. (2010a) 'Hospital-affiliated and hospital-owned retail clinics: strategic considerations and operational challenges', *Journal of Health Care Management*, 55(5): 325–329.

Kaissi, A. (2010b) 'The future of retail clinics in a volatile healthcare environment', *The Health Care Manager*, 29(3): 223–229.

Kaissi, A. and Charland, T. (2013a) 'How satisfied are hospital systems with their ownership of retail clinics?' *Journal of Health Care Management*, 58(2): 143–155.

Kaissi, A. and Charland, T. (2013b) 'Hospital-owned retail clinics in the United States: operations, patients and marketing', *Primary Health Care*, 3(1): 1–5.

Kaissi, A. (2014) *Flipping Health Care through Retail Clinics and Convenient Care Models*. Hershey: IGI Global Publishers.

Leppel, K. (2010). 'Factors influencing willingness to use convenient care clinics among baby boomers and older persons', *Health Care Manage Review*, 35(1): 13–22.

Lin, D. Q. (2008) 'Convenient care clinics: opposition, opportunity, and the path to system integration', *Frontiers of Health Services Management*, 24(3): 3–11.

Mehrotra, A., Wang, M. C., Lave, J. R., Adams, J. L. and McGlynn, E. A. (2008) 'Retail clinics, primary care physicians, and emergency departments: a comparison of patients' visits', *Health Affairs*, 5: 1271–1282.

Mehrotra, A., Liu, H., Adams, J. L. Wang, M. C., Lave, J. R., Thygeson, M., Solberg, L. I. and McGlynn, E. A. (2009) 'Comparing costs & quality of care at retail clinics with that of other medical settings for 3 common illnesses', *Annals of Internal Medicine*, 151: 321–328.

Merchant Medicine. (2013). The ConvUrgent Care Report, 6(2): 1–4.

Merchant Medicine (2015) [Online] Available from: http://www. merchantmedicine.com [Accessed Jan 21st, 2015].

Newbold, P. and O'Neil, M. J. (2008) 'Small changes lead to large effects', *Frontiers of Health Services Management*, 24(3): 23–27.

Paddock, K. (2007) 'AMA calls for investigation of retail health clinics', *Medical News Today*.

Patient Protection and Affordable Care Act [Online] Available at: http://www. healthcare.gov/law/full/index.html [Accessed on December 15th, 2014].

Pollack, C. E., Gindengil, C. and Mehrotra, A. (2010) 'The growth of retail clinics and the medical home: two trends in concert or in conflict?' *Health Affairs*, 29(5): 998–1003.

Pollert, P., Dobberstein, D. and Wiisanen, R. (2008) 'Jumping into the healthcare retail market: our experience', *Frontiers of Health Services Management*, 24(3): 13–21.

Rohrer, J. E., Angstam, K. B. and Furst, K. W. (2009) 'Impact of retail walk-in care on early return visits by adult primary care patients', *Quality Management in Health Care*, 1: 18–23.

Rohrer, J. E., Garrison, G. M. and Angstam, K. B. (2012) 'Early return visits by paediatric primary care patients with otitis media: a retail nurse practitioner clinic vs. standard medical officer care', *Quality Management in Healthcare*, 21(1): 44–47.

Schoen, C., Doty, M. M., Robertson, R. H. and Collins, S. R. (2011) 'Affordable care act reforms could reduce the number of underinsured US adults by 70 percent', *Health Affairs*, 30(9): 1762–1771.

Schumpeter, J. (1942) *Capitalism, Socialism, and Democracy*, 3rd edition. New York: Harper and Brothers.

Weinick, R. M., Burns, R. M. and Mehrotra, R. A. (2010) 'Many emergency department visits could be managed at urgent care centres and retail clinics', *Health Affairs*, 29(9): 1630–1636.

Wilson, A. R., Zhou, X. T. and Shi, W. et al. (2010) 'Retail clinics versus office setting: do patients choose appropriate providers?' *The American Journal of Managed Care*, 16(10): 753–761.

4
Institutional Logics and Micro-processes in Organizations: A Multi-actor Perspective on Sickness Absence Management in Three Dutch Hospitals

Nicolette van Gestel, Daniel Nyberg and Emmie Vossen

Introduction

Since healthcare organizations often have significant problems with the recruitment and retention of staff (McKee et al., 2008), preventing sickness absence and improving return-to-work processes are highly relevant for hospitals in order to deliver adequate services and ensure the quality and quantity of healthcare (Boselie et al., 2003). A high turnover of employees increases costs (e.g. recruitment and training) and potentially decreases patient care. Turnover can seriously affect both patients and other employees through higher error rates and increased workloads. In this chapter, we examine the implementation of new legislation aimed at preventing sickness absence and solving obstacles towards the return to work for sick-listed employees. We selected three hospitals in the Netherlands to study how national legislation for sickness absence management is understood and enacted locally by the involved actors.

The design of the change processes within the hospitals in addressing sickness absence focuses on cross-professional collaboration. Since their knowledge is complementary, supervisors, Human Resource (HR) managers and occupational health physicians (OHPs) are required to work together in applying the new legislation. For example, supervisors have the expertise to organize the work at the wards; HR managers have experience with relevant legal rules and procedures; and OHPs are able to determine the physical and mental capabilities of employees for work. Thus, teamwork between these professionals, with different disciplinary backgrounds, is deemed crucial for preventing and addressing employee health problems.

The new legislation for sickness absence management reflects a paradigm shift in European welfare states from 'welfare' to 'activation' (Kluve et al., 2007; Eichhorst et al., 2008; Weishaupt, 2011). In brief, the 'activation paradigm' implies a change in welfare states from 'passive' socio-economic protection (social benefit rights) to the 'activation' of benefit recipients to participate on the labour market (Van Oorschot, 2006). In theoretical terms, the activation paradigm can be perceived as an institutional logic, that is, a set of organizing principles that give direction and meaning to social behaviour. This chapter explores the micro-foundations of such an institutional logic, delving into the local processes that include a diverse range of actors (Powell and Colyvas, 2008: 276; see also Cooney, 2007; Suddaby et al., 2010; Thornton et al., 2012). We aim to understand how the new logic of 'activation' in national sickness absence policies is understood and enacted in the organizational setting of hospitals in the Netherlands.

We make two general contributions to the literature on institutional logics. First, we show that pressure towards adaptation of a new institutional logic does not necessarily lead to a change of professional roles and practices. It may even result in the maintenance of current practices. While the possibility of organizational maintenance despite institutional pressures to change has been suggested before (Lawrence and Suddaby, 2006; Edwards and Jones, 2008), we show *how* such a response is constructed locally in a multi-actor setting. Second, based on our analysis, we explain organizational maintenance by two interrelated mechanisms: (1) a reinforcement of professional boundaries and (2) a disconnection of practices. These mechanisms contribute to our understanding of the (non-)linkages between institutional logics and micro-processes in organizations, thus addressing a recognized gap in institutional theory (Cooney, 2007; Lounsbury and Crumley, 2007; Greenwood et al., 2011).

The chapter is structured as follows. We first review the literature on institutional logics in order to structure our analysis. Second, we describe the shift to the 'activation paradigm' in the context of Dutch sickness absence policies, which is followed by an outline of our research design and data analysis. Third, our findings explain how the new activation logic is supported by multiple actors, but not substantially enacted in the organizations. The findings thus explain organizational maintenance despite institutional pressures to change. Finally, we discuss how our findings contribute to the literature on institutional logics and suggest implications for future research.

Institutional logics and the performance of practices

Institutional logics are perceived as the organizing principles that shape the actions of field participants (Battilana, 2006: 656; Reay and Hinings, 2009: 631). Logics thus represent a shared understanding in a field of what goals to pursue and how to achieve them (Scott, 2008; Thornton et al., 2012). Research on institutional logics has long focused on shifting logics over time (Mazza et al., 2004; Lounsbury and Boxenbaum, 2013). More recently, the debate has moved to the interplay of multiple coexisting and/or competing logics (Greenwood et al., 2011). Despite the extensive study of (multiple/competing) logics and change, little is known yet of how logics interconnect with everyday practices within organizations (Suddaby et al., 2010; Lounsbury and Boxenbaum, 2013; Reay et al., 2013). In particular, we lack insights into how multiple actors with various professional backgrounds negotiate their understanding and enactment of a shift in an institutional logic *locally* (Greenwood et al., 2010; Goodrick and Reay, 2011).

Institutional theory suggests that logics and practices in a field are consistent with each other, or at least become consistent over time (Greenwood et al., 2002; Boxenbaum and Jonsson, 2008). Studies of the institutionalization process have focused on the stage of 'theorizing' institutional change, with a key role for actors to specify problems and justify solutions. For example, Greenwood et al. (2002) found that professional associations performed a major role in specifying problems and justifying solutions to implement a new logic in Canadian accounting firms. In contrast to the wide attention for the theorizing of a new logic, the enactment of logics into roles and practices is usually treated as a natural consequence, which is 'essentially leading to the "black-boxing" of practice' (Lounsbury and Crumley, 2007: 993).

Understanding the relationship between institutional logics and practices can depart from a macro- or micro-perspective. Some studies examined the creation of new practices at the micro-level as a basis for institutionalizing a new logic at the field level (Lounsbury and Crumley, 2007; Smets et al., 2012). For example, Smets and colleagues (2012) studied how the day-to-day enactment of banking practices in an Anglo-German law firm led to a change in the institutional logic prevailing in German law. The colliding English and German logics of banking were incorporated in practice through the lawyers' recognition of the novelty of the logics, a sense of urgency to get the job done and the consequences of failure in meeting deadlines. A new client–service practice was constructed, which spread to other law firms, and ultimately led to a macro-change in the logic of German law.

We take the opposite starting point to understand the relationship between logics and practices by focusing on how a new logic is enacted in local practices within organizations. Recent studies show that there is considerable room for interpretation in applying institutional logics (Greenwood et al., 2011). For example, a study of the Ontario fine wine industry (Voronov et al., 2013) demonstrated 'that institutional logics are not reified cognitive structures, but rather are open to interpretation' (p. 1563). The actors in this industry applied (two) different scripts in enacting an institutional logic, whereby their interpretations varied according to interactions with different audiences. Nevertheless, most studies of logic enactment have not performed an in-depth investigation of multiple actors in a micro-setting (Goodrick and Reay, 2011; Greenwood et al., 2011; Reay et al., 2013).

In this study, we address the issues of how and why multiple practitioners respond to a new logic in a local setting (Greenwood et al., 2010; Goodrick and Reay 2011). We take a further step in understanding the relationship between logics and practices by (1) studying a *multiplicity* of local actors and (2) *linking* the multiple actors' perceptions of a logic to their local practices. We thus go beyond solely investigating the actors' interpretations and perceptions of a logic and their intended responses (the level of ideas and cognition), by studying their roles and (inter)actions in enacting the logic, since the institutionalization of a new logic ultimately takes place in actual practices (Reay et al., 2013). This study thus aims to provide a more complete and in-depth understanding of the relationship between logic prescriptions, multiple actors and micro-practices.

A shift in focus from welfare to activation

Since the mid-1990s, there has been a shift in the dominant logic of European welfare states: from 'passive' welfare systems to 'activation policies' (Kluve et al., 2007; Eichhorst et al., 2008; Weishaupt, 2011). The turn to 'activation' in many areas of the welfare state (e.g. policies for social welfare, labour market, sickness absence) implies a shift in focus from people's inabilities to their capacities to work (James et al., 2002; Van Raak et al., 2005). This is in line with EU and national government aims to reduce public expenditures for social benefits and to increase labour market participation (Van Oorschot, 2006). Although the logic of activation has been first and foremost applied to the area of employment policies (Eichhorst et al., 2008), it has also affected other areas such as the laws and policies for sickness absence (and disability).

Governments across Europe have introduced guidelines and legislations to prevent health problems at work and to reduce absenteeism. Generally in EU countries, the financial responsibility for compensating sick-listed employees' income for employers is around four weeks. In contrast, the Dutch government introduced legislation that required employers to pay for their sick-listed employees during the first year of absence (since 1996). This obligation was later increased to two years in 2004. The Netherlands can therefore be seen as an extreme case of particular value to enlightening the sickness absence processes. The comparatively radical financial incentives underscore the aim of the Dutch government to prevent (long-term) sickness absence and improve the return-to-work process of sick-listed employees. Historically, the relatively strong activation measures in the Netherlands can be traced back to high numbers of social benefit recipients since the late 1970s and a relatively low labour market participation (Van Oorschot, 2006). The main differences between the old and the new logic in Dutch policies for sickness absence can be found in Table 4.1.

The shift from 'welfare' to 'activation' became even more obvious in the Netherlands with the Gatekeeper Improvement Act (2002), which introduced strict return-to-work procedures. For example, organizations are required to produce a problem analysis (diagnosis) and a plan for

Table 4.1 A shift from welfare to activation in sickness absence policies

Sickness absence policies	Welfare logic	Logic of activation
Focus	Inability for work	Capacity for work
Payment in case of illness	Collective funding (based on premiums)	Employers pay in case of illness (1996: one year; 2004: two years)
Return to work activities	Deficient	(Gatekeeper Improvement Act) 2002 (procedures and penalties)
Retain disabled workers	Not obliged by law	Employers are legally obliged to retain employees with >65% capacity after sickness absence (Work and Income according to Labour Capacity Act (2006))

return to work within six to eight weeks after an employee reported ill. The return-to-work plan is to be agreed upon by the employer, the sick-listed employee and the OHP. Regular follow-up conversations and actions (at least every six weeks) are legally required in order to implement this plan during the sickness absence period, up to two years. Collaboration of employers (supervisors, HR managers), employees and OHPs during this process is deemed crucial. Both employers and employees receive financial penalties if they cooperate insufficiently in line with the government procedures: sick-listed employees can be given a wage penalty, while employers' payment of sick-listed employee's salary can be extended beyond two years. Finally, with the new 'Work and Income according to Labour Capacity Act' (2006), the Dutch government introduced an obligation for employers to retain their personnel with a remaining work capacity of 65% or more after two years of sickness absence. This combination of laws and financial penalties in the Dutch national sickness absence policies, following the activation logic, aims to stimulate the prevention of health problems in organizations and to speed up return to work after sickness absence.

Research methods

This study is based on an analysis of how multiple local actors within three hospitals dealt with the shift to the activation logic in sickness absence policies and how they enacted it within their organizations. We studied 21 cases of long-term sick-listed employees (absent for more than six weeks) in three hospitals (see Table 4.2). For each case, we interviewed the line manager, the HR manager, the sick-listed employee and the OHP involved (and others, where relevant); in total, 81 interviews were conducted over a three-year period (September 2008–September 2011).

Given the explorative nature of our study, we selected the hospitals in our study on variation in size (3,500, 5,500 and 9,500 employees), category (an academic hospital and two top clinical hospitals) and location (different regions). In each hospital, we asked the occupational health service (OHS) to identify at least five cases of long-term sick-listed employees (> six weeks). The sick-listed employees' situations included a diverse range of health problems, such as muscular diseases, work stress or cancer, with often a combination of mental and physical illnesses. Most sick-listed employees in our study were women, employed as nurses, laboratory assistants or secretaries and aged over 45. According

Table 4.2 Summary of the data set

Hospital 1	Hospital 2	Hospital 3
5 cases	10 cases	6 cases
• 6 interviews: HR • 5 interviews: line manager • 5 interviews: employee • 5 interviews: OHP • 3 interviews: others (social worker, head of OHS, HR-team leader)	• 4 interviews: HR (re-integration officers) • 10 interviews: line manager • 10 interviews: employee • 3 interviews: OHP • 2 interviews: others (HR-team leaders)	• 6 interviews: HR • 6 interviews: line manager • 6 interviews: employee • 6 interviews: OHP • 4 interviews: others (head of OHS, 2 × social worker; relocation coordinator)
Total = 24 interviews	Total = 29 interviews	Total = 28 interviews

Notes: OHP – occupational health physician; OHS – occupational health service; HR: human resource.
Source: Authors' own.

to the OHS departments, the sample was representative of the hospitals' cases of long-term sickness absence.

In the interviews, we addressed the actors' adherence to the new logic of activation, their interpretation of the reasons for the sickness absence problems and their ideas about solutions for these problems. We further asked the actors for their view on their own role and the roles of the other actors in absence management. While the interviews started with discussing a particular case, the questions were broadened to the actors' experiences with other cases. The interviews lasted 60–75 minutes and were recorded (with a few exceptions) and transcribed.

In analysing the data, we developed case descriptions that summarized the different actors' views on problems, solutions and roles in sickness absence management for each case. Most actors spend considerable time during the interviews explaining the organizational problems that contributed to the sickness absence in the particular case and in the ward more generally, and they emphasized the importance of the logic of activation to prevent long-term illness and to allow for a return to work without a reappearance of illness and absence. We analysed their reflections on their own and others' roles and practices to prevent and solve these problems. From the interviews, core practices in absence management (i.e. diagnosis, prevention, HR policies) could be distinguished, and we analysed if and how these practices were connected. We verified our findings via presentations to the hospitals and discussions with academics and practitioners at (healthcare) conferences.

Understanding the relationship between logics and practices

The empirical material suggests that all involved actors support the new logic of activation as a positive change that stimulates the prevention of employees' health problems and creates better opportunities for (long-term) sick-listed employees to return to work (see Table 4.3). The obvious rationale behind this support is expressed by an OHP: 'Since organisations have to pay for sick-listed employees, they need to be more alert on the causes of absence and the opportunities for return to work'. The

Table 4.3   Supporting the logic of activation

Key elements of the logic of activation	Illustrations of the actor's support for the logic of activation
Focus on employees' capacity for work, instead of incapacity	*HR manager*: When I look at the past, the person was sick and had to recover first before he could come back to the workplace. Now, you should not spend one day at home because you get better at work. That's the idea, which is correct in my opinion. *Line manager*: I keep in contact with the employee on a weekly basis, and I really try to look at what she still *can* do, I believe that is important.
Employers have to pay the salary for the sick-listed employee, up to 2 years	*Line manager*: My interest is a financial interest. [...] My budget is based on a certain percentage of absenteeism what is used in the hospital as a standard. [...] If you're above it you will have a budget deficit. *HR manager*: Yes, there is a lot of attention because, yes, 1% less absenteeism will save you a lot of money.
Return to work procedures (Gatekeeper Improvement Act)	*HR manager*: At first of course it was much of 'what a bureaucratic mess and why should we fill in endless forms' [but] I'm actually quite happy with it. *Line manager*: You have mandatory contact moments as part of the Gatekeeper Improvement Act. The law stipulates more clearly what the obligations are. I am happy with it; otherwise it all becomes too informal.

Source: Authors' own.

HR managers in the hospitals support the new logic and express satisfaction with the national attention to sickness absence problems. The emphasis on 'activation' is clearly present, for example, with one HR manager suggesting that: 'employees should call their supervisor if they are sick and the manager must say: "come to work unless you miss both legs", so to speak'. The general support in the hospitals for the logic of activation includes a role change for line managers, who gained a new role as 'case manager' for the sick-listed employees. One line manager expresses his consent with the new policy accordingly: 'It feels good being responsible in the name of the hospital. [...] Roles and responsibilities are much clearer now'. Overall, the empirical material suggests that the logic of activation and the corresponding national laws and financial incentives receive support by the actors involved in sickness absence management.

However, despite the obvious support for the logic of activation, we found that the organizational problems that contribute to the illness of the employees, or restrict their return to work, are not substantially addressed. Exploring our data, we can identify two mechanisms that explain the maintenance of organizational practices: (1) while required to collaborate, the actors reinforce their professional boundaries, and (2) while the multiple actors often relate the employees' illnesses to organizational factors (work stress, psychical demands), they do not collaborate in changing the organizational reasons for absence and disconnect relevant practices, which leads to, for example, a lack of prevention. Below, we illustrate these two mechanisms in more detail.

Reinforcing professional boundaries

The logic of activation requires the actors (especially supervisors, HR managers and OHPs) to work across professional boundaries in order to reduce the health problems of employees and facilitate their return to work. In contrast, our study shows that the actors re-establish the divisions between their professional roles, thereby limiting their own role and waiting for other actors to solve the problems (see Table 4.4).

For example, most OHPs in our study limit their role to medical diagnosis and are not involved in designing a return-to-work plan. As one physician expresses: 'I can identify it [the sickness absence problem], but [to develop] real solutions or creating jobs, that is beyond my reach'. The physicians therefore frequently do not even know whether a return-to-work plan exists. Also the HR managers and line managers define their role as limited to a specific element. An HR manager expresses his focus as follows: 'My role is to monitor the legal procedures'.

Table 4.4 Reinforcing professional boundaries

Limited role descriptions	Illustrations
The OHPs restrict their role to the medical diagnosis. They recognize the organizational problems that contribute to sickness absence, but limit their role to signalling.	I have done my job, writing a problem analysis [diagnosis] for the cases. The solution must be found between line and employee. That is not something I need to find out. My job is about the medical aspects.
	In my problem analysis, I can see that she can lift up to 1 kilo, and she cannot handle heavy loads. But how to deal with that in the ward, that is an issue for the supervisor. That is not something I can imagine.
	My role is to analyse the sick employee and write down what the person can do and what he/she cannot do from a medical point of view. It is the line manager who has a central role in managing sickness absence.
The HR managers limit their role to monitoring procedures. They leave the solutions for (structural) sickness absence problems to line managers and do not provide HR policies.	It's up to the line these days. In the past, we did the absence management, but now the line manager is in the driver's seat. Our role [HR] is to keep up the files and monitor the process.
	I have no influence to change anything; the executives are responsible for solutions.
	I think the line managers should have the initiative [...]. I notice that they often literally sit back.
The line managers restrict their role to contacting employees. They emphasize their own role in absence management instead of teamwork.	I consider myself as the case manager. This means that I try to keep contact with the sick-listed employee, at least once a week.
	I have a regular contact with the OHP and the HR advisor but I take my own decisions. My role is to stay in touch with the employee.

Notes: OHP – occupational health physician; OHS – occupational health service; HR: human resource.
Source: Authors' own.

The line managers restrict their role to regular contacts with the sick-listed employees, without developing structural measures to prevent common health problems in their ward. All actors are thus limiting their roles to a delineated contribution: contacting the employee (line manager), medical diagnosis (OHP) and monitoring procedures (HR manager). As a result of the limited role perceptions and the following underdevelopment of collaboration, organizational problems related to absence are not addressed.

Both line managers and HR managers tend to blame each other for a lack of action. For example, one line manager complains about the lack of support from the HR department: 'This case is representative for our problems with an ageing workforce; but we need HR policies to do something about it'. Similarly, HR managers complain that line managers are reluctant to obtain the role of case manager in absence management. They do not aim to take this role themselves, since they are convinced that line managers are better positioned to do so. As one HR manager expresses: 'I do not really look forward to that; as a matter of fact, I do not have time for it'. Thus, while multiple actors recognize organizational problems as a frequent underlying reason of absence and support the logic of activation to address this situation, the reinforcement of professional boundaries prevents them from solving the problems.

Disconnecting practices

Following the logic of activation, sickness absence management is expected to be directly connected to other relevant practices in order to prevent and solve employees' health problems in a structural way. For example, through HR policies for an ageing workforce. Our study illustrates how the actors operate without connecting these practices (see for illustrations Table 4.5) and thus reproduce and maintain the organizational problems underlying the sickness absence.

In particular, the management of sickness absence is not connected to the prevention of health problems. A paradox underlying this disconnection is that the work pressure contributing to the absence problems in the first place, contributes to the line managers pushing ill employees for a quick return to work. As one line manager explains, while regretting his own actions: 'I think you should not put pressure on anyone to return to work more quickly, but sometimes I simply have to do it'. The line managers often point to the tension between their priority in running the ward and their responsibility for preserving employees' health. One line manager expresses this tension with regard to a person who became long-term ill and previously worked as a laboratory nurse: 'Because the workload [at radiology] was increasingly pressing, we made more use of her than was agreed in her contract. Yes, if you had no one else, you still had to ask her...and she never said no'. Similarly, the employees themselves neglect their health problems until sickness absence occurs, and continue working while being ill. One of the sick-listed employees explains why: 'It was always so busy

Table 4.5 Strategies of 'laissez faire', leading to a disconnection of practices

Key areas in disconnecting practices	Illustrations
Disconnection of health problems and measures for prevention	*Line manager*: The employee reported the flu very often, but she had just complaints...in the back...you saw five to six absences per calendar year...always a few days. But as a manager, I did not feel able to get control on it and reduce the problem... *Physician*: I was surprised to hear that the employee already had many complaints before she reported herself sick. *HR manager*: There is nothing done to prevent sickness absence [...]. Executives see that people work too hard and do a lot of shifts, but they say: as long as our employees continue working, we'll wait and see where it ends.
Disconnecting absence management to other practices, such as HR policies	*Line manager*: This case is representative for our problems with an ageing workforce; but we need HR policies to do something about it. *HR Manager*: I believe we have developed HR policies, for example, for ageing workers, but with the reorganization...I think, it must be somewhere in a drawer. *Physician*: If sickness absence is work-related, and the person cannot return to her job, then my experience in the hospital is: nobody really feels responsible.

Source: Authors' own.

at our department, I could not be absent, I could not let my patients and my colleagues down'. Thus, while the emphasis in the logic of activation is on the employees' health rather than on their illness, and on capacity rather than inability to work, the tension between the hospital's 'production' and the employees' well-being excludes prevention of employees' health problems.

A lack of strategic action at higher board levels in the hospitals reinforces limited role perceptions and the disconnection of relevant practices. For example, one OHP recalls sending a report on structural health problems to the departmental board months ago and still has not heard back about actions: 'The board invited me for a discussion; they completely agreed with my analysis, but I haven't heard about it since'. Most actors in our study recognize the adverse effects of not solving organizational causes underlying the sickness absence. As one physician expressed, referring to the regular meetings with supervisors and HR to discuss employees who called in sick, for example, for work stress or high physical demands: 'We don't make any progress and just exchange the information we already have. You feel so powerless, it's so inappropriate and ineffective'.

Discussion

The shift to a logic of activation in European welfare states, and the corresponding change of laws in the Netherlands, requires the collaboration of multiple local actors in solving sickness absence problems within organizations. We studied 21 cases of long-term sick-listed employees across three Dutch hospitals to explore how line managers, HR managers and OHPs dealt with this challenge. Our findings suggest that the logic of activation is highly recognized and supported by the multiple local actors, but the principles of the activation logic are not substantially enacted in their practices. In our data, we found two mechanisms that explain this discrepancy: (1) the actors' reinforcement of professional boundaries and (2) a disconnection of relevant practices. We now turn to how our findings contribute to the institutional logics literature.

The first contribution explains how the local enactment of a macro-logic may lead to organizational maintenance, despite an obvious cognitive support for change. The discrepancy between support for a new logic and a lack of new practice creation makes institutional change a much more complex process than most organizational (field) studies suggest (Scott, 2008; Reay et al., 2013). In particular, our findings question the dominant role of theorizing as the central stage of institutionalization (Greenwood et al., 2002). Our study highlights that the cognitive acceptance of ideas is only one part of the institutionalization process and not necessarily sufficient to translate new logics into practices (see also Reay et al., 2013). By studying the actors' roles and collaborations in enacting a new logic, we contribute to a more complete understanding of how a new logic is negotiated locally between multiple actors. Previous studies of institutional change have focused on one or a few macro-entrepreneurs in institutional change (i.e. the state, professional organizations) or on individual 'heroic' actors (Lounsbury and Crumley, 2007). Our findings suggest the value of studying the practices of multiple local actors in establishing collective responses to institutional pressures. The findings show how individuals support a new logic, while not *doing* the change by attributing the responsibility for connecting the relevant practices (i.e. diagnosis, prevention and HR policies) to other actors. We thus underline the importance of studying multiple actors' interpretations and practices to understand the impact of new logics in macro–micro linkages (see also Boxenbaum and Jonsson, 2008: 85–88).

Second, we contribute to the knowledge of the (non-)linkages between institutional logics and micro-processes in organizations. Our analysis assists in explaining two mechanisms leading to maintenance despite pressures to change: (1) a reinforcement of professional boundaries and strategies of 'laissez-faire', which lead to (2) a disconnection of relevant practices. The organizational maintenance in our case resulted in the continuation of organizational problems as a major cause of sickness absence. Our study further shows how the two mechanisms are mutually reinforcing: the demarcation of professional roles restricts the opportunity for collaborative practices in organizational change, and the disengagement of practices allows for protecting professional boundaries in justifying organizational maintenance. These findings respond to a recognized gap in institutional theory concerning the (non-)linkages between institutional logics and micro-practices (Cooney, 2007; Lounsbury and Crumley, 2007; Greenwood et al., 2011).

Based on our findings, we suggest distinguishing between *constructed* logics, developed in societal and economic discourses and articulated in national legislation, and *institutionalized* logics that have received a status of taken-for-grantedness in organizational practices. The latter may eventually counter the impact of the constructed logics. We can even question if a constructed logic (such as the activation logic) can be phrased as an institutional logic, as long as actors only *say* to support the ideas but *do not show* this in their actions. One reason for the manifested contradiction between logic recognition and following practices is the existence of other pressures, such as the marketization of healthcare. Competing logics may thus contribute to explaining the lack of practices prescribed by the activation logic. Another way of explaining the discrepancy between supporting and enacting a logic is that institutionalized practices are much more resilient than new ideas coming from a macro-level, implying that the design of change processes should better start with developing concrete alternatives on the floor, incorporating multiple local actors' experiences.

Given the limitations of our study to a particular logic and three hospitals in one country, it is not clear whether our findings are representative for other settings. Yet, we believe that they will be transferable to situations where implementation is dependent on multiple actors operating from different professional backgrounds and acting in a complex, hybrid context. We suggest that similar mechanisms (reinforcing professional boundaries and 'laissez-faire' strategies leading to a disconnection of practices) may occur in organizations engaged in, for example, (higher) education or social housing, where strong tensions exist between financial targets and societal goals for inclusion and equal opportunities. In future research, we hope to broaden our research to other settings, giving particular attention to the relationship between macro-institutional change and micro-processes in organizations.

References

Battilana, J. (2006) 'Agency and institutions: the enabling role of individuals' social position', *Organization*, 13(5): 653–676.

Boselie, P., Paauwe, J. and Richardson R. (2003) 'Human resource management, institutionalization and organizational performance: a comparison of hospitals, hotels and local government', *International Journal of Human Resource Management*, 14(8): 1407–1429.

Boxenbaum, E. and Jonsson S. (2008) 'Isomorphism, diffusion and decoupling', in R. Greenwood, C. Oliver, K. Sahlin and R. Suddaby (eds.), *Handbook of organizational institutionalism*. London: Sage, pp. 78–98.

Cooney, K. (2007) 'Fields, organizations, and agency. Toward a multilevel theory of institutionalization in action', *Administration & Society*, 39(6): 687–718.

Edwards, T. and Jones, O. (2008) 'Failed institution building: understanding the interplay between agency, social skill and context', *Scandinavian Journal of Management*, 24(1): 44–54.

Eichhorst, W., Kaufmann, O. and Konle-Seidl, R. (eds) (2008) *Bringing the Jobless into Work? Experiences with Activation Schemes in Europe and the US.* Berlin: Springer.

Goodrick, E. and Reay, T. (2011) 'Constellations of institutional logics: changes in the professional work of pharmacists', *Work and Occupations*, 38(3): 372–416.

Greenwood, R., Díaz, A. M., Li, S. X. and Lorente, J. C. (2010) 'The multiplicity of institutional logics and the heterogeneity of organizational responses', *Organization Science,* 21(2): 521–539.

Greenwood, R., Raynard, M., Kodeih, F., Micelotta, E. R. and Lounsbury, M. (2011) 'Institutional complexity and organizational responses', *The Academy of Management Annals*, 5(1): 317–371.

Greenwood, R., Suddaby, R. and Hinings, C. R. (2002) 'Theorizing change: the role of professional associations in the transformation of institutionalized fields', *Academy of Management Journal*, 45, 58–80.

James, P., Cunningham, I. and Dibben, P. (2002) 'Absence management and the issues of job retention and return to work', *Human Resource Management Journal*, 12 (2): 82–94.

Kluve, J., Card, D., Fertig, M., Góra, M., Jacobi, L., Jensen, P., Leetmaa, R., Nima, L., Patacchini, E., Schaffner, S., Schmidt, C. M., van der Klaauw, B. and Weber,

A. (2007) *Active Labor Market Policies in Europe: Performances and Perspectives.* Berlin/Heidelberg/New York: Springer.

Lawrence, T. and Suddaby, R. (2006) 'Institutions and institutional work', in S. Clegg, C. Hardy and T. Lawrence (eds.), *Handbook of Organization Studies*, 2nd edition. London: Sage, pp. 215–254.

Lounsbury, M. and Boxenbaum, E. (eds) (2013) *Institutional Logics in Action*, Part B (Research in the Sociology of Organizations, Vol. 39B, 37–61), Bingley, UK: Emerald.

Lounsbury, M. and Crumley, E. T. (2007) 'New practice creation: an institutional perspective on innovation', *Organization Studies*, 28(7): 993–1012.

Mazza, C. and Strandgaard Pedersen, J. (2004) 'From press to e-media? The transformation of an organizational field', *Organization Studies*, 25(6): 875–896.

McKee, L., Ferlie, E. and Hyde, P. (eds) (2008) *Organizing and Reorganizing: Power and Change in Health Care Organizations.* Basingstoke: Palgrave Macmillan.

Powell, W.W. and Colyvas, J. (2008) 'Microfoundations of institutional theory', in R. Greenwood, C. Oliver, K. Sahlin-Andersson and R. Suddaby (eds.), *The Handbook of Organizational Institutionalism*. Thousand Oaks, CA: Sage, pp. 276–298.

Reay, T. and Hinings, C. R. (2009) 'Managing the rivalry of competing institutional logics', *Organization Studies*, 30(6): 629–652.

Reay, T., Chreim, S., Golden-Biddle, K., Goodrick, E., Casebeer, A., Williams, B., Pablo, A. and Hinings, C. R. (2013) 'Transforming new ideas into practice: an activity based perspective on the institutionalization of practices', *Management Studies*, 50(6): 963–990.

Scott, W. R. (2008) *Institutions and Organizations: Ideas and Interests*, 3rd edition. Los Angeles, CA: Sage.

Smets, M., Morris, T. and Greenwood, R. (2012) 'From practice to field: a multi-level model of practice-driven institutional change', *Academy of Management Journal*, 55: 877–904.

Suddaby, R., Elsbach, K. D., Greenwood, R., Meyer, J. W. and Zilber, T. B. (2010) 'Organizations and their institutional environments – bringing meaning, values, and culture back in: introduction to the special research forum', *Academy of Management Journal*, 53(6): 1234–1240.

Thornton, P. H., Ocasio, W. and Lounsbury, M. (2012) *The Institutional Logics Perspective: A New Approach to Culture, Structure and Process.* Oxford: Oxford University Press.

Van Oorschot, W. (2006) 'The Dutch welfare state: recent trends and challenges in historical perspective', *European Journal of Social Security*, 8, 57–76.

Van Raak, A., De Rijk, A., Morsa, J. (2005) 'Applying new institutional theory: the case of collaboration to promote work resumption after sickness absence', *Work, Employment and Society*, 19(1): 141–151.

Voronov, M., De Clercq, D. and Hinings, C. R. (2013) 'Institutional complexity and logic engagement: an investigation of Ontario fine wine', *Human Relations*, 66(12): 1563–1596.

Weishaupt, J. T. (2011) *From the Manpower Revolution to the Activation Paradigm: Explaining Institutional Continuity and Change in an Integrating Europe.* Amsterdam, the Netherlands: Amsterdam University Press.

Part II

The Role of Professions in Change Processes

5

The Persistence of Professional Boundaries in Healthcare: A Re-examination Using a Theory of Foundational Values

Kathleen Montgomery, Wendy Lipworth and Louise Fitzgerald

Introduction

In this chapter, we draw on a theory of 'modest foundationalism' (Little et al., 2011, 2012; Little, 2014) as a means of shedding fresh light on the persistence of strict boundaries between the medical profession and other occupations, including other healthcare occupations such as nursing and allied health.

Little and colleagues have proposed a theory of foundational values. This theory, which might be said to underpin values-based medicine (VBM), was initially developed to augment medical school curricula, particularly in the area of medical ethics. It refers to three foundational values that people in all cultures agree upon – survival, security and flourishing – even when the principles and practices to express those values may vary substantially from culture to culture. Application of related values-based theories in the context of medical education has yielded enhanced understanding of ethical issues in healthcare and medicine, by providing a new perspective within which to approach ethical quandaries (Fulford et al., 2012). At the same time, values-based theories have not yet made their way in the literature on professional boundaries.

Here, we propose that the premises underpinning Little's version of VBM may be usefully applied in studying the structure of healthcare professions, including as a means of understanding the boundaries that persist between the medical profession and other health and non-health occupations. We seek to move beyond traditional explanations of the position of the medical profession in society that, at one extreme, draw on functional-based theories to justify the protections and high status afforded the medical profession; and, at the other extreme, draw on theories of power and self-interest to challenge the profession's elite status.

The medical profession has long been viewed as the prototypical example of professionalization, and its study has formed the basis of many general theories of the professions, including law, accounting, engineering, architecture and the clergy. Yet, while each of these professions may have the ability to affect the well-being of the people they serve, they do so in unique ways. Only medical professionals have the potential to affect people's well-being through physical interventions that are often intimate and sometimes extreme and which can mean the difference between life and death. We will argue that these fundamental ways in which the medical profession contributes to the attainment of the values of survival, security and flourishing help to explain the maintenance of the boundaries that the medical profession has carved out, even at a time when boundaries within and across other professions may be shifting (as shown, for example, in studies by Ramirez, 2009; Empson et al., 2013; Goretzki et al., 2013).

In presenting our argument, we do not wish to imply that there can never be any shifts in the boundaries of healthcare professions; and several recent studies have shown some movement towards greater task integration at the work group level (for example, Denis et al., 1999; Nancarrow and Borthwick, 2005; Sanders and Harrison, 2008; Goodrick and Reay, 2010). Nevertheless, we believe that the record demonstrates that the boundaries that distinguish the medical profession from other healthcare and non-healthcare professions have remained particularly stable over time, despite concerted efforts by, for example, nurses and physician assistants to shift these boundaries. (See studies by Fitzgerald and Ferlie, 2000; Degeling and Maxwell, 2004; Currie et al., 2009; Battilana, 2011; Currie et al., 2012; Powell and Davies, 2012; McCann et al., 2013). Our goal here is to offer a new values-based perspective about why that is so.

We begin by outlining what we mean by the concept of boundaries, followed by a brief review of sociological theories that have been employed to explain the vaunted position of the medical profession and the boundaries between medicine and other occupations. We then provide an overview of the main elements of the theory of foundational values, in which Little and colleagues identify three foundational values – survival, security and flourishing – that matter in any culture or society. Although the theory is positioned at a societal level, we will shift the analysis to a meso-level focus on the boundaries that exist among healthcare professions. With this approach, we propose that a deeper understanding may be achieved of why such boundaries endure – one that is neither an apology for the medical profession's unique and protected stature nor a criticism of it.

Sociological thought about professional boundaries

Boundaries play a key role in distinguishing social groups, including professions and organizations, from one another. Lamont and Molnar (2002) observe that boundaries represent *symbolic* and *socially constructed* distinctions that delimit both identity and domain. The first of these, symbolic boundaries, reflects a shared identity for members of an emergent group, in the form of shared cognitions that help the group to see itself as distinct from others on the basis of 'sites of difference' (Abbott, 1995: 863). Montgomery and Oliver (2007) emphasize that symbolic boundaries are a precursor to the development of socially constructed boundaries, while also serving to reinforce a sense of identity and community of practice (Brown and Duguid, 1991) once the group has been well established.

Socially constructed boundaries can take the form of rules regarding the group's membership and knowledge domain. Rules of membership often function as formalized 'rules of exclusion' to actors outside a group's knowledge and practice domain (Kogut and Zander, 1996: 515). The knowledge domain helps to distinguish the scale and scope of activities for which a group claims sole responsibility, including goals, authority structures, technologies and clients (Rao, 1988; Afuah, 2003).

In the case of professions, such as healthcare professions, rules of membership typically refer to requirements that a prospective member must attain a specified level of advanced education, accompanied by a state-granted license to practise within a particular knowledge domain. Specialization further delimits the knowledge domain to those who hold a credential of more focused expertise. Because of their exclusivity, such boundaries have been seen to contribute to the elevated status of healthcare professions, especially medicine (Freidson, 1970; Larson, 1977; Abbott, 1988).

Kerosuo's definition of socially constructed boundaries – 'distinctions and differences between and within activity systems that are created and agreed on by groups and individual actors over a long period of time' (Kerosuo, 2006: 4) – adds the important observation that these distinctions are *agreed on*, a point we return to at the end of the chapter. There are two broad views about how and why boundaries emerge and persist – a 'functionalist' approach and a 'power-based' approach.

The functionalist approach

During the first part of the 20th century, scholarship on the professions tended to characterize professions as a distinct type of occupational group, by delineating special 'traits' that set professions apart from other occupations and above them in status (Carr-Saunders and Wilson, 1933). For several decades thereafter, sociologists devoted much attention to articulating the distinguishing characteristics of professions, including an elevated ethical sensibility, an advanced body of knowledge and esoteric theoretical base, an altruistic orientation and a sense of professional community, among other traits (e.g. Parsons, 1939; Goode, 1957; Greenwood, 1957; Millerson, 1964; Vollmer and Mills, 1966). For the most part, these scholars maintained that such traits helped to identify worthy professionals and to justify the autonomy, status and power held by professionals in Western society.

Power-based explanations

An alternative line of thought emerged in the 1970s, dismissing the functionalist idea that the power and prestige of professionals is justified by their invaluable role in society. Sociologists also began to question the 'attribute approach' as little more than a 'mixture of unproven and often unexamined claims' for professional control and autonomy (Roth, 1974; Hafferty, 1988: 203). Instead, these scholars urged a shift from examining the functions that professional groups served to examining how the groups gained and maintained their power and prestige.

Freidson focused on the unique ability of professionals to 'exercise control over their work and its outcome' and to be the 'arbiters of their own work performance, justified by the claim that they are the only ones who know enough to be able to evaluate it properly' (Freidson, 1973: 30). His goal was to explain how such claims to professional autonomy and control were achieved and maintained. His seminal study of the profession of medicine (Freidson, 1970) laid out the stages through which the organized profession had historically engendered state support for barriers to entry, such as licensing, based on attainment of higher education and expertise. Larson subsequently described these efforts as 'professionalization projects' (Larson, 1977), which revealed the interdependence between professional claims to expertise and institutional reinforcement through state-supported 'labor market shelters' of licensing and credentialing (Freidson, 1986). Similarly, Abbott (1988) explored how professional groups established 'jurisdictional niches' – knowledge domains for which they claimed exclusive rights to practise – which in turn furthered the power and prestige of such groups.

Balancing functionalist and power-based perspectives

The popularity of the power-based approach quickly overshadowed the earlier functionalist explanations. Nevertheless, in recent years, there have been signs of a blending of the two perspectives: recognizing that professions can in fact be distinguished from other occupational groups and that their autonomy claims and concomitant power are not wholly unjustified (Crompton, 1990; Calnan and Gabe, 1991). Scholars have especially acknowledged this when examining the medical profession.

In his later writings, for example, Freidson (1994, 2001) espoused a more balanced view of professionals and professional powers, through what he labeled a 'third logic of professionalism' that has, at its core, a specialized knowledge that society values enough to want advanced and applied in socially useful ways. Importantly, he argued that this specialized and valuable knowledge largely justifies the jurisdictional protections and resulting professional power held by the medical profession.

Pilnick and Dingwall (2011) struck a similar chord, highlighting the enduring asymmetrical relationship between patient and physician; others have also emphasized this asymmetry, which provokes an inevitable need for trust and, with this, power and prestige (Mechanic, 1998; Hall et al., 2001; Broom, 2005). Dingwall drew from Adam Smith to illustrate the essence of trust in the medical profession and its relationship to prestige: 'We trust our health to the physician...Their reward must be such, therefore, as may give them that rank in society which so important a trust requires' (Smith, 1776/1976: 118). Dingwall concluded that 'the place of professions in the modern world...uses more colours in its palette than the monochrome of "occupational imperialism"' (2004: 10).

More recently, attention has been paid to the role of professions as 'institutional agents' (Scott, 2008) heavily involved in processes of institutional change, including within the organizational context of professional service firms (Muzio et al., 2013). This institutional approach has elements of both functionalist and power-based theory.

In the remainder of this chapter, we augment these classic and emerging perspectives on professional boundaries by demonstrating the role that boundaries play in fostering and preserving survival, security and flourishing, and thereby contributing to the overall well-being of individuals and society. We will argue that both functional-based and power-based theories of professions can be useful and that a valuable linking mechanism between the two can be found in the theory of foundational values and their expressions.

Foundational values and their expressions

Little (2014) and colleagues (Little et al., 2011, 2012) have proposed a theory in which they identify three foundational values (referred to as F-values) – survival, security and flourishing – that matter in all societies at all times. The three F-values are necessities for a society to continue and evolve. 'Survival' represents existence, without which a society would disappear. 'Security' represents the need for stability, in order to facilitate survival. Security needs constitute the basis of our willingness to trust and to accept some forms of social control in exchange for predictability. 'Flourishing' represents the need for self-development and self-expression beyond what is necessary for survival and security, which make life worth living for individuals and which contribute to a society's future.

On the surface, this theory resonates to some extent with Maslow's hierarchy of needs (1943), which grows from physiological needs and culminates in a need for individual self-actualization. Maslow's theory was formulated to explain individual motivation to achieve what he called 'deficiency' needs in a prescribed sequence. Subsequent efforts to test Maslow's theory have not yielded consistent support, especially in cross-cultural comparisons. In contrast, Little's theory focuses on a more limited set of foundational values important in *every* society, but which are enacted in very different ways over time and across communities and individuals, depending on the norms and associated practices within a particular context.

This theory is 'pre-normative' in that it identifies a social psychological phenomenon that is common to all societies (their need for survival, security and flourishing) and explains, but does not judge, particular expressions of these F-values. Normative judgements about the ways in which societies express F-values therefore have to be derived from outside the values framework. The three F-values help to explain our existence, as well as the specific patterns and institutions that give meaning to each society by enabling a sense of security and personal flourishing, without judging these phenomena.

While the three F-values exist in any context, their expression – that is, the beliefs, preferences and practices that flow from the F-values – will differ over time and across cultures and societies. Little argues that these expressions can be codified as axioms (A-values) and practices (P-values). Axioms (A-values) are generalized principles or 'truths' that are espoused by a particular group in society, often in the form of normative assertions derived from the three foundational F-values. They form the beginning of a societal ideology, or set of maxims, from which preferences and practices are derived.

We articulate some examples of axioms related to healthcare in Table 5.1, column B, to illustrate their connection to the values of survival, security and flourishing. Note that the three axioms are additive: that is, the first states a need for *help* in order to survive; the second states a need for *help* in the form of *accessible, reliable and expert healthcare* in order to feel secure; and the third states a need for *help* in the form of *a particular kind of accessible, reliable and expert healthcare* in order to flourish, both now and in the future.

Although different societies may embrace similar A-values, the manner in which A-values are enacted may vary substantially across cultures and over time. Little refers to these expressions as practical values (P-values), which represent translations of the A-values into actional 'shoulds' that reflect the preferences and policies of a particular culture or society at a particular time. To illustrate, we offer examples in Table 5.1, columns C and D, of some P-values that could flow from the axioms articulated in column B.

Applying the survival–security–flourishing framework to healthcare professions

In developing their framework, Little and colleagues aimed to explore the basic foundational values underpinning the provision of healthcare, values that may ultimately be manifested in a specific community or individual patient's idiosyncratic needs and wants (a major emphasis of the patient-centred care movement). In what follows, we will demonstrate how the same set of axioms can be expressed as practical actions (P-values) relevant to healthcare professions and the boundaries that distinguish them (Table 5.1, column E).

Survival. As shown in Table 5.1, a key axiom pertaining to survival is that 'People need help to deal with life-threatening illness and disease'.

Table 5.1 Healthcare-related F-values, A-values and P-values at the macrosocietal and meso (professional) levels

A. F-values	B. A-values (axioms)	C. General P-Values (practices)	D. Variable P-Values (context-specific practices)	E. Professional P-Values (practices espoused by healthcare professions)
Survival	• People need help to deal with life-threatening illness and disease	• A society should ensure that people receive the help they need to survive	• People with breast cancer should be treated with herbal medicine • People with breast cancer should be treated with radiation and surgery	• Professional entities should exist with the skill to manage life-threatening illness
Security	• People who become sick need access to healthcare from expert sources they can rely on and trust	• A society should ensure that there is an adequate source of trustworthy and expert healthcare providers	• People should have access to a 24-hour neighbourhood clinic • People should be able to see any healthcare provider they choose • People should have access to healthcare providers regardless of ability to pay	• Professions should establish educational, licensing and credentialing requirements to practise • Those without appropriate credentials should not be allowed to deliver healthcare • Professions should establish and enforce codes of conduct to ensure ethical behaviour of their members • Professionals should not take on roles for which they are not qualified
Flourishing	• People need the kind of healthcare that expresses their identities, that helps them to restore their capabilities for self-development and self-expression, and that enables them to trust that they will thrive	• A society should support advancement in knowledge to ensure that people receive healthcare informed by appropriate theories of care	• People should receive specialized healthcare informed by clinical trials and evidence-based medicine (EBM) • People should have access to healthcare in a way that addresses their preferences	• Professions should promote and pursue advancement in knowledge sufficient to respond to current and future health threats at the individual and societal level

Source: Authors' own.

Moving from the macro (societal) level to the meso (professional) level, it can be seen that the existence of a medical profession becomes the key mechanism for achieving this goal. Thus, a P-value might be articulated as follows: 'professional entities should exist with the skill to manage life-threatening illness'. This P-value has a dual purpose: First, it serves to provide a recognizable group to whom people can turn when they need help managing illness and disease, thereby reducing search costs and uncertainty for people when they need such help. Second, it opens a legitimate space within society that can be filled by healthcare professionals. Abbott (1988) would call this a 'jurisdictional niche'. At this level, the boundary that matters is that between healthcare professionals and laypeople, who lack even basic medical skills.

Security. The axiom pertaining to security – 'People who become sick need access to healthcare from expert sources they can rely on and trust' – reveals the importance of distinctions between different kinds of healthcare professions. Whereas the survival axiom refers in a general way to a need for help from any adequately trained healthcare professional, the security axiom addresses the need for 'reliable, expert, and trustworthy' healthcare providers and thus demands more skilled and specialized care, as well as the means to trust the competence of this care. P-values at this level would include those relating to the qualifications of medical and other providers, such as 'professions should establish educational, licensing, and credentialing requirements to practice'. These requirements serve as institutionalized signals that a minimum level of knowledge and competence has been achieved. Thus, through this P-value, the axiom of providing reliable and trustworthy sources is reinforced.

A corollary to this P-value would be that 'those without appropriate credentials should not be allowed to deliver healthcare'. This reflects an expectation that society should enforce clear and recognizable boundaries – marked by the possession of licenses and credentials – in order to delimit who can appropriately serve the needs of ill people in society, and who cannot. Two other relevant P-values expressing the need for security might be that 'professions should establish and enforce codes of conduct to ensure ethical behaviour of their members' and that 'professionals should not take on roles for which they are not qualified'. These P-values are indicators of the strength of professional norms, reflecting an expectation that healthcare professionals *themselves* should adhere both to the ethical standards of the profession and to the boundaries of care services that they are, and are not, trained and credentialed to perform.

Another security-level P-value might support the push for further specialization and credentials to signal greater expertise. An inevitable outcome of this is an additional layer of boundaries within the profession, to distinguish specialists from generalists and to distinguish one set of specialists from another.

Thus, we can see the link between the foundational need for security and the boundaries established to distinguish between different healthcare professions, such as nursing and medicine, and between more- and less-specialized professionals within each group. It is these basic underpinning values that help to explain why, despite criticisms and changing societal standards, the boundaries between the medical profession and other providers of healthcare persist.

Flourishing. The axiom pertaining to flourishing is that 'people need the kind of healthcare that expresses their identities, that helps them restore their capabilities for self-development and self-expression, and that enables them to trust that they will thrive'. It is here that individual identities and worldviews become most salient. While some context-specific professional P-values (column D) might emphasize scientific, evidence-based, uniform approaches to diagnosis and treatment, others might emphasize patient-centred care approaches that focus on patients' preferences. P-values might therefore demand substantial variation in the nature of healthcare services, accompanied by a growing set of boundaries within and between healthcare professions.

The trend towards specialization, accompanied by additional intra-professional boundaries, is relevant to flourishing as well as to security. For example, in the early days of the AIDS epidemic, it became important to stricken patients that they be seen by professionals with compassion for those who were infected, as well as expertise in treating people with the disease, who were in the best position to enhance patients' capabilities for flourishing (Lewis and Montgomery, 1992). Moreover, specialization within the nursing profession, with the emergence of certified midwives and nurse practitioners, also facilitates patients' preferences for particular kinds of nursing care and therefore enhances patients' capabilities for flourishing.

Also important at the level of flourishing are intergenerational considerations, reflecting Little's emphasis on the availability of opportunities for spiritual, aesthetic, moral, cognitive and physical growth for individuals that enables societies to resist the destruction of their cultures (Little, 2014). When individuals flourish, they, as well as their society, can thrive. In the context of healthcare, this P-value includes the expectation that the profession will promote and pursue advancement in knowledge sufficient to respond to current and future health threats.

Discussion

Little and colleagues have proposed that a set of three foundational values underpin a set of axioms or 'truths' that a group or society may adhere to, and from which more specific preferences and practices become articulated and embraced. Although the foundational values are stable regardless of the context, the axioms may be different across societies and over time, and the practices will vary to an even greater extent. We have drawn on the basics of this theory to explore the feasibility of employing a new lens through which to explain the persistence of professional boundaries in healthcare that extends beyond purely functionalist or power-based theories. In so doing, we have demonstrated how any society's need for survival, security and flourishing can be promoted when a group of experts provides the healthcare that is needed for the survival of individuals in the society; serves as an identifiable, reliable, expert and trustworthy source for such care; and provides care in a manner that is consistent with individuals' worldview and identity so as to promote individuals' self-development and that of future generations.

While this interpretation aligns most obviously with the early understandings of a medical profession advanced by functionalist thought, we also can employ the framework to see how the construction and maintenance of professional boundaries – along with associated jurisdictional niches, barriers to entry, and opportunities for specialization – align with those features identified by power-based theorists to explain professional power and its enduring autonomy and self-regulation. Boundaries delimit jurisdictional niches between professions and other occupations (at the survival level); between the medical profession and other healthcare professions and between more- and less-expert professionals (at the security level); and between specialists who represent different worldviews (at the flourishing level). At each level, boundaries serve not only as means of ensuring that patients survive, are secure and flourish but also as labour market shelters, by restricting entry to those who are appropriately educated and credentialed. As Freidson (1986) and Larson (1977), among others, have pointed out, the exclusivity of labour market shelters helps to heighten demand and preserve professional status and power over time, thereby promoting the survival, security and flourishing of the medical profession itself.

As noted above, many professions are in a position to enhance the well-being of individuals and a society, and they do so in different ways. However, professions within healthcare are in a unique position to do so because of their potential to affect people's survival, security and flourishing through highly intimate, and occasionally extreme, life-and-death interventions. We believe that this distinction helps to explain the persistence of strong boundaries, despite repeated challenges to these boundaries. A substantial factor in this persistence is the (often implicit) *acceptance* by society and individuals of such boundaries, consistent with Abbott's (1988) observation of the importance of boundary recognition in the public, as well as the legal spheres. This also resonates with Kerosuo's (2006) conceptualization of social boundaries as distinctions that are *agreed on* by groups and individual actors. Thus, we believe it is society's *need* to ensure the three foundational values that hinders the success of challenges to boundaries between medicine and other healthcare occupations and professions.

Conclusion and implications

There is a substantial literature examining boundaries between and across professional groups, but, for the most part, these studies have not explicitly brought a system of values into the discussion. We have drawn from a theory that identifies three foundational values that exist across societies and individuals, regardless of culture. We have demonstrated how the foundational values are expressed through axioms and practices that address individuals' needs for expert, reliable and trustworthy healthcare. We have then shifted the lens to the professional level and illustrated how these values and axioms can be expressed through practices that also address the profession's need for survival, security and flourishing. It is the complementarity of these practices that opens a new way to appreciate how and why professional boundaries persist.

Acknowledgements

The authors wish to thank Miles Little for encouraging our idea to expand his theory to the context of professional structure. We also appreciate the thoughtful feedback from participants at the 2014 Organisational Behaviour in Healthcare Conference. We gratefully acknowledge the institutional support from the University of California Academic Senate and the Edward A. Dickson Emerita Professor Fellowship (to KM), and the National Health and Medical Research Council (NH&MRC) Career Development Fellowship (to WL).

References

Abbott, A. (1988) *The System of Professions.* Chicago, IL: University of Chicago Press.

Abbott, A. (1995) 'Things of boundaries: defining the boundaries of social inquiry', *Social Research*, 62: 857–882.

Afuah, A. (2003) 'Redefining firm boundaries in the face of the Internet: are firms really shrinking?' *Academy of Management Review*, 28: 34–53.

Battilana, J. (2011) 'The enabling role of social position in diverging from the institutional status quo: evidence from the UK NHS', *Organization Science*, 22: 817–834.

Broom, A. (2005) 'Medical specialists' accounts of the impact of the Internet on the doctor/patient relationship', *Health*, 9: 319–338.

Brown, J. and Duguid, P. (1991) 'Organizational learning and communities of practice: towards a unified view of working, learning, and innovation', *Organization Science*, 2: 40–57.

Calnan, M. and Gabe, J. (1991) 'Recent developments in general practice: a sociological analysis', in J. Gabe, M. Calnan and M. Bury (eds.), *The Sociology of the Health Service.* London: Routledge, pp. 140–162.

Carr-Saunders, A. and Wilson, P. (1933) *The Professions.* Oxford: Clarendon.

Crompton, R. (1990) 'Professions in the current context', *Work, Employment and Society*, Special Issue, 4: 147–166.

Currie, G., Koteyko N. and Nerlich, B. (2009) 'The dynamics of professions and development of new roles in public services organizations: the case of modern matrons in the English NHS', *Public Administration*, 87: 295–311.

Currie, G., Lockett, A., Finn, R., Martin, G. and Waring, J. (2012) 'Institutional work to maintain professional power: recreating the model of medical professionalism', *Organization Studies*, 33: 937–962.

Degeling, P. and Maxwell, S. (2004) 'The negotiated order of health care', *Journal of Health Services Research*, 14: 36–48.

Denis, J.-L., Lamothe, L., Langley, A. and Valette, A. (1999) 'The struggle to redefine boundaries in health care systems', in D. Brock, M. Powell and C. R. Hinings (eds.), *Restructuring the Professional Organization.* London: Routledge, pp. 105–130.

Dingwall, R. (2004) 'Professions and social order in a global society', *Revista Electrónica de Investigación Educativa*, 6: 1–12.

Empson, L., Cleaver, I. and Allen, J. (2013) 'Managing partners and management professionals: institutional work dyads in professional partnerships', *Journal of Management Studies*, 50: 808–844.

Fitzgerald, L. and Ferlie, E. (2000) 'Professionals: back to the future?' *Human Relations*, 53: 713–739.

Freidson, E. (1970) *Profession of Medicine: A Study of the Sociology of Applied Knowledge.* New York: Dodd, Mead.

Freidson, E. (1973) 'Professions and the occupation principle', in E. Freidson (ed.), *The Professions and Their Prospects.* Beverly Hills: Sage, pp. 19–38.

Freidson, E. (1986) *Professional Powers*. Chicago: University of Chicago Press.

Freidson, E. (1994) *Professionalism Reborn*. Chicago: University of Chicago Press.

Freidson, E. (2001) *Professionalism: The Third Logic*. Chicago: University of Chicago Press.

Fulford, W., Peile, E. and Carroll, H. (2012) *Essential Values-Based Practice: Clinical Stories Linking Science with People*. Cambridge: Cambridge University Press.

Goode, W. (1957) 'Community within a community: the professions', *American Sociological Review*, 22: 194–200.

Goodrick, E. and Reay, T. (2010) 'Florence nightingale endures: legitimizing a new professional role identity', *Journal of Management Studies*, 47: 55–84.

Goretzki, L., Strauss, E. and Weber, J. (2013) 'An institutional perspective on the changes in management accountants' professional role', *Management Accounting Research*, 24: 41–63.

Greenwood, E. (1957) 'Attributes of a profession', *Social Work*, 2: 45–55.

Hafferty, F. (1988) 'Theories at the crossroads: a discussion of evolving views on medicine as a profession', *The Milbank Quarterly*, 66: 202–225.

Hall, M., Dugan E., Zheng B. and Mishra A. (2001) Trust in physicians and medical institutions: what is it, can it be measured, and does it matter?' *The Milbank Quarterly*, 79: 613–639.

Kerosuo, H. (2006) *Boundaries in Action: An Activity-Theoretical Study of Development, Learning and Change in Health Care for Patients with Multiple and Chronic Illnesses*. Helsinki: Helsinki University Press.

Kogut, B. and Zander, U. (1996) 'What do firms do? Coordination, identity, and learning', *Organization Science*, 7: 502–518.

Lamont, M. and Molnar, V. (2002) 'The study of boundaries in the social sciences', *Annual Review of Sociology*, 28: 167–195.

Larson, M. (1977) *The Rise of Professionalism: A Sociological Analysis*. Berkeley: University of California Press.

Lewis, C. and Montgomery, K. (1992) 'Primary care physicians' refusal to care for HIV-infected patients'. *Western Journal of Medicine*, 156: 36–38.

Little, M. (2014) 'Values, foundations, and being human', in M. Loughlin, (ed.), *Debates in Values-Based Practice*. Cambridge: Cambridge University Press, pp. 171–183.

Little, M., Lipworth W., Gordon J., Markham, P. and Kerridge I. (2011) 'Another argument for values-based medicine', *The International Journal of Person-Centered Medicine*, 1: 649–656

Little, M., Lipworth, W., Gordon, J., Markham, P. and Kerridge, I. (2012) 'Values-based medicine and modest foundationalism', *Journal of Evaluation in Clinical Practice*, 18: 1020–1026.

Maslow, A. (1943) 'A theory of human motivation', *Psychological Review*, 50: 370–396.

McCann, L., Granter, E., Hyde, P. and Hassard, J. (2013) 'Still blue-collar after all these years: an ethnography of the professionalization of emergency ambulance work', *Journal of Management Studies*, 50: 750–776.

Mechanic, D. (1998) 'The functions and limitations of trust in the provision of medical care', *Journal of Health Politics, Policy and Law*, 23: 661–686.

Millerson, G. (1964) *The Qualifying Associations: A Study in Professionalization*. London: Routledge and Kegan Paul.

Montgomery, K. and Oliver, A. (2007) 'A fresh look at how professions take shape: dual-directed networking dynamics and social boundaries', *Organization Studies*, 28: 661–687.

Muzio, D., Brock, D. and Suddaby, R. (2013) 'Professions and institutional change: towards an institutionalist sociology of the professions', *Journal of Management Studies*, 50: 699–721.

Nancarrow, S. and Borthwick, A. (2005) 'Dynamic professional boundaries in the healthcare workforce', *Sociology of Health and Illness*, 27: 897–919.

Parsons, T. (1939) 'The professions and social structure', *Social Forces*, 17: 457–67.

Pilnick, A. and Dingwall, R. (2011) 'On the remarkable persistence of asymmetry in doctor/patient interaction: a critical review', *Social Science and Medicine*, 72: 1374–1382.

Powell, A. and Davies, H. (2012) 'The struggle to improve patient care in the face of professional boundaries', *Social Science and Medicine*, 75: 807–814.

Ramirez, C. (2009) 'Constructing the governable small practitioner: the changing nature of professional bodies and the management of professional accountants' identities in the UK', *Accounting Organizations and Society*, 34: 381–408.

Rao, H. (1998) 'Caveat emptor: the construction of nonprofit consumer watchdog organizations', *American Journal of Sociology*, 103: 912–961.

Roth, J. (1974) 'Professionalism: the sociologist's decoy', *Work and Occupations*, 1: 6–23.

Sanders, T. and Harrison, S. (2008) 'Professional legitimacy claims in the multi-disciplinary workplace: the case of heart failure care', *Sociology of Health and Illness*, 30: 289–308.

Scott, W. R. (2008) 'Lords of the dance: professionals as institutional agents', *Organization Studies*, 29: 219–238.

Smith, A. (1776/1976) *The Theory of Moral Sentiments*. Oxford: Clarendon Press.

Vollmer H. and Mills, D. (eds.) (1966) *Professionalization*. Englewood Cliffs, NJ: Prentice Hall.

6

Medical Doctors and Health System Improvement: Synthesis Results and Propositions for Further Research

Jean-Louis Denis and G. Ross Baker

Introduction

Many efforts in different countries provide useful examples of new care models and broad strategies for improving population health, quality of care and patients' experiences while controlling costs (Baker et al., 2008). The successful strategies in these examples of health system improvement have relied on developing medical engagement and leadership as a critical element of transformative change (Baker et al., 2008; Baker and Denis, 2011; Ham, 2014). Recent policy initiatives in different jurisdictions also emphasize effective medical leadership and engagement. These include recent National Health System (NHS) reforms in the United Kingdom (Department of Health, 2010) and US efforts to develop accountable care organizations (Singer and Shortell, 2011). Yet, although the need to engage doctors seems to affect policy reforms and organizational change efforts, the issue of physician leadership and engagement has drawn only limited empirical attention.

Physician engagement and leadership refers to the role of physicians in formal executive positions and the engagement of doctors in activities 'within their normal working roles to [maintain] and [enhance] the performance of the organization...' (Spurgeon et al., 2008: 214). Leadership appears necessary for wider physician engagement, which refers to the active interest and participation of physicians in organizational (as well as individual professional) activities to improve care and services.

In this chapter, we discuss some institutional challenges for physician engagement and leadership. Then we explore various strategies to promote and support physicians' role in leading transformational change, concluding with implications for policy and research. Our analysis assumes that health system improvement cannot be achieved only through labour market regulation of professionals or funding reforms and that governments, healthcare delivery organizations and the medical profession must all be involved in achieving system improvement (Singer and Shortell, 2011). These assumptions also rely on observing that key contributing factors for failures in healthcare management and performance are inadequate clinical governance and limited physician engagement in managing quality and safety (Dwyer, 2010). The chapter situates the issue of physician engagement and leadership within the larger context of organized professionalism (Noordegraaf, 2011).

Competing logics and the dichotomy between medical and organizational worlds

Developing physician engagement and leadership for health system improvement implies the reconciliation of two distinct institutional logics: professional and organizational (Lounsbury, 2007). Institutional logics create norms and beliefs that organize the views of individuals and groups and provide a framework for decision-making (Dimaggio, 1997; Thornton, 2002), factors that are essential for improving health systems. The dominant professional logic for doctors rests on principles of self-regulation and individual clinical autonomy to guarantee clinical quality. Physicians' autonomy is exercised in the context of their accountability to patients and peers (Slater, 2001). By contrast, the organizational, or managerial, logic is based on the assumption that improving healthcare systems requires greater emphasis on management practices and incentives, including mechanisms of accountability, objective setting and continuous improvement (Ferlie et al., 1996). Combined with the policy and regulatory context and market forces, these two institutional logics provide the main organizing principles for the health sector (Friedland and Alford, 1991).

In a system characterized by great inertia (Coiera, 2011), the demand for increased physician engagement and leadership aligned with broader system/organizational goals implies reconciling the competing demands of these two distinct institutional logics (Reay and Hinings, 2009). Although some studies recognize an ongoing process of accommodation between the medical profession and organizations (e.g. Champagne et al., 1998; Kitchener et al., 2005), they do not illuminate how such accommodation can promote health system improvement. Closer examination of the various strategies used by health systems to engage doctors in achieving broader organizational and health system goals reveals the dynamics that result from efforts to reconcile the different institutional logics of the medical and organizational worlds.

Structural strategies for organizational or economic integration of physicians

Structural strategies include efforts to alter organizational designs and incentive systems to promote physician engagement and leadership for health system improvement.

A *first* stream of work in this category deals with structural determinants of physician engagement and leadership based on numerous empirical studies of hospitals and hospital systems mainly within the United States. The leading theme in this work focuses on creating formal organizational positions and new structures and policies (including formal executive positions for physicians, economic incentives to align physician interests with organizational/system interests and organizational structures to better integrate physicians) that influence physician engagement and leadership (Burns and Muller, 2008; Dickson, 2012; Metrics@Work et al., 2012; MSEQWG, 2012).

A variety of structures have been used by hospitals to integrate physicians within management (Denis et al., 2012). New organizational designs in various US organizations, including the Johns Hopkins Hospital and Health System, Kaiser Permanente, the Mayo Clinic and Intermountain Healthcare, have developed dyadic physician–manager leadership structures at multiple decision levels. These organizations typically also focus on strong physician engagement through economic integration and a commitment to view quality of care as the organization's core strategy, supported by well-developed information technology (Baker and Denis, 2011; Denis et al., 2011; Ham, 2014). Hybrid leadership structures that create physician leadership roles alongside other managers help in integrating clinical and non-clinical leadership, but such structures vary considerably across sites and are likely insufficient to enable broadscale improvement.

Other research has focused on using economic incentives for hospital–physician collaboration. In an extensive review of the US experience, Burns and Muller (2008) found only weak evidence supporting the impact of various models of economic integration used to link physicians with their organizations. These findings suggest the need for diverse organizational strategies to support better alignment of medical professional and organizational/system goals; successful strategies to engage physicians need to go beyond economic incentives.

Some work focuses specifically on the impact of having physicians in formal executive positions. Twenty years ago, Dunham et al. (1994) conducted a survey of US physician executives and other executives, which indicates the importance of physician executive contributions to organizational performance in all types of healthcare organizations. Physicians were seen as contributing to quality assurance activities, having effective relationships with medical staff and evaluating practice patterns to improve efficiency (MSEQWG, 2012). In the UK NHS, some observers saw little change in the traditional view of clinical autonomy following the creation of clinical director positions. Furthermore, physician executives' ability to implement sustainable improvements seemed limited (Ferlie et al., 1996).

Studies by Goes and Zhan (1995) in the 1980s and a recent survey of US hospitals (Goodall, 2011) conclude that using structural mechanisms (physicians as chief executive officers, on joint decision-making committees, etc.) to foster physician integration can positively influence the financial and organizational performance of hospitals or the quality of services provided. Moreover, hospitals where clinicians are engaged in strategic planning and decision-making perform better than hospitals where they are not engaged (Goldstein and Ward, 2004).

Overall, this stream of literature on physician leaders in formal leadership positions suggests such roles may contribute to improving clinical and system performance. Studies on structural determinants of physician integration emphasize the need to distinguish between situations where physicians are highly involved in senior level decision-making and governance without broader engagement, and situations where physicians are also strongly integrated within the organization and thus feel jointly accountable for its performance. The presence of physicians in leadership roles does not by itself guarantee broader physician engagement in the organization.

A *second* stream of structural research centres on the implementation of quality improvement initiatives in healthcare settings and the role of physician engagement and leadership in this process (Weiner et al., 2006; Wardhani et al., 2009). Many researchers have observed the crucial impact of physician involvement and support on successful quality improvement efforts (Lammers et al., 1996; Greer, 2008). Involving physicians in quality and safety initiatives often materializes through their involvement in dedicated structures and by the leadership they can exercise to enlist other physicians.

The broad range of research on structural determinants of physician engagement and leadership illustrates that many organizations/systems have adopted formal structural changes as the critical strategy for linking physicians and organizations more tightly. The evidence suggests that engaging physicians in dedicated structures for improvement is a valuable option. In addition, structural arrangements that formally integrate physicians within governance and management bodies and functions may plausibly contribute to improvement since such positions control the required resources and goal setting. However, the greater challenge rests in integrating physicians and simultaneously developing their sense of shared responsibility and accountability to organizations. Additional strategies seem necessary to supplement structural strategies to enable physician engagement and leadership.

Process strategies for physician engagement and leadership

We concentrate here on the critical dynamics of physician leadership and engagement in organizations identified as high performing and those involved in quality improvement initiatives (Dickson, 2012). We explore the role of organizational context, strategies and processes favouring the development of physician engagement and leadership for improvement.

Physician engagement does not just happen – organizations must develop strategies and work at their execution (Dickson, 2012). A multimethod study of a sample of US hospitals concluded that one key variable in promoting physician involvement is the level of trust between physicians and organizations (Zuckerman et al., 1998). Trust is important in better aligning physicians and hospitals and may help in designing and supporting proper incentives and clinical integration mechanisms (Kaissi, 2012; Metrics@Work et al., 2012). The importance of trust suggests the value of considering the broader organizational context and culture.

Spurgeon et al. (2008) reported on physician engagement in the United Kingdom using the Medical Engagement Scale. They found that higher medical engagement in hospitals was associated with higher scores on many quality indicators. Becher and Chassin (2002) and Goode et al. (2002) identified a series of conditions supporting physicians' engagement in quality improvement initiatives. These studies show that organizations can develop diversified strategies to engage physicians in improvement initiatives, including actions advancing trust and accountability. Effective physician engagement and leadership rely on the development of 'clinical governance' in the United Kingdom. Clinical governance is an umbrella concept that includes a set of management principles and tools (Department of Health, 2010) developed to reinforce clinicians' accountability for resource use and quality of care. Although the term is used more in the United Kingdom, Duvalko et al. (2009) discussed the development of performance improvement and clinical governance at Cancer Care Ontario, where strong emphasis on measurement and accountability helped create more effective physician engagement.

More broadly, Hockey and Bates (2010) identified performance measurement and transparency as critical contributors to physician engagement and improved performance, given stable and supportive organizational contexts. Organizations having stable leadership and good relationships with individual physicians appear able to translate organizational values into sound clinical practice.

Overall, these authors indicate that organizational leadership can play a key role in improving quality by providing medical staff with support systems and knowledge of quality improvement skills that promote improved care. More detailed discussion of four mechanisms for engaging physicians that result in higher performance will illustrate the ways in which such strategies help to engage physicians for improvement and leadership roles.

First, O'Hare and Kudrle (2007) discuss developing a physician 'compact', an explicit social contract between physicians as a group and the organization, as one mechanism to help clarify roles, expectations and accountabilities. Silversin (2009) worked with physician leaders and administrators to develop a compact guide to administrator–physician relationships. The new compact drove several key changes, and many areas showed improvements. A recent report on the Ottawa Hospital's experience with physician compacts also described success in using this mechanism for engagement (Scott et al., 2012). These examples suggest that such compacts may be effective means to enlist and align physician goals and activities, particularly in environments where physicians are relatively independent.

Developing a physician compact may be one way to deliberately act on the cultural dimensions of physician engagement often identified in research on quality improvement in healthcare organizations (Lammers et al., 1996; Ferlie and Shortell, 2001; Caldwell et al., 2008).

A second important mechanism focuses on the need for receptive organizational contexts. Physician leadership and engagement efforts must link to broader strategy to create this context. Physicians are motivated by efforts to create a more supportive culture for patient care quality and a better work life (Bohmer, 2012; MSEQWG, 2012). A study of leadership and strategic change in a large physician organization in the western United States (Caldwell et al., 2008) showed that intangible factors like support for a new strategy, group norms and leaders' actions can influence implementation, and the effects of these social processes are interactive. Effective leadership has the greatest impact when a group is positively oriented towards change, and adding support for a new strategy increases the success of implementation.

In a recent discussion of high-performing clinical systems, Bohmer (2012: 7) argues that 'leaders at the lowest level of delivery organizations, where clinicians and patients interact, have control over a set of organizational levers that have been shown to have a meaningful impact on both intermediate medical outcomes (e.g. adverse event and readmission rates) and longer term outcomes (e.g. mortality rates)'. Various studies support this point. Research on the effectiveness of quality improvement underlines the critical role of clinical microsystem leaders in improvement (Nelson et al., 2007). This work extends learning gained from quality improvement research that reveals the importance of organizational context (Blumenthal et al., 2012). More fundamentally, it provides a basis for understanding how organizational context can develop a powerful connection linking clinical improvement and physician engagement (Bohmer, 2011), as well as the nature of physician leadership that may be conducive to such improvement.

A third mechanism, based on the importance of physician leadership for improvement, has emerged in research on factors contributing to improved clinical performance and the type of leadership that can be developed to support physician engagement. For example, Albert et al. (2010) determined that a particular project was successful primarily because of physician leadership and assigning physicians trained as Six Sigma 'Green Belts' from project inception.

Different leadership appears necessary for various organizational situations (Shumway, 2004). Vina et al. (2009) showed that high-performing US hospitals had a chief medical officer who was more inclined to focus on adherence to quality indicators. Their study also showed the benefits of designating physicians as champions for specific clinical conditions as a strategy to improve quality of care. Ferlie and Shortell (2001) emphasized the role of transformational and transactional leadership in improving health systems.

One important message here is that, although senior leadership is key, its actions are not enough to support improvement and create the capacity to act. Responsibilities for improvement need to be delegated across the organization to create agents of change within different spheres of influence (within teams and among clinical staff in general) (Lammers et al., 1996; Caldwell et al., 2008).

A fourth mechanism in this literature centres on the value of teams and team leadership in developing a favourable context for physician engagement and leadership and organizational improvement (Metrics@Work et al., 2012). In quality improvement, teams of professionals and other staff are selected to improve care processes in hospitals and other settings. Managing multiple processes and developing collaboration is critical to achieving high team performance (Lammers et al., 1996; Shumway, 2004). Typically, quality improvement initiatives are carried out by quality improvement teams (Lammers et al., 1996; Caldwell et al., 2008). Team development (teamwork or team dynamics, team leadership, team building) therefore provides an important avenue for physician engagement and quality improvement implementation (Brand et al., 2007). Physicians are seen as having a pivotal role in developing team effectiveness (Jain et al., 2008). However, some authors (Jain et al., 2008; Weller et al., 2010) argue that organizational contexts may help to promote both effective teams and the key role of physician leaders in team effectiveness. Physician leaders are well positioned to foster transient task-specific leadership, positive team context and adoption of a patient-oriented posture (Jain et al., 2008). They can also liaise between clinical teams and the broader organizational environment. The presence of engaged physicians on quality improvement teams is assessed as contributing to the impact of such teams (Weiner et al., 2006; Wardhani et al., 2009).

In primary care settings, Wolfson et al. (2009) found that physicians saw leadership and teamwork as crucial to performance improvement. Furthermore, practices that succeeded in quality improvement had office cultures that valued teamwork and shared responsibility and also featured routine, co-operative interaction among physicians and between doctors and support staff. Financial incentives were not viewed as important. The study illustrates the interaction of factors and the key role of broader organizational context in developing physician engagement and leadership for improvement.

Developing a physician compact, a receptive organizational context, more collective and distributed forms of leadership and team-based organizations appear to be valuable elements in promoting physician engagement and leadership for improvement. A similar list of factors was identified in a study by Taitz et al. (2012) of ten high-performing US hospitals that examined the engagement of physicians in quality improvement and patient safety. The studies in this section all highlight the critical role of physician engagement and leadership in improving performance. They also suggest that leadership is needed at both microsystem and organizational levels and that supportive organizational contexts which set goals and provide information and support to front-line teams can have a reinforcing, enabling effect on engagement and leadership. Managing the interdependencies among these different factors appears essential to developing physician engagement and leadership. Organizational and system contexts that facilitate recruiting physicians into various governing and decision-making bodies, mobilizing front-line physicians in improvement efforts and focusing on measurement and performance management may also favour the development of more distributed, collective forms of leadership.

Policy and research implications

This review provides insights on strategies used by healthcare organizations to promote physician engagement and leadership for health system improvement. Whereas efforts to involve physicians in organizational affairs and improvement initiatives once focused mostly on structural strategies, they now increasingly emphasize process strategies. Process strategies focus on generating a facilitative context for engagement, leadership and improvement, moving beyond a transactional approach to physician involvement with broader organizational/system goals. They encourage a shift from viewing physicians primarily as customers of hospitals or healthcare organizations to seeing them as partners in healthcare system management and improvement. This review also highlights the dialectic nature of physician engagement and physician leadership for improvement. Healthcare organizations face a continuing challenge in connecting the clinical, operational world with the strategic apex. Leadership for improvement is necessary at all organizational levels to mobilize physicians around wider organizational goals. Simultaneously, a strategy that creates a facilitative context for broader engagement provides fertile ground for developing physician leaders. The need to balance structural and process strategies for physician engagement and leadership is a clear finding from this review.

   The literature also conveys a sense of movement towards a tighter coupling of interests, both psychologically and financially, between the medical profession and hospitals/organizations (Taitz et al., 2012).

This closer connection resonates with recent research on organized professionalism, a contemporary concept that contrasts with the traditional view of professions focused on occupational control. Organized professionalism is defined as situations where organizations become important anchors for producing standards and identities and where professional practices are embodied in an organizational, or system, logic (Noordegraaf, 2011). The emergence of organized professionalism in healthcare systems can be discerned from two observations from studies on health systems and improvement: (1) physicians have unique expertise and influence on clinical microsystems and access to levers to support improvement and achieve broader organizational/system goals; and (2) because of the documented challenges in medical practice (including studies on appropriateness and safety of care), physicians and other health professionals need richer organizational contexts to develop and sustain high standards of practice and care. There are still challenges about how best to stimulate physician involvement to capitalize on the development of organized professionalism in the light of the limitations of structural strategies. Some of the literature covered in this review provides emerging answers to this challenge.

From a policy perspective, health organizations and systems must develop strategies to provide organizational support for developing clinical microsystems where physicians can have 'engaging experiences' in their day-to-day work (Nelson et al., 2007; Snell et al., 2011). In addition, organizations need to create a facilitative context for physicians who may want to seek more formal leadership positions.

This view of developing leadership and engagement from the top to the bottom of the system is increasingly endorsed in many healthcare systems. For example, a model of shared leadership is the basis of the Medical Leadership Competency Framework in the United Kingdom (NHS Institute and AoMRC, 2010). Clark (2012: 438) describes the NHS as moving from a model of general management supported by medical representatives 'to one of greater distributed leadership with many doctors at all levels and across all parts of the system engaged in priority setting and decision-making, particularly around models of care, quality and safety'.

This approach to physician leadership also finds support in contemporary research that sees leadership more as a process and set of practices performed by numerous individuals throughout organizations than as a single individual in a formal position of authority (Denis et al., 2010; Metrics@Work et al., 2012). Such research shifts the emphasis from individual traits and behaviours to more distributed, collective forms of leadership (Denis et al., 2001). The collective property of leadership denotes the sharing of leadership roles among a set of actors in a complementary manner. These groups of organizational leaders combine diverse expertise, skills and sources of legitimacy to respond to system challenges (Denis et al., 2001). Distributed leadership refers to the degree to which such roles are spread across a system (Buchanan et al., 2007). Because of the fundamental characteristics of healthcare organizations, leadership needs to be widely distributed. The challenge is to harness these various sources of leadership to improve care and services, making cohesion and co-operation among leaders crucial.

Our review also stresses the critical nature of a receptive organizational context supporting physician leadership and engagement. Simply developing new positions or structures for greater physician participation does not create leadership. Instead, leadership needs to be developed in a context that values physician participation and encourages physician commitment to a culture of continuous improvement and teamwork. Thus, effective leadership thrives in an environment linking clinical activities with senior-level decisions and builds upon group norms and an organizational culture that enables a supportive work environment and values efforts to improve the quality of care and services provided.

The emphasis on organizational culture, group norms and distributed leadership has implications for the use of economic incentives to improve performance. Burns and Muller (2008) noted the growing use of payment reforms and economic incentives to improve hospital–physician collaboration. They concluded that these efforts had limited impact on improving quality and containing costs, partly because the economic incentives did not address clinical integration and the development of more effective relationships. New payment reforms that address these issues may be more successful, but the larger issue is that economic incentives alone may be insufficient if the core concern is creating shared purpose, commitment to common organizational norms and alignment of actions, both within and across organizations.

This review also has some limitations that may be used to guide future research. Most of the studies focused on well-structured environments like hospitals. The challenge of engaging physicians and developing leadership in less structured environments, such as networks of care providers across organizations, has been addressed less frequently. Although there are numerous scholarly works on networks, they rarely consider the engagement and leadership of physicians within such environments. The growing role of formal and informal networks in contemporary healthcare systems highlights the need to understand effective strategies to engage physicians in such contexts.

Another issue warranting further investigation involves the strategies needed to facilitate cultural change supporting improvement. Although the literature provides many insights on physician involvement in improvement initiatives, it provides less specific insights on how physicians and, more broadly, organizational leaders can develop strategies to renew organizational and professional norms. The work on physician compacts underscores the importance of group and organizational norms in renewing professionalism but provides only limited insights on how to deliberately act upon organizational contexts for cultural change.

Finally, the reviewed literature downplays the importance of organizational power and politics in shaping opportunities or limitations for physician engagement and leadership. Beyond the literature on competing institutional logics in organizations, studies on physician engagement and leadership pay little attention to how pressures for a more 'organized professionalism' challenge existing positions and behaviours and may induce resistance. Some research on clinical governance underlines the political dynamics around the renewal of clinical microsystems (Currie et al., 2012). However, the literature is largely silent on the kind of countervailing powers that may represent enabling forces to challenge the status quo and the limitations of a model of professionalism based on occupational control.

Acknowledgements

This chapter evolved from a paper presented at the SHOC's 9th International Organizational Behaviour in Healthcare Conference in Copenhagen, Denmark, in April 2014, which was based on a synthesis report (Denis et al., 2013) supported by a Canadian Institutes of Health Research grant. Details on the synthesis methodology are available in the report.

On behalf of the research team: Charlyn Black, Professor, School of Population and Public Health, University of British Columbia; Ann Langley, Professor, Department of Management, HEC Montréal; Bernard Lawless, Assistant Professor, Physician, St. Michael's Hospital, University of Toronto; Diane Leblanc, Organizational Psychologist, Capital District Health Authority, Halifax; Maria Lusiani, Postdoctoral Fellow, HEC Montréal; Charlotte Moore Hepburn, Assistant Professor, Department of Paediatrics, Faculty of Medicine, University of Toronto; Marie-Pascale

Pomey, Associate Professor, Université de Montréal; Ghislaine Tré, Post-doctoral Fellow, St. Mary's Hospital. Montreal. Members of the team have not reviewed the chapter.

References

Albert, K., Sherman, B. and Backus, B. (2010) 'How length of stay for conges-tive heart failure patients was reduced through six sigma methodology and physician leadership', *American Journal of Medical Quality*, 25(5): 392–397.
Baker, G. R. and Denis, J.-L. (2011) 'Medical leadership in health care systems: from professional authority to organisational leadership', *Public Money and Management*, 31(5): 355–362.
Baker, G. R., MacIntosh-Murray, A., Porcellato, C. et al. (2008) *High Performing Health Care Systems: Delivering Quality by Design*. Toronto: Longwoods.
Becher, E. C. and Chassin, M. R. (2002) 'Taking health care back: the physician's role in quality improvement', *Academic Medicine*, 77(10): 953–962.
Blumenthal, D. M., Bernard, K., Bohnen, J. et al. (2012) 'Addressing the leader-ship gap in medicine: residents' need for systematic leadership development training', *Academic Medicine*, 87(4): 513–522.
Bohmer, R. (2012) *Instrumental Value of Medical Leadership: Engaging Doctors in Improving Services*. London: The King's Fund.
Bohmer, R. M. J. (2011) 'The four habits of high-value Health Care Organizations', *New England Journal of Medicine*, 365(22): 2045–2047.
Brand, C., Ibrahim, J., Bain, C. et al. (2007) 'Engineering a safe landing: engaging medical practitioners in a systems approach to patient safety', *Internal Medicine Journal*, 37(5): 295–302.
Buchanan, D. A., Fitzgerald, L. and Ketley, D. (2007) *The Sustainability and Spread of Organizational Change: Modernizing Healthcare*. New York: Routledge.
Burns, L. R. and Muller, R. W. (2008) 'Hospital-physician collaboration', *Milbank Quarterly*, 86(3): 375–434.
Caldwell, D. F., Chatman, J., O'Reilly, C. A. et al. (2008) 'Implementing strate-gic change in a health care system: the importance of leadership and change readiness', *Health Care Management Review*, 33(2): 124–133.
Champagne, F., Denis, J.-L. and Bilodeau, H. (1998) 'Les intérêts médicaux et hos-pitaliers: la réconciliation sera-t-elle possible?' *Ruptures, revue transdisciplinaire en santé*, 5(1): 53–61.
Clark, J. (2012) 'Medical leadership and engagement: no longer an optional extra', *Journal of Health Organization and Management*, 26(4): 437–443.
Coiera, E. (2011) 'Why system inertia makes health reform so difficult', *BMJ*, 342: 3693.
Currie, G., Lockett, A., Finn, R. et al. (2012) 'Institutional work to maintain pro-fessional power: re-creating the model of medical professionalism', *Organization Studies*, 33: 937–962.
Denis, J.-L., Baker, G. R., Black, C. et al. (2013) *Exploring the Dynam-ics of Physician Engagement and Leadership for Health System Improve-ment: Prospects for Canadian Healthcare Systems*, GETOSS/ENAP, Avail-able from: http://www.getoss.enap.ca/GETOSS/Publications/Lists/Publications/Attachments/438/Expedited_Synthesis_CIHR_2013-04-10-Final.pdf

Denis, J.-L., Davies, H., Ferlie, E. et al. (2011) *Assessing Initiatives to Transform Healthcare Systems: Lessons for the Canadian Healthcare System*. Ottawa: Canadian Health Services Research Foundation.

Denis, J.-L., Lamothe, L. and Langley, L. (2001) 'The dynamics of collective leadership and strategic change in pluralistic organizations', *Academy of Management Journal*, 44(4): 809–837.

Denis, J.-L., Langley, A. and Rouleau, L. (2010) 'The practice of leadership in the messy world of organizations', *Leadership*, 6(1): 67–88.

Denis, J.-L., Langley, A. and Sergi, V. (2012) 'Leadership in the plural', *The Academy of Management Annals*, 6(1): 211–283.

Department of Health (United Kingdom) (2010) *Equity and Excellence: Liberating the NHS*. London: The Stationery Office.

Dickson, G. (2012) *Anchoring Physician Engagement in Vision and Values: Principles and Framework*, Research paper prepared for the Regina Qu'Appelle Health Region.

Dimaggio, P. J. (1997) 'Culture and cognition', *Annual Review of Sociology*, 23: 263–287.

Dunham, N. C., Kindig, D. A. and Schulz, R. (1994) 'The value of the physician executive role to organizational effectiveness and performance', *Health Care Management Review*, 19(4): 56–63.

Duvalko, K. M., Sherar, M. and Sawka, C. (2009) 'Creating a system for performance improvement in cancer care: cancer care Ontario's clinical governance framework', *Cancer Control*, 16(4): 293–302.

Dwyer, A. (2010) 'Medical managers in contemporary healthcare organisations: a consideration of the literature', *Australian Health Review*, 34: 514–522.

Ferlie, E., Ashburner, L., Fitzgerald, L. et al. (1996) *The New Public Management in Action*. Oxford: Oxford University Press.

Ferlie, E. B. and Shortell, S. M. (2001) 'Improving the quality of health care in the United Kingdom and the United States: a framework for change', *Milbank Quarterly*, 79(2): 281–315.

Friedland, R. and Alford, R. R. (1991) 'Bringing society back in: symbols, practices, and institutional contradictions' in W. W. Powell and P. J. DiMaggio (eds.), *The New Institutionalism in Organizational Analysis*. Chicago: University of Chicago Press.

Goes, J. B. and Zhan, C. (1995) 'The effects of hospital-physician integration strategies on hospital financial performance', *Health Services Research*, 30(4): 507–530.

Goldstein, S. M. and Ward, P. T. (2004) 'Performance effects of physicians' involvement in hospital strategic decisions', *Journal of Service Research*, 6(4): 361–372.

Goodall, A. H. (2011) 'Physician-leaders and hospital performance: is there an association?' *Social Science & Medicine*, 73(4): 535–539.

Goode, L. D., Clancy, C. M., Kimball, H. R. et al. (2002) 'When is "Good Enough"?' The role and responsibility of physicians to improve patient safety', *Academic Medicine*, 77(10): 947–952.

Greer, A. L. (2008) *Embracing Accountability: Physician Leadership, Public Reporting and Teamwork in the Wisconsin Collaborative for Healthcare Quality*, The Commonwealth Fund, Available from: http://www.commonwealthfund.org/Publications/Fund-Reports/2008/Jun/Embracing-Accountability–Physician-

Leadership–Public-Reporting–and-Teamwork-in-the-Wisconsin-Coll.aspx [Accessed December 9, 2014].

Ham, C. (2014) *Reforming the NHS from Within: Beyond Hierarchy, Inspection and Markets*, London, England: The King's Fund.

Hockey, P. M. and Bates, D. W. (2010) 'Physicians' identification of factors associated with quality in high- and low-performing hospitals', *Joint Commission Journal on Quality & Patient Safety*, 36(5): 217–223.

Jain, A. K., Thompson, J. M., Chaudry, J. et al. (2008) 'High-performance teams for current and future physician leaders: an introduction', *Journal of Surgical Education*, 65(2): 145–150.

Kaissi, A. (2012) *A Roadmap for Trust: Enhancing Physician Engagement*, Research paper prepared for the Regina Qu'Appelle Health Region.

Kitchener, M., Coronna, C. A. and Shortell, S. M. (2005) 'From the doctor's workshop to the iron cage? Evolving modes of physician control in US health systems', *Social Science & Medicine*, 60: 1311–1322.

Lammers, J. C., Cretin, S., Gilman, S. et al. (1996) 'Total quality management in hospitals: the contributions of commitment, quality councils, teams, budgets, and training to perceived improvement at Veterans Health Administration Hospitals', *Medical Care*, 34(5): 463–478.

Lounsbury, M. (2007) 'A tale of two cities: competing logics and practice variation in the professionalizing of mutual funds', *Academy of Management Journal*, 50(2): 289–307.

Metrics@Work Inc., Grimes, K. and Swettenham, J. (2012) *Compass for Transformation: Barriers and Facilitators to Physician Engagement*, Research paper prepared for the Regina Qu'Appelle Health Region.

MSEQWG: Medical Staff Engagement in Quality Working Group (2012) *A Model for Medical Staff Engagement in Quality*, Report prepared for Alberta Health Services.

Nelson, E. C., Batalden, P. and Godfrey, M. M. (eds) (2007) *Quality by Design: A Clinical Microsystems Approach*, 1st edition. San Francisco: Jossey-Bass.

NHS Institute for Innovation and Improvement and Academy of Medical Royal Colleges (2010) *Medical Leadership Competency Framework*, 3rd edition. Coventry: NHS Institute for Innovation and Improvement.

Noordegraaf, M. (2011) 'Risky business: how professionals and professional fields (must) deal with organizational issues', *Organization Studies*, 32(10): 1349–1371.

O'Hare, D. and Kudrle, V. (2007) 'Increasing physician engagement. Using norms of physician culture to improve relationships with medical staff', *Physician Executive*, 33(3): 38–45.

Reay, T. and Hinings, C. R. B. (2009) 'Managing the rivalry of competing institutional logics', *Organization Studies*, 30: 629–652.

Scott, C. G., Thériault, A., McGuire, S. et al. (2012) 'Developing a physician engagement agreement at the Ottawa hospital: a collaborative approach', *Healthcare Quarterly (Toronto, Ont.)*, 15(3): 50–53.

Shumway, J. M. (2004) 'Components of quality: competence, leadership, teamwork, continuing learning and service', *Medical Teacher*, 26(5): 397–399.

Silversin, J. (2009) 'Engaging the head and heart: leading change', *Healthcare Quarterly*, 13 Spec. No.: 49–53.

Singer, S. and Shortell, S. M. (2011) 'Implementing accountable care organizations: ten potential mistakes and how to learn from them', *JAMA: Journal of the American Medical Association*, 306(7): 758–759.

Slater, B. (2001) 'The new politics of medical regulation', *Social Science & Medicine*, 32: 871–883.

Snell, A. J., Briscoe, D. and Dickson, G. (2011) 'From the inside out: the engagement of physicians as leaders in health care settings', *Qualitative Health Research*, 21(7): 952–967.

Spurgeon, P., Barwell, F. and Mazelan, P. (2008) 'Developing a medical engagement scale (MES)', *International Journal of Clinical Leadership*, 16: 213–223.

Taitz, J. M., Lee, T. H. and Sequist, T. D. (2012) 'A framework for engaging physicians in quality and safety', *BMJ Quality & Safety*, 21(9): 722–728.

Thornton, P. H. (2002) 'The rise of the corporation in a craft industry: conflict and conformity in institutional logics', *Academy of Management Journal*, 45(1): 81–101.

Vina, E. R., Rhew, D. C., Weingarten, S. R. et al. (2009) 'Relationship between organizational factors and performance among pay-for-performance hospitals', *Journal of General Internal Medicine*, 24(7): 833–840.

Wardhani, V., Utarini, A., van Dijk, J. P. et al. (2009) 'Determinants of quality management systems implementation in hospitals', *Health Policy*, 89(3): 239–251. doi: 10.1016/j.healthpol.

Weiner, B. J., Alexander, J. A., Baker, L. C. et al. (2006) 'Quality improvement implementation and hospital performance on patient safety indicators', *Medical Care Research and Review*, 63(1): 29–57. doi: 10.1177/1077558705283122.2008.06.008.

Weller, J., Thwaites, J., Bhoopatkar, H. et al. (2010) 'Are doctors team players, and do they need to be?' *New Zealand Medical Journal*, 123(1310): 109–117.

Wolfson, D., Bernabeo, E., Leas, B. et al. (2009) 'Quality improvement in small office settings: an examination of successful practices', *BMC Family Practice*, 10: 14.

Zuckerman, H. S., Hilberman, D. W., Andersen, R. M. et al. (1998) 'Physicians and organizations: strange bedfellows or a marriage made in heaven?' *Frontiers of Health Services Management*, 14(3): 3–34.

7
The Role of the Quality Coordinator: Articulation Work in Quality Development

Marie Henriette Madsen

Introduction

Quality development in healthcare has undergone a movement from processes led by the medical professions to processes increasingly regulated by nationally formulated frameworks that consist of increased systematics, transparency and data-driven quality development (Power, 1997; Wiener, 2000; Timmermans and Berg, 2003; Knudsen et al., 2008; Knudsen, 2011). As part of this change, quality development has become a consolidated and permanent part of healthcare, with its own institutions, organizations and practices. In that respect, it has become a distinct, formalized field and a part of the hospital organization in its own right, occupying a considerable space in the hospitals in terms of tasks, methods, technologies and assigned employees. As part of this development, organizational positions in the hospital are changing and new organizational positions have been introduced in order to address the increasing demands for quality development (Kirkpatrick et al., 2009, 2011).

This study was sparked by an interest in this new and distinct field of hospital life, especially the way the practices of this field unfold in relation to the rest of the hospital organization. Practice should here be understood as what people do in everyday life, and as a set of socially organized activities that both constitute and are constituted in the interactions of people and their environment (Miettinen et al., 2009; Schmidt, 2014). Within healthcare, the interest in the organization and the ordering of practices has primarily been concerned with clinical work. In studies of the organization of medical work by Strauss and colleagues (Strauss et al., 1997), medical work is framed as '... several different kinds of work, and their relationships, that go to make up the bundle known as medical-nursing care' (ibid, xv). This work has inspired studies of the organization of illness trajectories across, for example, physical distances (Færgemann et al., 2005; Reddy et al., 2006) and different temporalities (Reddy et al., 2006) and through the support from new technologies of communication (Reddy et al., 2001). However, when it comes to the organization of quality development, very little has been said.

This is not to say that the field of quality development in healthcare remains uninvestigated. On the contrary, the continuous efforts to regulate healthcare using methods and technologies that are developed to affect efficiency, transparency and patient involvement have attracted the attention of a great number of researchers. Among these, there has been an interest in the changes in existing work practices, professional autonomy and divisions of labour (Allen and Pilnick, 2005; Zuiderent-Jerak and Berg, 2010). It is, however, striking that these studies foreground methods and technologies in an attempt to unpack how their underlying ideologies and practices may result in unintended consequences that throw into question whether and how quality is improved (Wiener, 2000; Bowker and Star, 2000; Timmermans and Berg, 2003; Vikkelsø, 2005; Pinder et al., 2005; Waring, 2007; Zuiderent-Jerak and Berg, 2010). This study is based on an ethnographic field study performed in a hospital organization. Here, every department had at least one formally assigned person, a so-called quality coordinator (QC), responsible for the planning and implementation of the many processes inherent in quality development. According to the QCs themselves, their department managers and the hospital's quality manager, the position as QC grew directly out of the increasing amount of tasks related to development. The QC's tasks and positioning in the department organizations varied, but many of these tasks were directly related to national demands for quality development. More specifically, the QCs were responsible for the planning and execution of various types of quality assessments, the maintenance of different quality technologies and the surveillance and communication of quality-related focus areas in the departments. Despite the close relation to mandatory frameworks of quality development, the QCs were positioned in a service function (Mintzberg, 2001) and hence without managerial influence or integration with the clinical parts of the hospital. Since quality development is loaded with controversies related to changes in professional autonomy and work, the workload, relevance and the effects of the present frameworks for quality development, this 'in-between' position was described as a challenge by the QCs themselves. In this chapter, however, I attempt to provide a different view on the possibilities for QCs to contribute to the processes of quality development by asking how they may do this from an organizational position, outside both management and clinical work. With a two-part analysis, I show, firstly, that quality development projects constitute a new, yet time-limited, arena of negotiations and, secondly, how QCs have the possibility of framing and supporting this new arena through their specific abilities to move in between organizational layers and professional boundaries.

Outline of the chapter

The remainder of this text is structured in five sections. As a continuation of the above framing of quality development as a particular type of hospital work, I begin with a description of the theoretical underpinnings and the specific theoretical concept of articulation work. This is followed by a brief introduction to the methods used in this study and the empirical material, after which I introduce the empirical case used in the analysis, specifically a case of a 'care pathway'. In the third section, I present the analysis of the case, in which particular attention is paid to the emergence of a new arena of negotiations related to the care pathway process, and how they enable the QCs to contribute to the progress of the process. Finally, in the conclusion, I elaborate on the wider consequences of the emergence of QCs as organizational figures in healthcare in terms of their contribution to both quality development and their interactions with other professional groupings in the hospital.

Theoretical framework: Paying attention to articulation work

In the analysis, I consider quality development a distinct and consolidated part of hospital life, with its own agendas, assigned actors and tasks. It therefore requires its own form of organizing. At the same time, the stated goal of quality development is to improve other types of hospital work, which necessitates an awareness of how other types of hospital work are organized. It is in these intersections between quality development and other types of hospital work that this study of the QC's abilities to contribute to processes of quality development is positioned.

Theoretically, the analysis draws on the concept of articulation work originally developed by Anselm Strauss and colleagues (Strauss et al.,

1997). Through a study of the organization of medical work, they identified different types of work that add up to what they term 'an arc of work'. Strauss defines an arc in the following way:

> An arc for any given project consists of the totality of tasks arrayed both sequentially and simultaneously along the course of a trajectory or a project.
>
> (Strauss, 1985: 4; Strauss et al., 1997)

As this definition reveals, an arc is constituted by a variety of tasks, and these tasks are allocated in time and performed either simultaneously or in sequence. In the case of Strauss and colleagues, an arc of work refers to the illness trajectory, that is, the organized work done over the course of an illness. More generally speaking, it refers to any project of organized actions centred on a given product. Additionally, there is an assigned actor for every task that may entail persons, groups of persons, or units of organizations (Strauss, 1985).

In order to make these building blocks (of tasks, clusters of tasks and various actors to perform those tasks), cohere requires an additional type of work. Strauss and colleagues termed this *articulation work*. Articulation work is a concept that provides an understanding of how a plurality of work practices can merge into a totality (Strauss, 1985). Suchmann has defined it as the work that is required '[...] in order to bring together discontinuous elements – of organizations, of professional practices, of technologies – into working configurations' (Suchmann, 1996). Hence, articulation work constitutes a distinct type of work concerned with the fact that arcs of work do not automatically arrange themselves into coherent sequences. Strauss calls articulation work a 'supra-type of work' and defines it as follows:

> Articulation work amounts to the following. First, the meshing of the often numerous tasks, clusters of tasks, and segments of the total arc. Second, the meshing of efforts of various unit-workers (individuals, departments etc.). Third, the meshing of actors with their various types of work and implicated tasks.
>
> (Strauss, 1985: 8)

Taking both the tradition of symbolic interactionism and an interest in the studies of human interaction as a point of departure, Strauss emphasizes that cooperation between actors cannot be perceived as given, but rather as a result of an effort. Each and every actor will engage in the interaction based on their own perspectives on the subject matter, and if they wish to cooperate, these actors will have to engage in an effort to align their actions with each other. They have to engage in a process of *articulation* through which they can agree upon the purpose of their mutual actions, who does what, when and to what level of quality. In many situations, interactions are based on routines, for instance, as a result of frequent interactions or 'standard operational procedures'. However, when new or unexpected things emerge (Strauss et al., 1997), or when new tasks or circumstances appear (Casper, 1998), the actors have to adjust or engage in negotiations to make new agreements that re-align their actions within this new situation.

Strauss emphasizes that articulation work is performed by everyone whose work interrelates with other types of work. An important part of articulation work is communication and, thus, both the reception of information about the work of others and the provision of information about one's own work to others. Some actors will only need to communicate with the actors closest to them, whereas others – often actors positioned in functions that encompass planning and coordination of wider structures of work – depend on a broader overview (Strauss et al., 1997: 152). In relation to the question of communication as a means of articulation work, the use of various technologies of communication has attracted the attention of many researchers (Schmidt and Bannon, 1992; Fitzpatrick and Ellingsen, 2013). In her study of articulation work in an airport, Lucy Suchmann has, for instance, investigated the capabilities provided by technologies of communication to support the articulation of interrelated work that are separated by large distances (Suchmann, 1996). Here, Suchmann describes how actors engaged in articulation work receive and translate messages about the work of others via computer screens, monitors and windows and, subsequently, translate these inputs into new messages that they can send back and forth between other involved actors. However, the articulation worker's insights are restrained by the available technologies of communication – she is not able to see everything – and the technologies of communication as providers of support in articulation work only manifest in the articulation worker's abilities to use and adapt them to the situation at hand. Furthermore, Suchmann suggests that the ability of *reading the scene* is a necessary trait of articulation workers, and that this requires *knowledge about past, present and future events* combined with *timely communication* (Suchmann, 1997).

In the forthcoming analysis, the concept of articulation work and its inherent emphasis on coherent work being dependent on negotiated orders, as well as the necessity of communication, constitute the analytical framework. This is an empirical sensitivity towards who and what becomes part of the negotiations, what their controversies are about and through which sources and actions of communication the subject of negotiations is revealed and framed. Nevertheless, I do not consider articulation work to be negotiations and communications that are solely fixed around direct interactions or technologies of communication. Rather, I pay attention to the QC's ability to move information, and hence communication and negotiations, around the hospital organization as a particular resource in the articulation work related to quality development.

Method and empirical material

The analysis is based on ethnographic fieldwork that was conducted in a Danish hospital in the Copenhagen area. Here, observations were performed in a Surgical Department and a Medical Department. In the study, two QCs were shadowed (Czarniawska, 2007) in time-limited periods over two years. Furthermore, semi-structured interviews were performed with the QCs, the managers of the hospital departments as well as the hospital directors. This particular analysis is, as mentioned above, related to a specific process initiated in the Medical Department in relation to a mandatory description of a care pathway. This process unfolded over a period of six months in the summer and fall of 2013 and included observations of both formal and informal meetings and conversations, workshops and the translation and coupling of information from different sources. Additionally, the empirical material consists of my own informal and clarifying conversations with participants involved in the process, as well as project documents, that is, various versions of project descriptions and working documents composed during workshops.

The empirical case: A care pathway for medical infections

This analysis revolves around a particular case of quality development related to a particular type of process: the description of a care pathway for *medical infections*. In this section, I introduce the care pathway as a method in quality development and the specific details of the empirical case.

A care pathway is described as a multidisciplinary management tool that both maps key activities in a healthcare process and serves as a record of care that can be used as information for operational and strategic management. It was developed as a tool for rationalizing resource utilization but is now used in healthcare institutions all over the world to address a number of healthcare agendas, including quality development (Pinder et al., 2005; Allen, 2009). What makes a care pathway particularly interesting as a case of articulation work related to quality development is its stated goal of coherence across professionals, organizational units and so on. In Denmark, the use of care pathways as a tool for quality development is part of a general development that links the delivery of healthcare services of a high quality with coherence. This is, among other things, reflected in the formulated aims of The Danish Healthcare Quality Programme (DDKM),[1] which emphasizes the importance of coherent processes and structures in providing treatment and high-quality care (Institut for Kvalitet og Akkreditering i Sundhedsvæsenet, 2012). This emphasis on quality as being more than just qualified by medical or nurse professionalism is underscored throughout the programme material; quality is described as being dependent on the support of the organization and hence as a cross-organizational and cross-professional concern (ibid.). Additionally, the formulation of a specific standard in DDKM stating that the hospitals have to work out descriptions of the care pathways for the most frequent and/or complex diseases underscores this emphasis.

The particular care pathway process for medical infections was part of a goal formulated by the hospital administration to describe care pathways for 80% of their patients before 2015, meaning that each department had to choose one or two care pathways to describe. In order to support these processes, the hospitals had developed a framework guiding the departments through three workshops. In short, this framework, and hence the case described here, included an initial phase in which the department formulated a project description that included the most important areas to focus on within the chosen care pathway, after which the three workshops followed. At the first workshop, the current care pathway was described and the most suboptimal areas were pinpointed; at the second workshop, a prospective and more optimal care pathway was described and ideas to overcome the current obstacles were collected; and, finally, at the third workshop, they focused on how new ideas could be implemented. However, the negotiations and their communicative foundations were not limited to these formal events, and, hence, this analysis also pays attention to the more informal, unplanned actions and interactions.

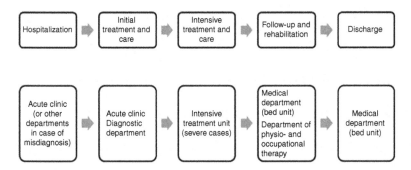

Figure 7.1 Illustration of the care pathway
Source: Adapted by the author from the original project description 'Care pathway for medical infections'.

In the first draft of the project description, the illness trajectory of medical infections, which covers diseases such as pneumonia, blood poisoning (sepsis) and meningitis, was described as *complicated, an area of high risk* and in *need of restructuring*. These descriptions served as justification for the specific choice of medical infections and, additionally, the many organizational units included in the pathway (see Figure 7.1 for the flow chart of the care pathway provided in the project description) made medical infections a difficult case to work with in terms of creating a coherent flow in treatment and care, especially in the first hours of hospitalization when the patient is diagnosed.

Patients that were referred to the hospital for possible medical infections entered the hospital via the Acute Clinic, where doctors (often younger doctors in a residency programme) performed a brief examination of the patient in order to decide which diagnostic tests should be performed. The ordering of diagnostic tests was communicated to the Diagnostic Department by the use of the digital information system, LABKA,[2] and this was also the site of communication when test results were returned to the Acute Clinic from the Diagnostic Department. When the test results were available, the doctor was able to make a preliminary diagnosis and refer the patient to one of the bed units in one of the hospital's specialized departments. In the case of a medical infection, this would be the bed section of Acute Examination and Internal Medicine (Medical Department) or in severe cases the intensive care unit (Anaesthetic Department). Here, the patients would receive treatment, care and training from the hospitals physio- or occupational therapists until their recovery.

As the forthcoming analysis illustrates, the different steps of the care pathway were not equally complicated, and it turned out that the first part of the pathway became the main focus of the process. More specifically, the cooperation between, firstly, the Medical Department and the Anaesthetic Department and, secondly, the Medical Department and the Diagnostic Department became subjects of negotiation with the assistance of the QC's supporting and framing activities.

Framing and supporting arenas of negotiations

In this section, I turn to the analysis of the empirical case described above. This analysis is divided into three sections: the first concerns the negotiation of 'the real' problems to pursue; the second elaborates on the care pathway as a new arena of negotiation; and the third emphasizes the QC's potential as an articulation worker.

Negotiating 'the real' problem(s)

In an initial meeting regarding the formulation of the project description, the QC presented statistics placing medical infections among the most common causes of hospitalization in the Medical Department. Present at this meeting were a radiographer, two nurses and a doctor, all of whom emphasized the importance of being attentive to medical infections. The doctor was even convinced that the available statistics underestimated the prevalence of medical infections, as patients were often hospitalized for something that later turned out to be an infection. This, and other similar meetings, revealed that the choice of medical infections as a subject of development was generally supported by both managers and staff. This support was based on statistical evidence showing a high prevalence of patients either suffering or dying from medical infections. Thus, the choice of medical infections required no or only minimal articulation work from the QC. However, in contrast to this seemingly consensual initial phase of the process, later events revealed that the specific content of *the complicated nature of the care pathway* and *the need of re-structuring* were much more heterogeneously understood. The exact areas in which to pursue improvements were still open for negotiation.

Concurrent with the preparations of the project on medical infections was another process of quality development pending in the hospital, which became constitutive for the further definition of the project. As part of a national campaign on patient safety, the hospital was preoccupied with the introduction of the systematic screening of pressure ulcers. International data had revealed a surprisingly large amount of undiscovered pressure ulcers among hospitalized patients, so the hospital initiated new standards for pressure ulcer screenings requiring all patients hospitalized for six hours or longer to be screened. How this became important for the project on medical infections is explained in the following text.

A few days after the initial meetings for the project took place, the QC met with the ward sister from the Acute Clinic to discuss an entirely different matter. At one point in the conversation, the ward sister brought up the problem of long waiting times in the Acute Clinic, which necessitated the pressure ulcer screenings and thus added to an already constrained time schedule:

> [...] it isn't uncommon that we're waiting many hours on the blood test results [...]. It's probably difficult to avoid such situations [where the screening has to be performed in the Acute Clinic].

> [...] It's a challenge that the younger doctors want to have all the test results before they refer the patients to the bed sections. They're afraid of [name of a senior doctor] and they want to have all the results as justifications for the relevance of their referral.

They then discussed different possible solutions to the problem of long waiting times, but without success. The next day, I met the QC at her office and she was angry. That same morning, the hospital's Unit of Quality & Development had circulated an email to every ward stating that *every* patient had to be screened for pressure ulcers before a date in the near future. She had already discussed this with the head nurse in the Acute Clinic, and the conclusion was clear:

> This will be a catastrophe for the Acute Clinic, because it's adding to an already busy procedure. In the Acute Clinic, they're taking many vital tests, and they don't have time to do much more. Screening for pressure ulcers is extremely time-consuming: The patient needs to be undressed and examined very thoroughly. One fifth of the patients in the Acute Clinic are already spending too much time in the ward because they're waiting on blood test results and doctors' decisions.

She explained that she had decided that the coming process of describing the care pathway for medical infections should pay specific attention to the procedures of blood testing and analysis. This would imply an attention towards the interrelation of the work performed by the Diagnostic Department and the Medical Department, as a way to reduce the waiting times that lead to the stipulated screenings for pressure ulcers in the Acute Clinic.

As the process proceeded and more participants representing other units involved in the trajectory of medical infections were included in the project, further nuances regarding the content of suboptimal coordination appeared. The other participants in the project drew attention to various types of work included in the course of treatment for medical infections – often through informal conversations with the QC. For instance, the QC confronted a senior doctor about the junior doctors' indecisiveness, which supposedly arose out of fear of the senior doctor's critique. This accusation was refuted as 'nonsense' by the senior doctor, who instead drew attention to a general inattentiveness among the junior doctors towards the existing clinical guidelines for the treatment of medical infections. She especially highlighted *sepsis* as an area where very clear criteria for both the diagnosis and treatment were formulated, and she argued persistently that an important part of the new and improved care pathway should include these criteria and that they should be known by healthcare professionals at every step in the care pathway. As such, this would eliminate every doubt among the junior doctors about the right course of action and, hence, also eliminate their reluctance to make decisions, the senior doctor argued. Moreover, she argued that the dynamics between the junior and senior doctors were less problematic within the Medical Department than between the junior doctors of the Medical Department and the senior doctors of the intensive care unit:

> I [as a senior doctor] know that it helps to insist that this patient needs intensive care and it maybe even helps getting really angry. It's much easier to reject a junior doctor, but it isn't right. Decisions of who should receive intensive care should not be based on who is able to insist the most.

In a similar way, the participants from the Diagnostic Department pointed back to the Medical Department when they were faced with critique of their lengthy response times, as described by the ward sister in the Acute Clinic. They explained how they were often unable to move on with the diagnostic tests because of inaccurate referrals (e.g. to MR- or CT scans), mislabelled blood tests (e.g. without the proper patient identification) or blood samples performed incorrectly (e.g. too small an amount of blood). In the Diagnostic Department, the response to these faulty referrals was a rejection communicated in LABKA, however, the doctors in the Medical Department did not encounter this system systematically and therefore missed the information on the rejected referrals. As the QC phrased it: *Then everybody is waiting, but what are they actually waiting for?*

These three positions revealed different suggestions of which parts of the care pathway needed to be changed or optimized and, on the same note, who (or what) needed to change their way of working. The alignment of actors and the construction of a consensus about the problems to pursue obviously required negotiations. These negotiations were to some extent framed by the hospital's general outline of care pathway processes, but, as I show in the following section, the QC was also participating in the framing of this *new* arena of negotiation.

A new arena of negotiation

Figure 7.1 depicts the care pathway as a linear sequence of work provided by actors from at least four departments in the hospital, and, as the case unfolds, we learn that it requires effort to align the different types of work performed with and around the patients in the Acute Clinic, Diagnostic Department and the Anaesthetic Department, respectively. Basically, the care pathway process sets out to clarify where coherence between the work of the involved actors and departments are suboptimal and how it can be improved – or, in other words, how articulation work can be supported within the given care pathway. However, this requires another kind of articulation work related to the specific care pathway process regarding the framing and supporting of negotiations about what the key problem actually is, and, thus, which activities of the care pathway are supposed to change.

Within the framings of the care pathway process, the involved actors are expected to align in order to draw a new and improved care pathway compared to the existing one. These actors are not unrelated or unfamiliar with each other's work, as they are all part of the same existing care pathway. The care pathway process constitutes, however, a *new* arena of negotiation because the object of work (Casper, 1998) is not a patient, but rather a generalized description of their own work. Additionally, this new arena has a time constraint and evaporates as soon as the care process ends, and there are no permanent structures or technologies to support or frame the progress of this negotiation. Each actor that is included in the care pathway process represents an organizational unit or a professional group, and they are asked to contribute with their understanding of the problem. These actors are then delivering resources to the project in terms of their particular 'insight' about the processes that need to be changed or improved. Each involved actor presents their own point of view, formulated from within the scope of their own position in the care pathway. Some of these points of view were juxtaposed in the workshops, but, as the situation with the ward sister from the Acute Clinic revealed, they were also invoked in unexpected situations far from the formal events of the care pathway process. Hence, a specific challenge was the supporting and framing of these negotiations to construct a coherent picture of the most pertinent problems to address in the future.

Mobility: A resource of articulation work

The QCs interviewed and observed in this study were themselves problematizing both their organizational as well as their physical positioning in the hospital. The QC job description defined them as offering a service function to the managers of the departments, and hence they were not directly part of any ward. Additionally, their offices were placed next to the managers' offices, away from the wards, inspiring one QC to use the metaphor of being placed on top of an iceberg, implying that there was something underneath her that she could not see. In terms of the above case, I would suggest that the loose coupling between the QCs and the clinical wards was not only a disadvantage but also a virtue that enabled the progression of the project.

As opposed to the staff who contributed information on the problem of coherence framed by their specialized, but rather narrow, focus, the QC was able to move between the different organizational units, tasks and staff that constituted the different parts of the care pathway. In that way, one part of her work consisted of *collecting* information on the different perspectives concerning what caused suboptimal coherence; and another part of her work in supporting the necessary negotiations within the care pathway process consisted of making *connections* between these different pieces of information provided by the participants.

The QC was in the possession of cumulative information about, for instance, time constraints or miscommunication. This information enabled her to depict an alternative version of where in the care pathway efforts should be made to optimize it, or, in other words, what should be the content of the negotiations of the particular care pathway process. Neither the QC's insights nor her choice of focus and priority came from anywhere. They were based on juxtapositions of earlier encounters with actors performing the tasks that made up the entire, and already-existing, care pathway; their information about a given situation; and her own interpretation of the available information. In that respect, the QC's capability as an *articulation worker*, and thus as a support for the progression of the care pathway process, relied on both her ability to interpret the information provided to her and her ability to interact with those who could provide her with the information. These interactions constituted an important source of information, but they could never reveal the 'big picture'. However, because the QC was not restricted to an enclosed corner of the department or to a specific clinical task, she was able to interact across professional and organizational boarders and grasp a picture that was different than each of the other participants. Additionally, by juxtaposing the involved actors' perspectives with each other, she facilitated a negotiation without necessarily requiring the actors to meet in person. Therefore, the limitations engendered by the QC's positioning in the hospital organization were counteracted by her ability to move between actors and the perspectives they provided.

Conclusion

This study investigated the question of how Quality Coordinators may contribute to the processes of quality development from an organizational position outside both management and clinical work. Characteristic of the process outlined in this chapter, as well as other quality improvement processes, is that it is a short-term project aimed at changing a delimited section of work. What makes the QC's work interesting to study is specifically grounded in this fluctuation: each new quality development project is a new situation where purposes and problems have to be defined and negotiated anew, and where the involved actors are not aligned beforehand.

Drawing on the notion of articulation work and with an emphasis on negotiations and communications as crucial parts of this work, I argued that the QC has a certain potential as an articulation worker in quality development processes. Precisely because of their position as outsiders in the hospital organization, the QC has the ability to move between the various organizational layers and professional groupings, and to both collect and connect a variety of information about 'suboptimality'. The QC is provided with a particular view on the quality development project under scrutiny, which covers the perspectives of several groups of staff and organizational units. Or, in other words, they are able to collect the *particular* perspectives and mesh them into an alternative perspective where new (organizational) types of quality problems are illuminated. Additionally, the QCs are able to usher perspectives along as they go, and in that respect they become a *mobile* source of that information, which feeds into the negotiations of both problems and their solutions. This ability allows them to both frame and support these negotiations via decisions about what should be negotiated and who should participate in them. The QCs depend on what inputs they receive from their interactions with other actors included in the quality development processes; their power to frame is not limitless. Though, with this analysis I have attempted to show how QCs, based on their organisational positioning and their delegated responsibility over quality development processes, are provided with the opportunity to place themselves among actors who want to set the agenda for regulation of hospital work.

Notes

1. *The Danish Healthcare Quality Programme (DDKM),* an accreditation programme consisting of 104 quality standards combined with pre-defined cycles of quality assessment (Institut for Kvalitet og Akkreditering i Sundhedsvæsenet, 2012).
2. LABKA is an information system developed for laboratories to support communication on requisitioning, analysis and response on laboratory tests.

References

Allen, D. (2009) 'From boundary concept to boundary object: the practice and politics of care pathway development', *Social Science & Medicine,* 354–361.

Allen, D. and Pilnick, A. (2005) 'Making connections: healthcare as a case study in the social organisation of work', *Sociology of health & illness,* 27(6): 683–700.

Bowker, G. C. and Star, S. L. (2000) *Sorting Things Out. Classification and Its Consequences,* 1st edition. Cambridge, MA: The MIT Press.

Casper, M. J. (1998) 'Negotiations, work objects, and the unborn patient: the interactional scaffolding of fetal surgery', *Symbolic Interaction,* 21(4): 379–400.

Czarniawska, B. (2007) *Shadowing and Other Techniques for Doing Fieldwork in Modern Societies.* Liber: Copenhagen Business School Press – Universitetsforlaget.

Færgemann, L., Schilder-Knudsen, T. and Carstensen, P. H. (2005) 'The duality of articulation work in large heterogenous settings – a study in health care', *ECSCW 2005: Proceeding of the Ninth European Conference on NComputer Supported Cooperative Work,* pp. 163–183.

Fitzpatrick, G. and Ellingsen, G. (2013) 'A review of 25 years of CSCW research in healthcare: contributions, challenges and future agendas', *Computer Supported Cooperative Work*, 22: 609–665.

Institut for Kvalitet og Akkreditering i Sundhedsvæsenet (2012) *Den danske kvalitetsmodel, DDKM* [Homepage of IKAS], [Online]. Available from: http://www.ikas.dk/DDKM.aspx [Accessed January 9, 2014].

Institut for Kvalitet og Akkreditering i Sundhedsvæsenet (2013) *Akkrediteringsstandarder for sygehuse (2. version)*, 2nd edition. IKAS: Aarhus.

Kirkpatrick, I., Dent, M. and Kragh Jespersen, P. (2011) 'The contested terrain of hospital management: professional projects and healthcare reforms in Denmark', *Current Sociology*, 59(4): 489–506.

Kirkpatrick, I., Kragh Jespersen, P. and Dent, M., Neogy, I. (2009) 'Medicine and management in a comparative perspective: the case of Denmark and England', *Sociology of health & illness*, 31(5): 642–658.

Knudsen, M. (2011) 'Forms of inattentiveness: the production of blindness in the development of a technology for the observation of quality in health services', *Organization Studies*, 32(7): 963–989.

Knudsen, J. L., Christiansen, M. E. and Hansen, B. (2008) *Regulering af kvalitet i det danske sundhedsvæsen.*, Nyt Nordisk Forlag Arnold Busck.

Miettinen, R., Samra-Fredericks, D. and Yanow, D. (2009) 'Re-turn to practice: an introductory essay', *Organization Studies*, 30(12): 1309–1327.

Mintzberg, H. (2001) 'The five basic parts of the organization' in J. M. Shafritz and J. S. Ott (eds.), *Classic of Organization Theory*. Orlando: Hartcourt College Publishers.

Pinder, R., Petchey, R., Shaw, S. and Carter, Y. (2005) 'What's in a care pathway? Towards a cultural cartography of the new NHS', *Sociology of health & illness*, 27(6): 759–779.

Power, M. (1997) *The Audit Society. Rituals of Verification*. Oxford: Oxford University Press.

Reddy, M. C., Dourish, P. and Pratt, W. (2001) 'Coordinating heterogenous work: information and representation in medical care', *Proceedings of the Seventh European Conference on Computer Supported Cooperative Work*, pp. 239–258.

Reddy, M. C., Dourish, P. and Pratt, W. (2006) 'Temporality in medical work: time also matters', *Computer Supported Cooperative Work*, 15: 29–53.

Schmidt, K. (2014) 'Praksisanalyse' in S. Vikkelsø and P. Kjær (eds.), *Klassisk og moderne organisationsteori*, 1. udgave, 1. oplag edn, Hans Reitzels Forlag, pp. 157–179.

Schmidt, K. and Bannon, L. (1992) 'Taking CSCW seriously: supporting articulation work', *Computer Supported Cooperative Work*, 1(1): 7–40.

Strauss, A. (1985) 'Work and the division of labour', *The Sociological Quarterly*, 26(1): 1–19.

Strauss, A., Faerhaugh, S., Suczek, B. and Wiener, C. (1997) *Social Organization of Medical Work*. New Brunswick, NJ: Transaction Publishers.

Suchmann, L. (1996) 'Supporting articulation work' in R. Kling (ed.), *Computerization and Controversy. Value Conflicts and Social Choices*, 2nd edition. Academic Press, pp. 407–421.

Suchmann, L. (1997) 'Centers of coordination. A case and some themes' in L. B. Resnick, R. Säljö, C. Pontecorvo and B. Burge (eds.), *Discourse, Tools and Reasoning: Essays on Situated Cognition*. Berlin: Springer-Verlag, pp. 41–62.

Timmermans, S. and Berg, M. (2003) *The Gold Standard. The Challenge of Evidence-Based Medicine and Standardization in Medicine.* Philadelphia: Temple University Press.

Vikkelsø, S. (2005) 'Subtle redistribution of work, attention and risks: electronic patient records and organisational consequences', *Scandinavian Journal of Information Systems,* 17(1): 3–30.

Waring, J. (2007) 'Adaptive regulation or governmentality: patient safety and the changing regulation of medicine', *Sociology of health & illness,* 29(2): 163–179.

Wiener, C. (2000) *The Elusive Quest. Accountability in Hospitals.* New York: Walter de Gruyter, Inc.

Zuiderent-Jerak, T. and Berg, M. (2010) 'The sociology of quality and safety in health care', in C. Bird, P. Conrad, A. Fremont and S. Timmermans (eds.), *Handbook of Medical Sociology,* 1st edition. Nashville: Vanderbilt University Press, pp. 324–337.

8
The Role of Outside Consultants in Shaping Hospital Organizational Change

Amit Nigam, Esther Sackett and Brian Golden

Achieving strategic change in hospitals, similar to other types of organizations, involves reorienting employees' interpretative frameworks – shared assumptions, narratives or cognitive schema that give meaning to organization members' experiences (Currie and Brown, 2003; Balogun and Johnson, 2004; Lockett et al., 2014; Nigam et al., 2014). Recent studies have begun to consider the social position of actors engaged in interpretative change activities (Battilana et al., 2009). For example, Lockett et al. (2014) show how actors' social positions in the National Health Service in England – as physicians or nurses and as staff in research-oriented tertiary care centres or in clinical care-oriented secondary care centres – shape their ability to envision strategic change. Prior research on social position and interpretive change focuses on the social positions of diverse insiders. Although external consultants often play a critical role in the change process in all types of organizations, including hospitals, our knowledge how they are able to bring about interpretive change remains unclear (Bartunek et al., 2011).

We examine practices that outside consultants engage in, in inter-action with insiders, to shape interpretive change in the context of strategic change in hospitals. Drawing on an ethnographic study of a performance improvement initiative in seven Ontario hospitals involving the use of outside consultants, we found that outsiders were able to precipitate schema change because they could gather and use comprehensive local and contextual knowledge that was superior in breadth to that available to insiders. Drawing on these findings, we turned to Simmel's (1971) account of the stranger to theorize how outside change agents accomplish interpretive change.

Theoretical context

An actor's social position 'mediates their relation to the environment in which they are embedded' (Battilana et al., 2009: 76). It shapes how they are embedded in the organization's social structures, cognitive or cultural environment, and political system (Dacin et al., 1999). The literature on social position and change provides mixed evidence on how insiders' structural, cognitive and political embeddedness might impact their ability to effect schema change. Insiders' structural embeddedness enhances their ability to catalyze change. Senior managers can use their formal authority and access to resources to impose change on an organization. Middle managers and other organization members without formal authority can draw on social networks to gather information and political support (Balogun and Johnson, 2004; Reay et al., 2006; Howard-Grenville, 2007). In healthcare settings, structural embeddedness is complicated by the status hierarchy among professional roles. Physicians have high status and cultural capital in healthcare settings (Abbott, 1988; Stevens, 2000; Battilana, 2011; Nigam, 2013; Lockett et al., 2014). In addition, they have decision-making authority over clinical decisions, and decisions that may have implications for clinical care. This decision-making authority has significant downstream impacts on resource use and on the work of other professional groups (Starr, 1982; Stevens, 2000). Nurses, in contrast, have more limited authority over clinical decisions, but may take on administrative roles that give them hierarchical authority and associated control over at least some financial resources (Battilana, 2011). Both physicians and nurses can potentially have social networks that cut across a range of professional groups. In contrast, outsiders lack the formal authority to impose change and have limited social networks or access to financial resources to mobilize support (Lockett et al., 2014).

Insiders' cognitive embeddedness can either enhance or inhibit their ability to catalyze change. On the one hand, insider's membership in an organization and experience may allow them to develop contextual knowledge that can allow them to craft change strategies that would be tailored to and uniquely effective in their local environment (Reay et al., 2006; Howard-Grenville, 2007). This was the case with advocates for a creating a nurse practitioner role in the Alberta healthcare system (Reay et al., 2006). On the other hand, insiders, absorbed in their day-to-day work, may be limited in their ability to conceptualize new ways of organizing and may become profession-centric in their thinking, only considering the perspective of their own professional group as physicians or nurses (Lockett et al., 2012; DiBenigno and Kellogg, 2014; Lockett et al., 2014). To the extent that outsiders have experience with alternate models of organizing and cultural frameworks, outsiders might be more able to envision alternative ways of doing things (Battilana, 2011).

Finally, political embeddedness can also have mixed effects on agentic possibilities of insiders. On the one hand, a climate of organizational silence, or a lack of psychological safety, might inhibit insiders from voicing support for their desired changes (Edmondson, 1999; Morrison and Milliken, 2000). In healthcare, this would suggest that members of lower-status professional groups would be less likely to speak up or challenge members of higher-status professional groups, that front-line professionals may be unwilling to exercise voice in the presence of more senior clinical administrators or that concerns about their image as competent professionals that are shaped by the broader climate or culture in an organization might inhibit individuals from speaking up, even to their peers (Morrison and Milliken, 2000; Kellogg, 2012). On the other hand, insiders may have knowledge of the political landscape and legitimacy that enhances their effectiveness as political actors (Reay et al., 2006; Howard-Grenville, 2007; Kellogg, 2011).

Data and methods

Empirical context

As part of its strategy to reduce surgical wait times ('wait time strategy') and increase the efficiency and accountability of hospitals, Ontario's Ministry of Health and Long Term developed a consultant-based programme to help hospitals improve perioperative efficiency. Perioperative care represents the full production processes of how surgical procedures are performed. As part of the programme, hospitals could request a visit by a team of consultants that would help them identify problems in the perioperative programme that are potential causes of inefficiency (Sherrard et al., 2009). Each consulting visit unfolded in three broad phases involving interviews and focus groups with stakeholders in the perioperative programme, issue prioritization and action planning where hospital physicians and staff agreed on specific change commitments.

Data and analysis

Our research draws on observation of seven consulting team visits over a six-month period. We engaged in a collaborative, inductive process of data analysis (Charmaz, 2006). We coded specific practices that the

Table 8.1   Data structure

First-order codes	Aggregate constructs	Meta-constructs
Ask questions grounded in familiarity with hospital operations	Access perspectives	Reading the organization
Probe to gather interpretations and opinions	Access perspectives	
Create safe space	Access perspectives	
Make self available as a target of issue selling	Learn the political landscape	
Triangulate perspectives to generate a response	Learn the political landscape	
Broker perspectives and information	Brokering	Brokering perspectives
Ask questions to raise awareness of decision-making processes/structures	Possibility of new actions	Provoking reflection
Ask questions to suggest new ways of thinking	Possibility of new actions	
Encourage brainstorming and creativity	Rethinking taken-for-granted	
Encourage actor to accept accountability	Rethinking taken-for-granted	
Frame responsibility for solving problems	Provide positioning advice	Orchestrating agency
Highlight political barrier to change	Provide positioning advice	
Offer advice on framing	Provide positioning advice	
Offer political advice	Building political capacity	
Recommend political coalition	Building political capacity	

Source: Authors' own.

consultants engaged in over the course of the consulting visit. Once the initial round of data coding was complete, each of the first three authors constructed narrative summaries for focused specifically on the practices the consultants drew on to influence change. We then engaged in a discussion of how we could group the first-order codes theoretical constructs (Charmaz, 2006). We developed a list of 15 codes, each of which identifies a specific practice, and grouped these codes into four meta-constructs. Table 8.1 presents our codes and shows how we grouped them into aggregate constructs and meta-constructs or themes. [1]

The strangers as change agent

Simmel describes the stranger as a distinct social position within a group that is simultaneously close and remote. He observes that 'the stranger is an element of the group itself... an element whose membership within the group involves being outside it and confronting it' (Simmel, 1971: 144). Like the outside change agents that we observe, Simmel describes the social position of the stranger as one defined by social interaction between the outsider and insiders to a community.

Building on Simmel's account of the stranger, we theorize a two-step process – involving four interaction practices – that explains how outside change agents are uniquely able to achieve interpretive change. First, through their interactions with insiders, outsiders *read* the organization to develop a comprehensive view of its issues and routines. As outsiders, the consultants were able to gain organizational commitments to change because they were better able to access information and perspectives from many, diverse insiders. Second, based on their reading outsiders use three additional interaction practices to alter insiders' schema: *brokering perspectives, provoking reflection* and *orchestrating agency*.

We elucidate the consultants' two-step process and four interaction practices by drawing on the vignette of nurse retention and satisfaction at Academic Hospital, one of the sites in our study,[1] to illustrate, in depth, how the consultants were able to generate the commitment of key stakeholders to change.

The unique abilities associated with the social position of the stranger were evident at Academic, where the consultants secured senior administration's commitment to proactively manage nurse retention and job satisfaction in the wake of negative fallout from a new staffing model. Academic had recently adopted a new staffing model that reduced the average number of registered nurses (RNs) in the operating room (OR) from 3 to 2.5, and introduced new paraprofessionals who took on tasks previously performed by RNs. While front-line nurses resented the new model, senior administrators were not willing to acknowledge a problem. The consultants were able to secure senior administration's commitment despite their initial reluctance to consider the issue.

The consultants were able to gather diverse perspectives regarding the effects of the new staffing model and form an independent assessment. Using this assessment, they brokered the perspectives of front-line staff to more senior administrators. In confronting senior administrators with the perspectives of front-line staff, the consultants were able to alter the administrators' interpretation, getting them to recognize gaps in perspectives between administrators and staff.

Reading the organization

At Academic, the consultants gathered opinions, experience and information from across the organization to gain a comprehensive understanding of the effects of the new staffing model. The chief of anaesthesia focused attention on the staffing model in the first meeting with the consultants, which included the CEO, medical chiefs and senior management team. He noted, 'There was a change in the staffing ratio in the OR to bring us in line with our peer hospitals. On the floor there's still sense that we are different [i.e. need more staff per room than other hospitals]'. The CEO followed up by asking if the consultants could validate the perception that there was a need for more staff.

Through their interactions with front-line nurses, physicians and nursing managers – middle managers who supervised front-line nurses for individual hospital units – the consultants were able to gain novel insight into diverse perspectives on the new staffing model from across the organization. For example, front-line nurses shared their perceptions that they were short staffed and that they could do anything demanded of them to increase efficiency if they had sufficient staff. Middle managers highlighted the pushback that they got from nurses in dealing with the change in the staffing model. One OR manager noted that she was surprised by the negative reaction to the new model, noting, 'The new staffing model, I thought it would work itself out after some months. We formed a team to see how to make it work, and are engaging them, but some are angry people'. The OR managers conveyed that there was a perception among the nurses that the new staffing model threatened patient safety. In addition, in a province with a severe shortage of RNs, one OR manager highlighted the impact of the new staffing model on retention, observing, 'It is not a safety issue, but I think it makes it difficult retaining nurses. You see migration [of nurses] to other hospitals and sister ORs'.

The consultants actively encouraged the frank sharing of information and perspectives by providing staff members with opportunities and encouragement to engage in issue selling. In addition, insiders often indicated that they recognized the consultants as potential issue selling targets, and used the facilitation visit to sell issues that might otherwise not get attention. For example, the OR Manager at Eagle Hospital tried to sell her plan to cross-train OR nurses as ICU nurses to the consultants noting: 'The need is there for ICU nurses, but VP Patient Care does not see it there. Maybe you can [nodding]...you know'. The OR Manager hoped that the consultant would communicate her plan to the VP of patient care. Finally, the consultants were able to gather and triangulate information by directly asking insiders to explain or justify current practices that might hamper organizational performance, often asking higher-status actors about practices that lower-status actors identified as problematic.

In their interactions with lower-status actors, the consultants attempted to access insiders' perspectives by presenting themselves, and the facilitation process, as a safe space for information sharing for actors who otherwise might feel inhibited in voicing their perspectives. For example, in introducing the purpose of the facilitation process at Eagle Hospital, one consultant highlighted: 'We want to find what are your issues, what would you like to fix...and identify some to work on as a team, with docs, labs etc...We meet with staff separately so they are free'.

As a result of their interactions with diverse organization members, the consultants collected significant information that they triangulated and integrated to develop comprehensive view. In triangulating perspectives from across the organization, the consultants drew two conclusions related to the new OR staffing model at Academic. First, they concluded that front-line nurses perceived the new staffing model as a loss that limited their ability to do their jobs effectively and that potentially threatened patient safety in an effort to cut costs. Second, they identified a gap in perspectives between front-line staff and senior administrators. For example, in a private meeting of the consulting team, one consultant noted, 'Managers and chiefs tend to be in alignment, but not necessarily the front-line nurses'.

Building on Simmel, we identified three reasons why outside change agents are able to more effectively read an organization than insiders. First, because of their social distance, outsiders paradoxically have contact with a broader cross-section of organization members. Noting that the stranger is a position characterized by mobility, Simmel observes that 'the purely mobile person comes incidentally into contact with *every* single element but is not bound up organically, through established ties of kinship, locality, or occupation, with any single one' (Simmel, 1971: 145). Second, organization members may be more willing to share information and perspectives with outsiders, who often receive 'the most surprising revelations and confidences, at times reminiscent of a confessional, about matters which are kept carefully hidden from everybody with whom one is close' (Simmel, 1971: 145). Third, outside change agent's social distance from the organization also creates a cognitive distance which can give them unique insight. Taken together, this social and cognitive distance makes outside change agents uniquely able to gain a comprehensive view of an organization, its issues or problems, and political landscape.

Altering insiders' schema

Outsiders used this comprehensive view developed through their reading of the organization to engage in three interaction practices: brokering perspectives, provoking reflection and orchestrating agency.

Brokering perspectives. Drawing on their ability to access uncensored views and perspectives from diverse organizational insiders, we observed that the consultants could influence interpretive change by brokering perspectives – sharing information and perspectives across different audiences in the organization. At Academic, the consultants began to broker perspectives as they engaged with a cross-functional group of insiders to discuss specific change commitments that would increase perioperative efficiency. An OR manager raised the issue of the new staffing model in a discussion of how the organization would develop a plan to better retain nurses and increase job satisfaction. The discussion included the director of perioperative care, three OR managers, medical chiefs and middle managers involved with perioperative care. One consultant suggested using a 'stop, start, continue' model for identifying changes that would improve nurse retention, explaining, 'Stop are things you do not like, start are things you want to do, and continue are things you do well'. Here, one of the OR managers responded, 'What if you ask the stop and it is something you cannot change? I know what it is. It is the 2.5 nurses [per room in the new staffing model]'. The director of perioperative care immediately attempted to downplay the impact of the new staffing model, saying, 'You won't get that from nurses who have just been here a few months'. Here, another consultant interjected to broker perspectives from the front-line staff, saying, 'When we asked nurses, in a perfect world, what would you want...It is staff'.

The exchange highlighted a clear gap in perspectives between front-line nurses and director of perioperative care, the senior manager for the perioperative programme. Middle managers were more aware of the perspectives of front-line staff. As middle managers, however, they would be reluctant to raise issues and perspectives if they perceived that senior managers were unsympathetic (Dutton et al., 1997). In this context, the consultants were able to broker perspectives across groups that otherwise were not shared. The consultants challenged the director of perioperative care's attempt to downplay the impact of the new staffing model on morale and job satisfaction. They also made her aware of different perspectives from within her own organization.

This attempt to broker perspectives, grounded in the comprehensive view that the consultants developed through their reading of the organization, influenced the schema of the director of perioperative care. Towards the end of the discussion, one of the consultants began to wrap up the conversation, stating, 'We had a very good discussion of what the issues are... things about perceptions, loss. You have people grieving'. In contrast to her earlier efforts to downplay the impacts of the new staffing model, at this point the director interjected, 'Yes we do'.

In emphasizing that the stranger's membership in a group 'involves being outside it and confronting it' (Simmel, 1971: 144), Simmel offers us insight into how outsiders are able to broker perspectives. As outsiders, the consultants were able to access perspectives from across the organization, at all levels of its hierarchy. Front-line staff or others organization members with limited power and authority may be more likely to honestly share their perspectives to consultants, even if they are reluctant to share the same views with others in their own organization. In addition, the consultants were able to, or even expected to, confront and challenge organization members. This ability to both gather information and confront insiders allowed the consultants to share perspectives with higher-status actors – senior managers and physicians – that would otherwise be censored.

Provoking reflection. The consultants attempted to provoke members of the organization to reflect on possible opportunities and means for altering routines related to the operating room. They did this by asking questions that were intended to provoke thought and generate new understandings of the taken-for-granted.

We observed two types of provoking. First, consultants provoked employees to see or become aware of practices that were taken-for-granted – what they referred to as 'sacred cows'. For example, at Academic a consultant asked the OR Managers a difficult, direct question, 'Are you feeling like what you are being asked to accomplish is jeopardizing the safety of the patient?' After a pause, two OR managers shook their head (no) and a third OR manager responded, 'The staff think so'. This prompted a longer conversation in which the OR managers discussed, criticized and reflected on current practices.

The second approach to provoking involved the consultants asking questions that required employees to identify the formal decision-making structures of the organization. The consultants challenged employees to articulate how decisions were made (or not), and to consider what role they could play in current or potentially new decision-making processes that would bring about desirable change. In doing so, the consultants provoked members of the organization to think about concrete ways they could effect change. At Academic, a consultant asked the site chief – the chief of surgery for one of the hospitals in the Academic system – 'What one thing do you think you can do to make a difference?' The site chief had, for several minutes prior to this question, been complaining about the 'hardship' of the new nursing model. The consultant's question provoked the site chief, an actor with relatively significant formal and informal authority, to think about how he might be able to intervene in this situation to alleviate this hardship for himself and others.

Outsiders, the consultants, asked questions that provided insiders with potential clues and suggestions for how they could use established mechanisms to make change in the organization. They were able to ask provocative questions because they first developed an understanding of how the organization functioned and the political landscape of the organization.

Orchestrating agency. The consultants also drew on their comprehensive view of the organization to advise insiders on how they could more effectively sell issues and build political support for specific changes. Prior research highlights that insiders improve their issue selling effectiveness slowly over time, as they accumulate formal authority, relationships, expertise and normative knowledge of the schema held by diverse groups within the organization (Howard-Grenville, 2007). In contrast, our research suggests that outsiders are uniquely positioned to acquire normative knowledge of the schema of diverse organizational insiders quickly through their reading of the organization. They use this knowledge to offer insiders advice on how to improve their issue selling effectiveness and intra-organizational coalitions.

At Academic, one consultant offered the director of perioperative care advice on how to appeal to the schema of front-line nurses. Mid-way through the discussion among hospital insiders, she reiterated her perspective and proposed a potential solution to the problem – engaging a facilitator to deal specifically with the issue of the new staffing model in the hopes of achieving a common understanding of the issue:

> One way [to address the issue] is to formally acknowledge issues in structured way, to say we all agree these are the issues. What are the

strategies and what is the data that we need to have as a metric for resolving the issue?

In asking the director and middle managers whether they wanted to engage with the issue, she offered her thoughts on how focusing attention on the issue now, and engaging in a facilitated discussion could resonate with the schema of front-line nurses, noting, 'It can signal "I hear you. I value what you say"'. The consultants' advice to engage in a facilitated discussion with nurses draws on their reading of the organization, in which they identified the gaps in perception between front-line nurses and more senior administrators – something the nurses themselves pointed out in highlighting that they felt excluded from decision-making in organization.

We identified two ways that outsiders were able to offer political advice to insiders. First, as illustrated in the examples above, they offered advice on how to frame issues or problems to appeal to the schema of others within the organization. In addition, they offered political advice, recommending coalitions of potential supporters to insiders or other advice on how to overcome potential political barriers to change. The consultants were able, because of their reading of the organization, to identify the parties who could support and drive change related to particular issues and the parties who would contest or challenge such change. Seeing, from their position as outsiders, the potential forces both in favour and against an issue, they engaged actors in each of these categories and challenged their potential.

In the case of supporters, this challenge was intended to direct and fortify their efforts. For example, the consultants not only encouraged individual actors to demonstrate change agent behaviour ('You are a leader. You are a champion of change just by your initiative'.) but also ensured that these actors were aware of each other. In the case of detractors, this challenge was intended to weaken their resistance. At Academic, a VP argued that the new RN staffing model was conservative and, in fact, even fewer than 2.5 nurses were needed. A consultant challenged this actors' resistance to acknowledge the pressing issue of nurse retention, explaining,

> You need to stabilize this first move [the new staffing model]. You have a strategy ... to get people onto the same page. It is difficult on [the middle-] managers. Every day they get pushback. Stabilize this situation and get on same page ... Once it is stabilized you can then have the other discussions.

Discussion and conclusion

Our chapter develops theory specifying the resources and practices that outsiders can draw on to effect interpretive change. We build on and extend the small, but growing, literature examining the role of social position of insiders (Balogun and Johnson, 2004; Maitlis, 2005) – to examine the resources and practices that outside change agents draw on to catalyze schema change.

Drawing on Simmel's account of the stranger, we identify a two-step model, including four social interaction practices, theorizing how outsiders are able to bring about schema change leading to organizational change commitments.

First, we theorize that outsiders, because of their position as strangers who are both close to and remote from the organization, were able to effectively read the organization. They develop a comprehensive view of the organization's problems, perspectives and political landscape. Outsiders are able to develop this comprehensive view because of their unique access to actors and information from across the organization. In the healthcare setting for our research, it was likely critical that the outside facilitators were insiders to clinical context and professional roles prevalent in the perioperative care setting. That the teams of outsiders who acted as strangers were made up of clinical administrators, nursing managers and a physician was critical in allowing them to gather the information needed to read the organization. That said, this breadth of perspective combined with their critical distance from entrenched conflicts or frames also allowed them to see through entrenched conflict in organizations to identify areas of common interests and perspectives.

Second, grounded in their reading of the organization, outsiders are able to draw on brokering perspectives, provoking reflection and orchestrating agency as three practices for accomplishing schema change. Brokering takes place when outsiders relay information from within the organization that is surprising or novel to a particular insider. In hospitals, the tendency of individuals to see things from the perspective of their own professional role, and the fact that surgeons and anaesthetists are less likely to experience the full range of the perioperative care process in their day-to-day work, makes the potential for brokering higher. Outsiders provoke reflection on the part of insiders when they ask questions that motivate insiders to rethink existing processes and routines, or to consider and rethink the decision-making processes that can lead to change or performance improvement. They also orchestrate agency, making insiders aware of how they can form political coalitions and frame their change proposals, and getting them to reconsider their role in the change process. Here, our findings contrast with the literature on insider change agents, which emphasizes that local knowledge of work processes, organizational systems and the political landscape, gained through experience, is critical in allowing insiders to see opportunities for change, craft effective discursive arguments to gain support and build political coalitions.

Outsiders are able to both provoke reflection and orchestrate agency because of their ability to read the organization, as well as the cognitive and political distance they have from the organization. As outsiders who were nevertheless familiar with the perioperative care process in their own work, they could provoke reflection, in part, because they were able to see practices or problems that insiders take for granted. In addition, because of outside consultants' lack of a political stake in the outcome of change efforts, insiders may be more inclined to see outsiders as objective, increasing the likelihood that they will appreciate outsiders' advice.

By examining the resources and practices of outside change agents, we make two basic contributions to extant research. First, in focusing on how outsiders' social position makes available specific resources and practices because of their role as strangers, we develop theory to explain how social position – in addition to discursive practices or the persuasiveness of sense-giving efforts – plays an important role in the schema change process. Outsiders were able to craft specific discursive practices because their social position as outsiders allowed them to effectively read the organization. Their discursive practices were effective, in part, because of the perceived neutrality of their role as strangers. Second, in explicitly theorizing the role of outsiders, we help develop more complete knowledge of the range of resources and practices associated with diverse change agents in organizations. While highlighting the importance of outsiders in shaping change in hospitals, our research also suggests some limitations to their effectiveness. First, not all outsiders are equal. The outsiders that we observed had legitimacy in part because of the professional roles they held in their own organizations. Second, the outsiders were not uniformly successful in achieving commitments for all of the changes that they perceived would be useful (Nigam et al., 2014). Our data suggest that outsiders less more effective in making changes that challenged surgeons' or anaesthetists' jurisdictional authority, or that would have forced changes in clinical care. This suggests that outsiders may be less effective than insiders, particularly physician opinion leaders, in making changes that impact physicians' core clinical work (Lomas et al., 1991; Ferlie and Shortell, 2001; Ferlie et al., 2005).

Note

1. We changed hospital names to protect anonymity.

References

Abbott, A. D. (1988) *The System of Professions: An Essay on the Division of Expert Labor.* Chicago: University of Chicago Press.

Balogun, J. and Johnson, G. (2004) 'Organizational restructuring and middle manager sensemaking', *Academy of Management Journal,* 47: 523–549.

Bartunek, J. M., Balogun, J. and Do, B. (2011) 'Considering planned change anew: stretching large group interventions strategically, emotionally, and meaningfully', *Academy of Management Annals,* 5, 1–52.

Battilana, J. (2011) 'The enabling role of social position in diverging from the institutional status quo: evidence from the UK National Health Service', *Organization Science,* 22: 817–834.

Battilana, J., Leca, B. and Boxenbaum, E. (2009) 'How actors change institutions: towards a theory of institutional entrepreneurship', *The Academy of Management Annals,* 3: 65–107.

Charmaz, K. (2006) *Constructing Grounded Theory: A Practical Guide through Qualitative Analysis.* London: Sage.

Currie, G. and Brown, A. D. (2003) 'A narratological approach to understanding processes of organizing in a UK hospital', *Human Relations,* 56: 563–586.

Dacin, T., Ventresca, M. and Brent, B. (1999) 'The embeddedness of organizations: dialogue and direction', *Journal of Management,* 25: 317–356.

Dibenigno, J. and Kellogg, K. C. (2014) 'Beyond occupational differences: the importance of cross-cutting demographics and dyadic toolkits for collaboration in a US hospital', *Administrative Science Quarterly,* 375–408.

Dutton, J. E., Ashford, S. J., O'Neill, R. M., Hayes, E. and Wierba, E. E. (1997) 'Reading the wind: how middle managers assess the context for selling issues to top managers', *Strategic Management Journal,* 18, 407–423.

Edmondson, A. (1999) 'Psychological safety and learning behavior in work teams', *Administrative Science Quarterly,* 44, 350–383.

Ferlie, E., Fitzgerald, L., Wood, M. and Hawkins, C. (2005) 'The nonspread of innovations: the mediating role of professionals', *Academy of Management Journal,* 48, 117–134.

Ferlie, E. B. and Shortell, S. M. (2001) 'Improving the quality of health care in the United Kingdom and the United States: a framework for change', *Milbank Quarterly,* 79, 281.

Howard-Grenville, J. A. (2007) 'Developing issue-selling effectiveness over time: issue selling as resourcing', *Organization Science,* 18, 560–577.

Kellogg, K. C. (2011) 'Hot lights and cold steel: cultural and political toolkits for practice change in surgery', *Organization Science*, 22, 482–502.

Kellogg, K. C. (2012) 'Making the cut: using status-based countertactics to block social movement implementation and microinstitutional change in surgery', *Organization Science*, 23, 1546–1570.

Lockett, A., Currie, G., Finn, R., Martin, G. and Waring, J. (2014) 'The influence of social position on sensemaking about organizational change', *Academy of Management Journal*, 57, 1102–1129.

Lockett, A., Currie, G., Waring, J., Finn, R. and Martin, G. (2012) 'The role of institutional entrepreneurs in reforming healthcare', *Social Science & Medicine*, 74, 356–363.

Lomas, J., Enkin, M., Anderson, G. M., Hannah, W. J., Vayda, E. and Singer, J. (1991) 'Opinion leaders vs audit and feedback to implement practice guidelines: delivery after previous cesarean section', *The Journal of the American Medical Association*, 265, 2202–2207.

Maitlis, S. (2005) 'The social processes of organizational sensemaking', *Academy of Management Journal*, 48, 21–49.

Morrison, E. W. and Milliken, F. J. (2000) 'Organizational silence: a barrier to change and development in a pluralistic world', *Academy of Management Review*, 25, 706–725.

Nigam, A. (2013) 'How institutional change and individual researchers helped advance clinical guidelines in American health care', *Social Science & Medicine*, 87, 16–22.

Nigam, A., Huising, R. and Golden, B. R. (2014) 'Improving hospital efficiency: a process model of organizational change commitments', *Medical Care Research & Review*, 71, 21–42.

Reay, T., Golden-Biddle, K. and Germann, K. (2006) 'Legitimizing a new role: small wins and microprocesses of change', *Academy of Management Journal*, 49, 977–998.

Sherrard, H., Trypuc, J. and Hudson, A. (2009). 'The use of coaching to improve peri-operative efficiencies: the Ontario experience', *Healthcare Quarterly*, 12, 48–54.

Simmel, G. (1971) *Georg Simmel on Individuality and Social Forms*. Chicago: University of Chicago Press.

Starr, P. (1982) *The Social Transformation of American Medicine*. New York: Basic Books.

Stevens, R. (2000) *In Sickness and in Wealth: American Hospitals in the Twentieth Century*. New York: Basic Books.

Part III

Leadership and Organizational Change

9
NHS Managers: From Administrators to Entrepreneurs?

Mark Exworthy, Fraser Macfarlane and Micky Willmott

Health service managers have long been involved in organizational restructuring, notably in the apparent 'transition' narrative from public administration to 'new public management' (NPM). More recently, debates have focused on entrepreneurialism.

Over the past 30 years, the National Health Service (NHS) in England has undergone multiple reorganizations with increasing rapidity. The number of reforms affecting organizations and managers and the associated processes and discourses have been equally significant. In this period, NHS managers have been faced with the introduction of quasi-markets, greater competition, new performance regimes, greater decentralization and reorganizations. This chapter explores the ways in which NHS managers have navigated their way through organizational restructuring and policy reforms. We examine the actions and reactions of managers to these institutional and policy changes, in terms of career paths, identities and role enactment.

The chapter examines the heuristic stages of development of health service management, before presenting empirical evidence from interviews with 20 NHS managers. It concludes by considering the extent to which entrepreneurial NHS managers are emerging from recent health policy reforms.

From administration to new public management and beyond?

As the NHS has responded to changing political and social expectations (Klein, 2010), the way in which its organizations have been 'run' has involved apparent shifts from administration to (new public) management and, arguably, to entrepreneurialism. These shifts also reflect substantive changes in the identities and careers of managers. (Others suggest 'leaderism' as an alternative evolution beyond NPM (Martin and Learmonth, 2012)). Parallel shifts are apparent as the NHS shifts from a monolithic institution to a fragmented series of increasingly autonomous organizations.

Bureaucracy

The bureaucratic characterization represents the NHS between its formation in 1948 and 1983 when the NHS corresponded closely to Weber's (1946) notion of bureaucracy, characterized by fixed spheres of competence, defined hierarchy of positions and careers for officials, inter alia. This approach stressed the personal/individual aspects of bureaucracy (Pollitt and Bouckaert, 2004). Staff thus only occupied office to serve the interests of the organization, although bureaucracies often served their own interests (Niskanen, 1971).

This long period was marked by continuity in terms of the roles played by 'administrators'. Despite modest reforms, the structure of the NHS remained static. Hierarchical control was rarely exercised, not least because such powers were weak due to professional dominance (Harrison and McDonald, 2008). The institutional structure of the NHS hospitals, general practice and local government (in place since 1948) was reformed in 1974; hospitals were run by 'consensus teams'. Such teams comprised a medical officer, a nursing officer, a financial officer and an 'administrator' who acted as a 'diplomat' (Harrison, 1988). They had no veto over the decisions of clinical colleagues and a remit to 'manage consensus' (Day and Klein, 1983).

NPM

The dominant narrative suggests that the bureaucratic model was usurped by NPM in the mid-1980s in the United Kingdom and elsewhere (Ferlie et al., 2005). NPM was associated with the decline in growth of government, privatization, marketization, expanding IT applications and growing internationalization (Hood, 1991). NPM needed to be staffed by a cadre of 'managers' who occupied roles in the decentralized 'business' units.

The stability of the 'bureaucratic' period in the NHS was ended by the Management Inquiry (Griffiths, 1983). It was emblematic of the shift in fiscal policy and political ideology, associated with the Conservative government, elected in 1979 (Greener, 2001). The inquiry diagnosed an institutional stalemate of the consensus team and proposed an end to the administrators and consensus teams and their replacement by managers who were to adopt a 'bias for action'. Managers (with executive functions over clinicians and others) would necessarily need to manage conflict (Day and Klein, 1983).

It was intended that many managers would be recruited from the commercial sector or other public sector spheres (e.g. military). By 1986, 60% of the most senior managers were ex-NHS administrators, 19% were doctors, 10% were nurses and only 8% came from outside the NHS (Petchey, 1986, quoted in Cox, 1991). Harrison (1988) argues that, in transforming the 'administrator' into a 'manager', their role had also changed from a 'diplomat' to a 'scapegoat' for failings of the NHS and to being an agent of central government policy.

The NPM emphasis shifted further towards market mechanisms in the 1990s and 2000s. With some public services deemed not suitable for privatization (Flynn, 2002), market-style mechanisms introduced a form of competition (Saltman and von Otter, 1992). Initially, markets were introduced through the outsourcing of 'ancillary' services (e.g. catering and laundry). Later, the market was applied to clinical services, some of which were more amenable to marketization than others. However, the 'market' remained heavily regulated.

Several features symbolized this 'NHS quasi-market' period. Former unitary organizations (such as District Health Authorities, covering populations of about 250,000) were split into purchasers and providers (hospitals and other providers). Purchasers included health authorities (which commissioned most clinical services) and general practice fund-holders (i.e. primary care providers who were given budgets to purchase certain secondary care services) (Robinson and Le Grand, 1994). Providers were given some decision-making autonomy. Purchasers and providers were run much more along business lines (Ferlie et al., 1996). NHS managers were 'separated' into either purchaser or provider organizations. Despite such separation, social and institutional networks between purchaser and providers remained, often because of their geographical proximity and organizational interdependence (Flynn et al., 1996; Exworthy, 1998). With relatively weak market incentives in the 1990s, persistent networks and a strong hierarchy, the NHS quasi-market did not deliver the gains that had been expected (Le Grand et al., 1998).

Entrepreneurialism

Notwithstanding some use of the term 'entrepreneurial' (Weber, 1946; Mintzberg, 1979), the idiom 'entrepreneur' and its cognate terms increasingly signify risk-taking, innovation and 'breaking' (or manipulating) the rules (Llewellyn et al., 2007). These categories extend the definition proposed by Currie et al. (2008), which focused on 'the process of identifying and pursuing opportunities' (p. 988; *cf.* Lapsley, 2008) or using 'locally contextualised change agency to tailor and embellish policy mandates' (McDermott et al., 2013: S93). In terms of individuals, Courpasson (2000) argues that entrepreneurs are

> actors who are capable of playing with the existing rules of the organization, of taking risks. (pp. 144–145)

Some have applied the 'entrepreneurial' term to the NHS quasi-market reforms of the 1990s (Schofield, 2001); others have drawn attention to the search for 'additional value' from existing resources (Greener, 2008: 205). Martin and Learmonth (2012) argue that the 'turn' towards leadership has sought to co-opt 'managers' (and others) into the reforms' purpose and discourse, thereby diffusing overt opposition. McDermott et al. (2013) note a continuum of responses to policy mandates, not simply acceptance *or* resistance.

Whilst the extent of public entrepreneurialism is debatable, it might be contradictory to NPM. Public entrepreneurialism presents challenges for managers in balancing 'personal visions of the future' with public accountability (Lapsley, 2008). Currie et al. (2008) examine these tensions in terms of competing roles for public managers: political, stakeholder and entrepreneur.

The quasi-market reforms of the 1990s carried weaker incentives that might be associated with the NHS reforms implemented since 2001 (Le Grand et al., 1998; Mays et al., 2011). Nevertheless, the term 'modernization' in the 2000s signified the shift towards entrepreneurialism (Powell, 2008). The emergence of entrepreneurialism, in the last decade or so, combines features of the previous modes of governance, but with a more extensive application of market-style mechanisms, more organizational autonomy and a greater emphasis on user responsiveness. It is debatable when this mode became evident but the defining document might have been the NHS Plan (DH, 2000). It prompted the introduction of 'patient choice' policy (allowing patients a greater choice of provider of their secondary care), performance-based 'star ratings' for NHS organizations, the use of performance targets, the inspectorate Commission for Health Improvement (and its subsequent incarnations), a prospective payment system, Independent Sector Treatment Centres (designed to stimulate provider diversity) and the introduction of autonomous Foundations Trusts (FTs; Mays et al., 2011). NHS (provider) organizations (which were already classified as 'high performing') were eligible to apply for FT status (Allen et al., 2012). FTs were supposed to 'unleash a degree of innovation' through their ability to alter staff terms and conditions, raise private capital and reinvest savings, inter alia. Despite their autonomy, constraints remained; many FT managers were inured to centralization and felt their 'freedoms' were illusory (Hoque et al., 2004), or lacked capacity to act entrepreneurially. Some FT managers remained risk averse in the still highly politicized environment (Exworthy et al., 2011; King's Fund, 2011).

The 'rise' of entrepreneurialism is associated with post-bureaucratic organizations (Ferlie et al., 2005; Morris and Farrell, 2007). However, the definition and existence of post-bureaucracy is disputed (Du Gay, 2005). Hoggett (1996) summarizes post-bureaucratic organizations in terms of decentralized units within centralized systems of control, competition and performance management and monitoring. Arguably, these features are more indicative of NPM in the 1990s than what has now come to be seen as post-bureaucracy. Pollitt (2009) argues that a post-bureaucratic organization refers to the 'conscious replacement [of] a traditional bureaucracy' (p. 200). Characteristics of post-bureaucratic organizations include flattened hierarchies, networks beyond the organization, variable arrangements for staff employment, less certain career path, more career moves, hierarchical rules softened and traditional staff controls weakened.

Does this post-bureaucratic thesis fit with the recent experience of the NHS? The NHS has experienced a rapidity of health reforms (Walshe, 2010). In Britain, the first major reform came 35 years after the inception of the NHS, whilst the second came eight years later and the third came a further nine or so years after that. Between 1997 and 2010, the NHS was subject to 26 Green and White Papers and 14 Acts of Parliament (Thorlby and Maybin, 2010: 8). The Coalition Government's Health and Social Care Act (2012) established a further reorganization with greater incursion of private sector organizations in the NHS, a more widespread application of their techniques and greater incentives for entrepreneurial behaviour by NHS managers (Department of Health, 2010; Pollock and Price, 2011). Consequences of this constant reform include churn in managerial tenure and performance indicators. On average, NHS chief executives are in post for two years, four months (Sergeant, quoted in Foreword to Hoggett-Bowers, 2009: 2). Entrepreneurial behaviour might thus be less apparent than a coping strategy of maintenance or defence (possibly for the individual and the organization).

Entrepreneurialism and post-bureaucracy appear interrelated. As NHS managers adjust their notions of risk and redirect their efforts (Currie et al., 2008; Macfarlane et al., 2011), the organizations within which they work are becoming increasingly disaggregated from the NHS 'family' through decentralization and competition. The causation between these two factors is, however, hard to establish. Lapsley (2008) argues that the evolution of NPM discourses and practices into new archetypes has been constrained by professional boundaries, embedded social institutions and the limitations of the performance culture. Moreover, some argue that the bureaucratic model has not disappeared but rather has been reinvented. The intensification of bureaucratic practices has been termed 'neo-bureaucracy' (Morris and Farrell, 2007). The coexistence of these roles challenges public managers to reconcile (often contradictory) policy and organizational imperatives (McDermott et al., 2013). Arguably, managers (*qua* managers) have always had to reconcile competing pressures, but the ability of managers to draw upon previous certainties and identities is increasingly limited.

Entrepreneurial managers in the NHS?

To explore how managers understood and negotiated their careers through the changing NHS, we conducted an empirical study of managers' accounts. We identified managers through institutional networks, their own published 'stories' of their careers and 'recommendations' from previous interviewees. We recruited 20 NHS managers and former NHS managers in England. The sample comprised maximum variability by managerial experience (in different types of organizations), gender, professional background (general manager, clinical manager) and functional area (e.g. human resources or finance). We sought to recruit managers from a black or minority ethnic background but were unsuccessful. Interviewees had joined the NHS between the mid-1960s and the mid-1980s, and those still working in the NHS were towards the end of their career. In total, the sample of 20 comprised 6 women, 12 chief executives and 2 individuals with clinical backgrounds.

Most interviews were conducted face-to-face and were recorded with verbal consent. Due to time pressures, three participants elected to give taped telephone interviews and one gave an untapped interview. Interviews lasted, on average, between 50 and 60 minutes. Wengraf's (2001) biographical narrative life interview method was adapted to explore how respondents had perceived and responded to major reforms in the NHS. This approach sought to explore career histories, influence of triggers on career decisions and setbacks to their career.

We adopted the 'Framework' approach to data analysis (Ritchie and Spencer, 1995). All recorded interviews were transcribed and annotated with contemporaneous field notes. The authors read all transcripts independently and coded responses. Each item within the data was compared data to establish analytical categories; negative cases that contradicted the emerging themes were used to refine these themes. Consensus of thematic coding was achieved iteratively through discussion and rereading of transcripts; representative quotes were selected to illustrate these. Quotes from interview respondents are used here to illustrate the themes discussed above. Managers have been ascribed pseudonyms.

We appreciate the methodological difficulties in conducting such research (Pollitt, 2009), including recall bias and post hoc rationalization. Other data sources might have also been deployed, but the resources and scope of the study prevented this. It was deemed out with the remit of the NHS research ethics committee at the time; ethical approval was obtained from the University of Surrey Research Ethics Committee.

We present findings from this case study in terms of three themes: risk, innovation and autonomy; networks and careers; balancing competing roles.

Risk, innovation and autonomy

For much of their career, these managers had been working within an institutional structure which did not overtly foster entrepreneurial traits of risk-taking, innovation and autonomy. Whilst interviewees accepted this caricature, NHS managers, individually, also sought to exercise discretion, which portrayed a heroic career narrative.

> I've got a risk taking profile so I've had to learn how to protect myself and my career and my organisation from inappropriate risk taking but still take risks.
>
> (Barbara)

> I think I was able in nearly all those roles to introduce some form of change and innovation and stimulate a bit of different way of doing things.
>
> (Harry)

Indeed, managers were expected to show a 'bias for action', according to the 1983 Griffiths Report. One manager recognized that his identity was *meant* to be 'innovative'.

> One of the big things that was supposed to be a distinguishing feature was that you should have innovative views about how you should manage your people.
>
> (Bob)

However, these accounts were moderated by recognition of the local and national constraints within which they were working. The politicized nature of the NHS, some felt, already exposed them as managers to a high degree of risk. They recognized that some hierarchical control was always likely in the NHS.

> You can understand their [politicians'] reaction on the back of Maidstone and Tunbridge Wells [an NHS organisation whose management had been criticised for the handling of an infection outbreak in the mid-2000s in which about 90 people died] for wanting to make sure that doesn't happen elsewhere but I actually think the way to do that is through empowering the organisation to put in place their own response plan, not by saying 'you must have completed a thorough deep clean of your hospital by the 31st March' when actually there aren't the contractors to do it ...
>
> (Rebecca)

Managers were thus more circumspect than the entrepreneurial narrative might denote.

> Political risk will trump and financial risk or even clinical risk.
>
> (Chris)

Pressure to conform and risk-aversion remained strong traits among NHS managers.

Networks and careers

The traditional NHS 'management' career path was 'managed' in what interviewees referred to as the 'planned movement' or the 'golden pathway' (Steve). Senior managers would oversee the 'transfer' of junior managers between organizations, to ensure that individuals acquired a breadth of appropriate experience. (Several interviewees had been part of the NHS Graduate Management Training Scheme.) This pathway encouraged junior managers to adopt practices and behaviours which might elicit the patronage of senior managers. Managers displaying conformance would thus be recruited and prosper in this regime.

> What people call the golden pathway . . . that's the sort of classic, you know, you're a trainee, you go and work in one of the teaching hospitals, you go out and work in the provinces for a bit and DGH [District General Hospital] experience and you move to be a Chief Exec and that's the pathway that I followed.
>
> (Steve)

However, this process effectively reduced managers' allegiance and loyalty to a single organization but rather fostered social ties across the NHS; this might contradict the significance of autonomous organizations and entrepreneurial behaviour.

One consequence of the 'planned movement' was the ability to relocate the 'problem' or 'failing' manager. This did not solve the problem but moved it to another part of the NHS. One effect was to avoid managers leaving the NHS altogether. This created a strong sense of belonging and being 'looked after'; a more entrepreneurial regime might lose this aspect. Barbara and Steve describe their career 'problems':

> I was a successful chief executive at a district general hospital but then had a huge career accident. I was put on gardening leave that lasted for 18 months . . . I had to make the biggest career decision: should I get out of the NHS?
>
> (Barbara)

> It was a really hard time. I think my fundamental belief system was . . . stayed very strong throughout it; I don't . . . I never really thought about really doing something else, [but] I was very concerned that my career was over.
>
> (Steve)

Both stayed in the NHS.

The role of the mentor was crucial in brokering local managerial solutions for 'failing' managers such as finding a safe 'haven' elsewhere. With stronger performance incentives and media attention, managerial 'failures' are becoming more conspicuous (Calkin, 2012; Francis, 2013) and yet, with the removal of superordinate organizations, the (formal) oversight role has been lost.

The loyalty to the NHS might have been undermined by the recruitment of managers from outside the service. Generally, these managers did not last long in the service.

> Quite a few people were brought in from industry and I can't think of any who were successful apart from [Luke] around this South East area... one or two other parts of the country...
>
> (Chris)

> At the time, there was a lot of, you know, sniffiness about these people and actually to be fair many of the people from the private sector and the [armed] forces were not hugely successful...
>
> (Oliver)

Interviewees claimed that 'external' managers did not understand or the organizational culture of the NHS, notably medical power – what Chris referred to as 'concrete slabs':

> If you went with outsiders' way of behaviour... the concrete slab would come down on top of you and I was trying to work out where these concrete slabs were.

Some of our interviewees had retired from their NHS career to become a 'consultant', most frequently to NHS organizations. These managers enjoyed the flexibility of such positions.

> I left and moved into consultancy/academic type work... What I recognise is that I love variety so I'll be here one or two days a week, you know, what is a great project and very intellectually challenging, great people...
>
> (Oliver)

These ex-NHS managers highlight the erosion of traditional career pathways and illustrate more entrepreneurial ones which enable looser network-based forms of employment.

Balancing competing roles

Interviewees sought to balance their competing roles as NHS managers. The political, stakeholder and entrepreneurial roles were evident in terms of the emphasis managers placed on their own personal agendas and their support for (or resistance to) national policy.

All managers recognized the constraints of their role within the NHS and its public accountability, but they also demonstrated their commitment to the values and principles of the NHS. However, there were differences in terms of managers' views about the appropriateness of new entrepreneurial reforms and practices. On the one hand, some felt that the NHS needed a 'public service orientation', rather than entrepreneurialism.

> The NHS isn't a thing... it's a system or an organisation idea, it isn't an entity and therefore it has some similar characteristics wherever you are but equally it has local differences that are the product of their own history and their own people. I resist the notion that you can describe it universally... You can't manage it or lead it effectively unless you understand it so to that extent it's true that it's special.
>
> (Bob)

On the other hand, others felt that the distinction between public and private management was blurred and that entrepreneurialism might thus be embraced.

> The interesting thing is we mustn't fall into the assumption that NHS culture and values are somehow inimical to that sort of thing [clash of culture between NHS and private sector]... In the NHS, there are some fairly toxic tendencies, in terms of competitiveness, in terms of class system, in terms of individualist as opposed to corporatist behaviour, all of which a Chief Executive has to handle. And then of course outside the health system we shouldn't assume that all values are bad.
>
> (Nick)

Managers valued managerial autonomy within their organizations but balanced this with a commitment to wider NHS goals. Len implied that national imperatives should be accepted but they should not prevent the pursuit of local/personal agendas:

> If you deliver all the targets, you don't argue. There's no point in arguing... Basically you just get on and do whatever they want you to do, however stupid it is, and you deliver all of that... I mean I'm not stupid, I don't put my career at risk, you know, I do what's expected of me but having done enough to keep it off my back then I go on championing the things I believe in.
>
> (Len)

Managers also needed to balance national imperatives with local capabilities, a role which Rachel felt had been given insufficient time in recent reforms:

> Did we allow, sort of, the . . . managers sufficient time and story-telling about the [reforms]? What was the thinking, what are we trying to achieve – to help them to make decisions about the local situation and their own positions?

(Rachel)

Discussion and conclusions

Managers have been central to recent NHS reforms and are emblematic of recent public sector restructuring. Thus, accounts of their experiences can help gauge whether entrepreneurialism has taken root in the NHS and if so, how far. (Similar questions could be asked of clinicians, some of whom accept entrepreneurial behaviour (McGivern et al., 2015).) These questions can be answered in terms of individuals, institutions and ideas (Exworthy and Halford, 1999). First, as individuals, our interviewees have been described as administrators, managers and most recently entrepreneurs and leaders, terms which have become 'construed as an alternative identity' (O'Reilly and Reed, 2010: 968). Our sample of 20 interviewees did not present a heroic narrative of their career (Learmonth, 2001; Greener, 2004), although such 'presentation of self' was apparent on occasion. Second, the institutional framework within which these managers worked has shifted from the ideal-typical Weberian bureaucracy towards the post-bureaucratic organization. However, ongoing hierarchical control and the socialization of managers to the exigencies of the centre have created persistent legacy effects which may have dampened entrepreneurial dynamism. Third, the managerial discourse privileges managers' roles. Managers have often internalized these managerial (or sometimes, entrepreneurial) discourses. This will become increasingly significant as many managers (recruited in the past 20 or so years but not in our sample) will have only ever known the marketized NHS.

This study of NHS managers has shown that entrepreneurialism has pervaded managerial discourses but largely not in ways which have been described in the literature. This might beget a reinterpretation of entrepreneurialism. For example, the ambiguity of managers' competing roles has been most acutely felt in managing in/across networks in the past decade (Ferlie et al., 2011). Whilst networks can provide 'stable professionalised leadership' (Ferlie et al., 2011), managers have not been absolved from their political accountabilities. Their role (as stakeholder) has become changed in being the problem ('excessive bureaucracy') and/or the solution ('stimulating improved performance'). However, managers have long seen their role as being one of taking risks and being innovative (Courpasson, 2000). Indeed, these skills were honed by managers' need to cope with the exigencies of ongoing reform processes and multiple stakeholders. Yet, such activities have usually related to managing inter-/intra-organizational relations (Greener, 2008), rather than exploiting (commercial) opportunities (inter alia). However, this balance is now being brought into sharper relief by the incursion of private sector organizations into NHS service delivery, only some of whose managers may possess a public service ethos (Hall et al., 2015). Thus, NHS managers will need to negotiate constant reorganizations, possibly through the acquisition and enactment of entrepreneurial skills. Their career 'survival' will depend on their ability to internalize the discourses of these reforms. Previously, sacked NHS managers have not always left the NHS but have been relocated elsewhere (Greer and Jarman, 2007); now, such 'rescue' is less likely as management numbers have been cut and functions been outsourced to the private sector.

Many factors that shaped these social and institutional relations are still prevalent and may even be exacerbated by recent reforms which herald a new phase for managers under the guise of decentralizing resources to clinicians on the 'front line'. NHS managerial careers thus face significant uncertainty. As some clinicians may be unwilling to assume their new powers, this may enable greater incursion from private organizations to take on managerial functions (Allen et al., 2012).

In any event, based on this evidence, the consequence is likely to be increased ambiguity of managers in balancing their competing roles and managing multiple stakeholders. The notion of agency will thus be critical in shaping the extent of entrepreneurialism. Further investigation is merited in terms of whether a larger sample of managers 'adopt' entrepreneurial behaviours and whether they reluctantly accept it or actively resist it (McDermott et al., 2013). Equally, to what extent are managers (in traditional NHS organizations, in private companies or in social enterprises) able to draw on the learning and knowledge from previous NHS regimes? Do transitions create enduring changes in managerial identity and role?

As the latest NHS reforms are unlikely to be the last, the 'incessant restructuring' (Pollitt, 2009: 214) will continue to shape the trajectory and character of the NHS and, thus, managerial careers. Vestiges of the *ancien regimes* will be manifest alongside glimpses of emerging entrepreneurial role. Therefore, the already-complex picture of the NHS is undoubtedly becoming more intricate.

Acknowledgements

We are grateful to the Nuffield Trust for funding this study and to the managers who were interviewed. An earlier version of this paper was presented to the OBHC conference (Copenhagen, 2014).

References

Allen, P., Turner, S., Bartlett, W., Perotin, V., Matchaya, G. and Zamora, B. (2012) 'Provider diversity in the English NHS: a study of recent developments in four local health economies', *Journal of Health Services Research and Policy*, 17(1) (suppl): 23–30.

Calkin, S. (2012) 'Hunt backs new standards for NHS managers', *Health Service Journal*, November 7. Available from: http://www.hsj.co.uk/news/workforce/hunt-backs-new-standards-for-nhs-managers/5051528.article [Accessed August 4, 2015].

Courpasson, D. (2000) 'Managerial studies of domination: power in soft bureaucracies', *Organization Studies*, 21: 141–161.

Cox, D. (1991) 'Health service management – a sociological view: Griffiths and the non-negotiated order of the hospital', in J. Gabe, M. Calnan and M. Bury (eds.), *The sociology of the health service*. London: Routledge

Currie, G., Humphreys, M., Ucbasaran, D. and McManus, S. (2008) 'Entrepreneurial leadership in the English public sector: paradox or possibility?' *Public Administration*, 86(4): 987–1008

Day, P. and Klein, R. (1983) 'The mobilisation of consent versus the management of conflict: decoding the Griffiths report', *British Medical Journal*, 287: 1813–1816. December 10.

Department of Health (2000) *The NHS Plan*. London: DH.

Department of Health (2010) *Equity and Excellence: Liberating the NHS*. London: DH.

Du Gay, P. (ed) (2005) *The Values of Bureaucracy*. Oxford: Oxford University Press.

Exworthy, M. (1998) 'Localism in the NHS quasi-market', *Environment and Planning C: Government and Policy*, 16: 449–462.

Exworthy, M., Frosini, F. and Jones, L. (2011) 'Are NHS foundation trusts able and willing to exercise autonomy? "You can take a horse to water…" ', *Journal of Health Services Research and Policy*, 16(4): 232–237.

Exworthy, M. and Halford, S. (eds) (1999) *Professionals and the New Managerialism in the Public Sector*. Buckingham: Open University Press.

Ferlie, E., Ashburner, L., Fitzgerald, L. and Pettigrew, A. (1996) *The New Public Management in Action*. Oxford: Oxford University Press.

Ferlie, E., Lynn, L. and Pollitt, C. (eds) (2005) *Oxford Handbook of Public Management*. Oxford: Oxford University Press.

Ferlie, E., Fitzgerald, L., McGivern, G., Dopson, S. and Bennett, C. (2011) 'Public policy networks and "wicked problems": a nascent solution?' *Public Administration*, 89(2): 307–324.

Flynn, N. (2002) *Public Sector Management*. Harlow: Prentice Hall.

Flynn, R., Williams, G. and Pickard, S. (1996) *Markets and Hierarchies: Contracting in Community Health Services*. Buckingham: Open University Press.

Francis, R. (chair) (2013) *Report of the Mid Staffordshire NHS Foundation Trust Public Inquiry*. Volume 1: analysis of evidence and lessons learnt. HC-898-1. London: The Stationery Office.

Greener, I (2001) 'The ghost of health services past revisited', *International Journal of Health Services*, 31(3): 635–646.

Greener, I., (2004) 'Talking to health managers about change: heroes, villains and simplification', *Journal of Health Organization and Management*, 18(5): 321–335.

Greener, I. (2008) 'Decision making in a time of significant reform: managing in the NHS', *Administration and Society*, 40(2): 194–210.

Greer, S. and Jarman, H. (2007) *The Department of Health and the Civil Service: From Whitehall to Department of Delivery to Where?* London: Nuffield Trust.

Griffiths, R. (chair) (1983) *NHS Management Inquiry*. London: HSMO.

Hall, K., Miller, R. and Millar, R. (2015) 'Public, private or neither? Analysing the publicness of health care social enterprises', *Public Management Review*, doi: 10.1080/14719037.2015.1014398. Published online 24 February 2015.

Harrison, S. (1988) *Managing the National Health Service: Shifting the Frontier?* London: Chapman and Hall.

Harrison, S. and McDonald, R. (2008) *The Politics of Healthcare in Britain*. London: Sage.

Hoggett, P. (1996) 'New modes of control in the public service', *Public Administration*, 74: 9–32.

Hoggett-Bowers (2009) *NHS Chief Executives: Bold and Old*. London: Hoggett-Bowers. http://www.hoggett-bowers.com/_images/_adverts/Final_NHS_Report-June_09.pdf

Hood, C. (1991) 'A public management for all seasons?' *Public Administration*, 69: 3–19.

Hoque, K, Davis, S. and Humphreys, M. (2004) 'Freedom to do what you are told: senior management team autonomy in an NHS Acute Trust', *Public Administration*, 82(2): 355–375.

King's Fund (2011) *The Future of Leadership and Management in the NHS: No More Heroes*. London: King's Fund.

Klein, R. (2010) *The New Politics of the NHS: From Creation to Reinvention*. Oxford: Radcliffe Publishing.

Lapsley, I. (2008) 'The NPM agenda: back to the future', *Financial Accountability and Management*, 24(1): 77–96.

Learmonth, M. (2001) 'NHS trust chief executives as heroes?' *Health Care Analysis*, 9(4): 417–436.

Le Grand, J., Mays, N. and Mulligan, J.-A. (eds) (1998) *Learning from the NHS Internal Market: A Review of Evidence*. London: King's Fund.

Llewellyn, N., Lewis, P. and Woods, A. (2007) 'Public management and the expansion of an entrepreneurial ethos', *Public Management Review*, 9(2): 253–267.

Macfarlane, F., Exworthy, M., Wilmott, M. and Greenhalgh, T. (2011) 'Plus ça change, plus c'est la même chose: senior NHS managers' narratives of restructuring', *Sociology of Health and Illness*, 33(6): 914–929.

Martin, G. P. and Learmonth, M. (2012) 'A critical account of the rise and spread of "leadership: the case of UK healthcare"', *Social Science and Medicine*, 74: 281–288.

Mays, N., Dixon, A. and Jones, L. (eds) (2011) *Understanding New Labour's Market Reforms of the English NHS*. London: King's Fund.

McDermott, A., Fitzgerald, L. and Buchanan, D. (2013) 'Beyond acceptance and resistance: entrepreneurial change agency responses in policy implementation', *British Journal of Management*, 24: S93–115.

McGivern, G., Currie, G., Ferlie, E., Fitzgerald, L. and Waring, J. (2015) 'Hybrid manager-professionals' identity work: the maintenance and hybridisation of professionalism in managerial contexts', *Public Administration*, 93(2): 412–432, published online: January 23, 2015; doi: 10.1111/padm.12119.

Mintzberg, H. (1979) *The Structuring of Organizations*. Englewood Cliffs, NJ: Prentice Hall.

Morris, J. and Farrell, C. (2007) 'The "post-bureaucratic" public sector organization. New organizational forms and HRM in ten UK public sector organizations', *International Journal of Human Resource Management*, 18(9): 1575–1588.

Niskanen, W. (1971) *Bureaucracy and Representative Government*. Chicago: Aldine Atherton.

O'Reilly, D. and Reed, M. (2010) 'Leaderism: an evolution of managerialism in UK public service reform', *Public Administration*, 88(4): 960–978.

Pollitt, C. (2009) 'Bureaucracies remember, post-bureaucratic organizations forget?' *Public Administration*, 87(2): 198–218.

Pollitt, C. and Bouckaert, G. (2004) *Public Management Reform: A Comparative Analysis*. Oxford: Oxford University Press.

Pollock, A. and Price, D. (2011) 'How the secretary of state for health proposes to abolish the NHS in England', *British Medical Journal*, 342: 1695 (March 22, 2011).

Powell, M. (ed.) (2008) *Modernising the Welfare State: The Blair Legacy*. Bristol: Policy Press.

Ritchie, J. and Spencer, L. (1995) 'Qualitative data analysis for applied policy research', Chapter in A. Bryman and R. G. Burgess (eds.), *Analysing qualitative data*. London: Routledge, pp. 173–194.

Robinson, R. and Le Grand, J. (eds.) (1994) *Evaluating the NHS Reforms*. London: King's Fund Institute.

Saltman, R. B. and von Otter, C. (1992) *Planned Market and Public Competition: Strategic Reforms in Northern European Health Systems*. Buckingham: Open University Press.

Schofield, J. (2001) 'The old ways are the best? The durability and usefulness of bureaucracy in public sector management', *Organization*, 8(1): 77–96.

Thorlby, R. and Maybin, J. (eds.) (2010) *A High Performing NHS? A Review of Progress 1997–2010*. London: King's Fund.

Walshe, K. (2010) 'Reorganisation of the NHS in England', *British Medical Journal*, 341: 3843 (July 16).

Weber, M. (1946) *From Max Weber: Essays in Sociology*. Translated by H. H. Gerth and Wright Mills. New York; Oxford University Press.

Wengraf, T. (2001) *Qualitative Research Interviewing: Biographic Narrative and Semi-Structured Methods*. London: Sage.

10
Opportunity Does Matter: Supporting Doctors-in-Management in Hospitals

Marco Sartirana

Introduction

The introduction of professional–manager 'hybrid' roles has been seen as a solution to 'bridge the gap' between the two competing worlds of medicine and management (Freidson, 2001; Noordegraaf, 2007) at the organizational level. In particular, in a number of Western countries we observe doctors being involved in management as head of clinical directorates, which have become a popular object of analysis for management scholars (Fitzgerald and Dufour, 1998; Kitchener, 2000; Marnoch et al., 2000; Llewellyn, 2001; Kirkpatrick et al., 2009; Witman et al., 2011; McGivern et al., 2015). Clinical directorates are intermediate management units formed around either a broad medical specialty or a support service grouping a number of smaller specialties. They were introduced in order to increase the governance of clinical services, pool resources, favour inter-specialty integration and support the top management in the strategy making (Chantler, 1993; Kirkpatrick et al., 2013).

However, after the formal introduction of clinical directorates, doctors were not always effective in taking up management roles (Kitchener, 2000; Llewellyn, 2001; Lega, 2008, Neogy and Kirkpatrick, 2009; Numerato et al., 2011; Ham and Dickinson, 2012). This has raised the interest, among academics and practitioners, in understanding the determinants or antecedents of doctors' hybridization, which has been mainly explored with reference to the individual level, by looking at how professionals respond (and often resist) management logics. For instance, Forbes et al. (2004: 171) identify the personal attitudes of 'investors', defined as directors 'who came into management with a specific agenda...they saw themselves as natural leaders and innovators...for them management concepts were seen as being easily acquired'. On the other hand, they find the 'reluctants', those who 'felt pushed into accepting a clinical director role...the decision to accept the role either came from their reservations about being managed by someone they objected to or from a perceived need to defend their specialty...and felt no need to develop a managerial self'. Similar clusters were identified by McKee et al. (1999), Llewellyn (2001) and McGivern et al. (2015).

In this study, a complementary perspective is explored and looks at how organizational practices, such as management systems and the support provided by top (non-medical) managers, by interacting with determinants at the individual level, influence the process of CDs' managerial role taking. This enables understanding of the complex managerial context of hospitals, organizations characterized by a continuous interplay of rational and political logics in between professional and managerial domains.

Theoretical framework

The roles of the contextual factors at an organizational level, such as the hospital structure, management systems or the support provided by top (non-medical) managers, have rarely been addressed in the literature on professional–managerial hybrids, because they have often been considered as a control variable rather than a direct object of inquiry. Only a few studies in the field of healthcare management have analysed how the opportunities to perform provided by the organizational context interact with professional logics to determine CDs' managerial role taking. A recent work by McGivern et al. (2015) argues that career paths and formal management training do not appear to have significant impact on hybridization, but hint at the role of peers and mentors in supporting the process of identity formation. Fitzgerald and Dufour (1998) found that the quality of relationships across professional boundaries facilitate the involvement of professionals in management and describe effective organizational arrangements supporting CDs. Hoff (2001) shows how elements of the work environment and situational factors, such as the socialization of CDs in the management role, favour the development of a positive dual commitment, both to the profession and to the organization. McKee et al. (1999) acknowledge the importance of facilitating factors like talented and experienced business managers and nurse managers, a proper design of directorates in terms of scale, nature of the business and presence of a clear strategic mandate, and finally the proactive support from the chief executives in terms of provision of review mechanisms, training initiatives and creation of managerial structures which draw CDs into the broader organization. Thorne (1997) highlights the role played by the organization in sustaining the individuals who struggle to perform this role, while Lega (2008), focusing on Italian CDs, also shows the relevance of contextual factors at the organizational level, like tenure, appointment process and directorate design.

In order to increase our understanding of how the hospital organizational context influences the behaviours of doctors-in-management, I make use of the conceptual framework of individual performance commonly referred to as 'ability-motivation-opportunity', or 'AMO' (Blumberg and Pringle, 1982; Boxall and Purcell, 2011). This comprehensive framework, which is grounded on the work of Peters and O'Connor (1980) on situational constraints, sheds light on the importance of the interaction between the opportunity provided by the context and the capacity and willingness of the individual, which do not stand in isolation but are embedded in a social order which might act as a hindrance or a facilitator of individual behaviour. Opportunity is defined as 'the particular configuration of the field of forces surrounding a person and his or her task that enables or constrains that person's task performance and that is beyond the person's direct control' (Blumberg and Pringle, 1982: 565). A broad range of variables, related to the features of the organizational environment and the actions of others, can be included in this construct, such as organizational procedures that favour information sharing and delegation, budgetary support or the interaction with supervisors and co-workers.

According to the interactive nature of the model, the lack of opportunity to perform inhibits personal motivation, while when opportunity to perform is provided, ability and motivation can also develop and are further strengthened by the positive performance experienced personally. The model also explains that the interaction among these variables is not static but rather occurs in a process which develops over time. Furthermore, from this perspective, it can be understood why some types of opportunities might have different impacts on different groups of subjects as 'those highly able and highly motivated individuals predicted to have their performance most strongly affected by the presence of constraints will also be the most frustrated and dissatisfied under high constraint conditions' (Peters and O'Connor, 1980: 393). This comprehensive model has effectively been adopted by recent research in order to explain a wide array of behaviours including teamwork (Gould-Williams and Gatenby, 2010) and knowledge sharing (Siemsen et al., 2008).

Referring these notions to the case of CDs allows to fully take into account the complexity of organizational contingencies which, by interacting with individual determinants and the determinants at a professional group level, impact the behaviour of doctors-in-management in hospitals. By doing this, the AMO model is applied in a way which differs from those contributions, especially in the HRM field (Appelbaum et al., 2000; Boselie, 2010), which adopts a more positivist approach to study and quantify the causal link between the three variables and the individual performance of line workers. Rather, I make use of its analytical categories for drawing a conceptual framework which, by describing how individual and organizational dynamics are intertwined, allows a more thorough understanding of the determinants of individual behaviours.

Methods

The study was designed to make sense of individual and collective experiences of CDs within their specific organizational context, with its non-formalized facets, tacit power arrangements and off-the-record information flows. For these reasons, the empirical evidence for this analysis was gathered through qualitative research and, in particular, through the case study methodology (Yin, 2009). This approach was adopted because, through accessing multiple sources of evidence, it allows us to capture the richness and diversity of professionals' sense making during the process of managerial role taking and to develop a deep comprehension of the complex social phenomena which take place in the hospital setting. For the same purposes, similar qualitative methodologies were successfully used by a number of previous studies on doctors-in-management (e.g. Kitchener, 2000; Marnoch et al., 2000; Witman et al., 2011).

Case study context

The case study was carried out in a large tertiary hospital in Italy. The Italian experience is particularly relevant as doctors have historically been involved in management in the Italian health system. Since the royal law on hospital organization of 1938, unit chiefs have been in charge of formal responsibilities over human resources and physical resources like operating rooms and beds; and, in the 1990s, they also became accountable for reaching production and financial targets. Moreover, there is a unit run by the so-called hygienists in every hospital, that is, doctors specialized in hospital organization taking care of operations management responsibilities. These factors also contributed to a limited presence, especially if compared with other systems like the NHS, of non-medical managers, who usually work in centralized offices (for instance, human resources, finance, budget and control, quality, ICT) rather than being based in directorates or clinical divisions. CD roles were introduced in all Italian hospitals at the end of the 1990s and were intended to participate in strategy making, foster clinical and organizational integration and pool resources. By law, CDs must be selected from among the units and work on a part-time basis, maintaining their role at the specialty unit level. They are appointed by the hospital chief executive officer (CEO) and take part in the 'council of directors' board meetings.

With its 1,000 inpatient beds, the hospital is one of the largest providers in its area; it offers both general services for the local population and highly specialized care. It employs almost 4,000 staff and has a budget of over €400 million. For the purpose of the study, it represents a critical case for two main reasons: (1) it is a hospital which has been exposed to relevant managerial reforms for the last 15 years and (2) it introduced CD roles back in 1998. At the time when the study was conducted, the organizational chart identified 11 'managerial' clinical directorates and five 'support' clinical directorates (Figure 10.1). Each 'managerial' directorate included an average of five specialty units, ranging from a minimum of two to a maximum of ten.

In 2011, a new top management team (CEO, medical director and administrative director) was appointed which decided to increase the involvement of CDs in hospital management and decision making.

Data collection and analysis

The study, which took place in 2012, is based on direct interviews with the staff, observations of hospital board meetings over a six-month period and the analysis of archival material. Different categories of respondents were identified and multiple interviewees were selected in each category. The researcher had the unique opportunity to interview all CDs of the hospital,[1] the hospital CEO and the other members of the top management team, the chief hygienist (operations manager)

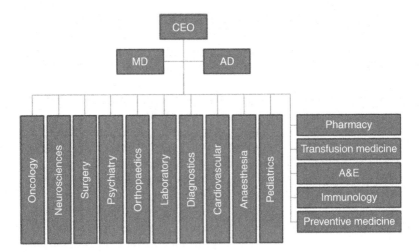

Figure 10.1   Hospital clinical directorates
Notes: CEO – Chief Executive Officer; MD – Medical Director; AD – Administrative Director;
A&E – Accident and Emergency.
Source: Author's own.

and the hospital chief nurse in depth. The presence of all hospital key informants afforded the gathering of valuable insights on CDs' actual managerial behaviours through the combination of a plurality of perspectives. The analysis was completed with the interview of the hygienists in charge of the budget negotiations and with two directorate nurse managers. In total 21 interviews were conducted, 16 with a medical background and five with a nursing or administrative background. Interviews were conducted with guarantees of anonymity and confidentiality; they took place on site and their average length was of one hour.

The interview protocol was prepared by the author analysing existing literature on doctors-in-management and was developed and fine-tuned after the discussion of the results of a pilot interview. The interviews were framed by a number of core question areas, including the content of the managerial activity; the reasons for moving into management and the attitudes towards the job; the relationship with non-medical managers and nurses; and the interaction with the organization and how it changed over time. Each theme was subdivided into specific interview topics; however, in order to empower respondents and increase their propensity to give narrative accounts, interviews were kept as open as possible. The question order was not rigid and follow-up questions were added if necessary. Interviews were conducted by the author, recorded and summarized in order to condense the most important meanings emerging from the answers (Weiss, 1994; Kvale and Brinkmann, 2009). Participant observation took place at four monthly hospital board meetings, lasting about three hours each; the author observed the meetings in order to understand the most frequent topics of the discussions, the style of the hospital top managers, the verbal and non-verbal behaviours through which each CD participated in the discussion of performance management issues and/or strategic issues. Finally, the dataset was completed with the analysis of relevant hospital documents like the statute, the organizational charts and the résumés of all CDs.

The initial conceptualization of data was made through the analysis of theory, developing themes that were enriched by categories emerging from the words and ideas expressed by the interviewees. Identification of patterns for interpretation and understanding of causal relationships then took place in an iterative process from data to theory and from theory to data.

Findings

The vast majority of CDs were the 'natural' candidates for the position: highly influential clinicians, presidents of scientific societies, sitting on the editorial boards of international journals or pioneers of new techniques at a national level. They had the professional legitimacy to occupy the position and the respect from colleagues. They were also aware that in order to maintain that legitimacy, both within the directorate and in the medical community at large, they needed to continue their clinical practice. All of them had been unit chiefs for years and were used to solving operational management issues, managing resources and directing people. And they had been exposed to the notion of medical management for years, both directly – as many had worked in the United States in the early phases of their career – and indirectly, through personal international networks. However, CDs' engagement in management changed consistently, according to both the individual capacity and willingness to step into management and the degree of opportunity to perform provided by the hospital.

The old days: Unsupported and unbacked

Although the hospital introduced clinical directorates back in the early 1990s, for a number of years CDs were not put in the position to really make a difference in managerial terms. The council of directors, initially presented to the organization as a management board, was summoned only four times a year and was intended as the place in which decisions were communicated one-way; discussions mostly took place with reference to clinical issues, such as the adoption of accreditation criteria, guidelines or quality standards. An extensive system to assign targets and monitor the financial performance was indeed introduced, and the pharmacy started providing reports about the drug consumption and the planning of expenses, the hygienists supported doctors in operations management issues. However, CDs had limited power in managing the budgets of specialty units, and when problems arose, often 'unit chiefs knocked on the CEO door to be listened to' (CD10) and they solved problems directly by bypassing CDs. Therefore, the opportunity to exercise managerial activities mostly came in terms of financial issues at the level of their own specialty unit.

Although in such context doctors' contribution to the hospital management was quite modest, different individual responses to management were present. A first group of CDs was composed of individuals who initially had the least interest in management, as they entered the role primarily with the hope to favour one's clinical group: 'I believed in my area of practice and I could not stand the risk of being governed by someone who did not care too much about it' (CD5); 'at the beginning, I wanted to be in a place to move my specialty forward' (CD4). They opted for conservative strategies; they continued to exercise their organizational power to access resources and managed to prevent the advent of undesired colleagues. They referred to the their managerial activities in the early years as a matter of controlling the achievement of financial targets, which required participation in setting the caps of the units and acting as supervisors in case of overspending: 'I understood that in order to be a good doctor you have to deal with financial management too' (CD4). Thanks to the exposure to monthly reports, frequent interactions with the staff of the CFO and discussions with the head of pharmacy, they had been acquiring competence in finance: 'it is really about administration, finance, and dealing with the pharmacy' (CD1). Accordingly, interactions with unit chiefs in the directorate were often focused on financial issues and took place on an occasional basis, and communication with the nursing staff was modest: meetings with the nurse directorate manager were non-frequent, often unscheduled and usually for administrative issues or small-scale operational problems: 'the only interactions were when we had to sign papers' (Nurse Manager (NM) 1).

The situation was rather different for a second group of CDs. They were those who entered the role with more of a positive attitude towards management, with the aim to make a difference and to change things. They had also been performing their role as budget controllers and had frequent exchanges with hospital accountants and pharmacists. At the same time, these directors reported being very much willing to address those few small-scale operational problems they were faced with: they held monthly directorate meetings with doctors and other professionals to foster discussion with colleagues and two-sided information sharing, and frequently mentioned the role of the nurse manager – with whom they held frequent interactions – as a key player in the directorate life. Apart from finance management they described their initial activity as a matter of fostering collaboration to share human or physical resources and clinical governance. Overall, they liked the managerial role, but they felt that their expectations had been betrayed by the limited scope of their involvement, by limited power they were provided with: 'they pretended to involve us' was one of their comments.

The last two years: Fostering the involvement and the emergence of the differences

Interviewees reported how in recent years a substantial change occurred in how their managerial role was supported by the hospital. In the managerial accounting system, some resources were pooled in order to be planned and managed collaboratively by the units under the director's supervision, and directors were asked to take active part in all the budget negotiations of the units. The new top management team asked unit chiefs to talk directly to CDs when organizational problems arose, therefore reinforcing their legitimacy. The council of directors became a monthly meeting, and the discussion of activity and performance data took the first place in its agenda: reports were analysed on a directorate basis, and directors had to openly respond to the CEO for gaps or missed goals, therefore increasing mutual control. Most importantly, the new CEO was openly sharing concerns and thoughts asking for suggestions and comments before taking final decisions.

This new approach had different impacts on CDs' behaviours on the basis of their degree of managerial ability and willingness. Those in the first group were indeed aware of the change: 'now we have to pay attention to the top management, and we are really responsible for the achievement of the directorate financial targets' (CD2), but were maintaining a conservative orientation, not taking possibly unpopular decisions which could compromise the status quo. The approach to managing organizational problems of the other units within their directorate could be described as 'live and let live'. When issues were openly raised, they tried to avoid tackling them directly and rather 'tossed the potato up' to the operations manager or the medical director. During the council of directors meetings, they rarely intervened and did not make proposals with long-term perspectives, nor on issues related to the directorate or the hospital as a whole. They were not very interested in dealing with the new opportunities to engage in medical management that the organization was offering, and it was also clear to them that their main focus was the clinical work: 'that is the job I really like, where I really have fun' (CD4).

The second group of CDs, on the contrary, was making use of the new organizational space which had been provided and got involved in hospital-wide thinking on issues such as performance management, cross-directorate collaboration and service reorganization. During the directorate meetings, they were actively interacting with the top management team offering suggestions and proposals, for instance on the strategies to attract patients from abroad or to set up a district hospital network. Some of their comments were, 'Now they know what we think about things' and 'at the beginning the board was only a place to get to know each other, and to discuss problems of clinical quality, now it is different'. These directors greatly appreciated the new course of the events; and at the time of the interviews, they were willing to increase their engagement, to move from consulting to a decision making role and to broaden the scope of their involvement by contributing to the development of partnerships with local institutions or to fundraising initiatives. And they complained when the agenda of the council of directors meetings was driven by the discussion of short-term performance data: 'of course short term performance targets are important, but we should not talk only about these things, especially in the council of directors ... we should discuss things like internationalisation, research strategies, strategic repositioning in our catchment area, criteria to select unit chiefs' (CD9).

Discussion

CDs' managerial behaviours emerged to be strongly influenced by the interaction between ability, motivation and the opportunity to perform provided by the organization. This situated account from a large Italian hospital shows how the poor engagement of doctors-in-management is not only a problem of scarce professionals' willingness to engage in management, but by and large it is due to lack of investment in these roles and by the lack of effective support from the top management.

This Italian case study confirms the findings of previous research on doctors-in-management as CDs, according to which managerial behaviours vary significantly on the basis of the ability of the individual in terms of people management competencies and strategic/entrepreneurial mindset. Also, the motivation to enter in the role, in terms of perceived congruence between professional and managerial values and culture, intention to make a difference and desire to achieve recognition, has a major impact on the dynamics and effectiveness of the role taking. Two types emerged: one of reluctant professionals who entered mainly for defensive reasons and did not want to engage in management; and a second group of enthusiastic doctors willing to take up the new managerial role, yielding similar results to the studies by McKee et al. (1999), Forbes et al. (2004) and McGivern et al. (2015) on CDs in the NHS.

However, CDs' managerial behaviours were also strongly influenced by the role of the opportunity to perform provided by the organization. The group of doctors who reported interest and willingness to engage in management complained the most about the lack of involvement granted by the former top management team. Therefore, the analysis confirmed the value of the AMO framework to explain the behaviour of doctors-in-management: as claimed by Peters and O'Connor (1980) performance cannot be improved if the 'ceiling on potential performance' determined by severe constraints is not raised. When provided with greater support and higher degrees of freedom instead, they started performing the intended CD role and made a visible difference in managerial terms. The problems with medical management, therefore, not (only) are a matter of professional resistance but are also to an important extent due to the behaviour of non-medical managers, who resist delegation and involvement of doctors for fear of losing organizational control. The analysis enables identification of two main organizational factors that offer doctors opportunities to perform in the managerial role: firstly, the support provided by the top management in the involvement in decision-making, for example in terms of frequency and content of board meetings, which gives the occasion to openly discuss hospital strategies but also represents a context for positive social control among professionals; secondly, the delegation of organizational power, the endowment with management leverages and effective backing, which strengthen CDs' authority in front of their former colleagues.

This support is necessary to overcome the sources of resistance to medical management in the Italian NHS, which are due to a number of factors such as the short top management mandates, the scarce amount and quality of managerial support staff or the historical status and influence of unit chiefs (Sartirana et al., 2014). However, it seems plausible that similar dynamics can be found outside of Italy in other European systems, at either the institutional or organizational level. These findings are in line with the research on the models of clinical directorates and their impact on the effectiveness of clinical management. Fitzgerald and Dufour (1998) found that the presence of leadership trios or duos heading CDs, as those that are in place in the United Kingdom or Canada, increase professionals' involvement in management through inter-professional co-operation and mutual support. Hospitals in other countries might learn from these experiences and invest more in the quality of the staff which supports medical managers.

Finally, as stated by previous research on doctors-in-management, according to which managerial behaviours vary significantly on the basis of personal features, when motivation and ability are low, then performance will also be low, and an increase in the single dimension of opportunity to perform will have limited impact on doctors' managerial behaviours and therefore on the managerial performance. This was confirmed by the first group of directors, who self-reported an initial lack of interest for management and intended their role as a matter of understanding financial management and keeping costs under control. They were content with their role and not calling for greater involvement in management. And when the opportunity to perform a broader managerial activity was provided, to engage in more strategic, long-term and outward-oriented initiatives, they did not exploit it.

Limitations and conclusion

The research has limitations linked to the nature of the methods used. The case study methodology proved to be particularly effective in offering an in-depth understanding of political dynamics taking place in the hospital organizational context; however, the analysis has an explorative nature and uses cross-sectional information from a single organization. Therefore, future research could make use of multiple and/or longitudinal case studies.

Research on doctors-in-management has looked for the reasons of professionals' (un)willingness or (in)capacity to engage in management by exploring either the individual responses to the professional–managerial dilemma or by understanding how professionals can acquire and preserve the legitimacy to lead their peers. However, the time has probably come to look at the complex organizational settings in which these processes take place. The chapter, by bridging the literature on medical management hybrids with contributions from theories on the impact of the organizational context on individual performance, has shown how the different organizational support, which (non-medical) managers offered to CDs, over time played a major role in determining the different managerial performance of those highly motivated and capable individuals.

Implications for policymaking and managerial practice are numerous. Firstly, if health policymakers in Western countries really want to increase professionals' involvement in management they should probably address top managers more than doctors. Secondly, if top managers are determined to assign CDs a strategic mandate, they should not fear to delegate and involve them in resource management and decision-making. Thirdly, organizational support to CDs' managerial role taking should be targeted to the needs of individuals: one size does not fit all. For the support to be effective in developing hybrid roles such as doctors-in-management, the amount and nature of training, involvement in decision-making and delegation of responsibilities should match the capacities and willingness of the different professionals. Accordingly, it is necessary to identify and understand the differences between a variety of forms of medical management, unveiling the multiple facets of a concept which, as argued by Glouberman and Mintzberg (2001: 57), 'is not one homogeneous process but several, usually quite distinct from one another'.

Acknowledgements

The author thanks Mirko Noordegraaf and Paul Boselie for the time put into the review of this manuscript, and Federico Lega, Ian Kirkpatrick, Gianluca Veronesi and the book editors for their valuable comments and suggestions. I also deeply thank all healthcare professionals involved in the research and Regione Lombardia – Programma Dote Ricerca Applicata for its financial support.

Note

1. Thirteen clinical directors were interviewed out of 16 directorates (one directorate was vacant, one director was the *pro tempore* head of two directorates and the preventive medicine directorate was excluded as, due to the specific nature of its activity, it was considered not relevant for the analysis).

References

Appelbaum, E., Bailey, T., Berg, P. and Kalleberg, A. (2000) *Manufacturing Advantage: Why High-Performance Work Systems Pay Off.* Ithaca: Cornell University Press.

Blumberg, M. and Pringle, C. D. (1982) 'The missing opportunity in organizational research: some implications for a theory of work performance', *The Academy of Management Review,* 7(4): 560–569.

Boselie, P. (2010) 'High performance work practices in the health care sector: a Dutch case study', *International Journal of Manpower,* 31(1): 42–58.

Boxall, P. and Purcell, J. (2011) *Strategy and Human Resource Management,* 3rd edition, Basingstoke and New York: Palgrave Macmillan.

Chantler, C. (1993) 'Historical background: where have CDs come from and what is their purpose?' in A. Hopkins (ed.), *The Role of Hospital Consultants in Clinical Directorates. The Syncromesh Report.* London: Royal College of Physicians.

Fitzgerald, L. and Dufour, Y. (1998) 'Clinical management as boundary management, a comparative analysis of Canadian and U.K. healthcare institutions', *Journal of Management in Medicine,* 12(4/5): 199–213.

Forbes, T., Hallier, J. and Kelly, L. (2004) 'Doctors as managers: investors and reluctants in a dual role', *Health Services Management Research,* 17(3): 167–176.

Freidson, E. (2001) *Professionalism: The Third Logic.* Chicago: University of Chicago Press.

Glouberman, S. and Mintzberg, H. (2001) 'Managing the care of health and the cure of disease–part I: differentiation', *Health Care Management Review,* 26(1): 56–69.

Gould-Williams, J. S. and Gatenby, M. (2010) 'The effects of organizational context and teamworking activities on performance outcomes: a study conducted in England local government', *Public Management Review,* 12(6): 759–787.

Ham, C. and Dickinson, H. (2008) *Engaging Doctors in Leadership: What We Can Learn from International Experience and Research Evidence?* London: NHS Institute for Innovation and Improvement.

Hoff, T. J. (2001) 'Exploring dual commitment among physician executives in managed care', *Journal of Healthcare Management,* 46(2): 91–111.

Kirkpatrick, I., Bullinger, B., Lega, F. and Dent, M. (2013) 'The translation of hospital management reforms in European health systems: a framework for comparison', *British Journal of Management,* 24: S48–61.

Kirkpatrick, I., Jespersen, P. K., Dent, M. and Neogy, I. (2009) 'Medicine and management in a comparative perspective: the case of Denmark and England', *Sociology of Health and Illness,* 31(5): 642–658.

Kitchener, M. (2000) 'The "Bureaucratization" of professional roles: the case of clinical directors in UK Hospitals', *Organization,* 7(1): 129–154.

Kvale, S. and Brinkmann, S. (2009) *Learning the Craft of Qualitative Research Interviewing.* California: SAGE Publications.

Lega, F. (2008) 'The rise and fall(acy) of clinical directorates in Italy', *Health Policy,* 85(2): 252–262.

Llewellyn, S. (2001) 'Two way windows: clinicians as medical managers', *Organization Studies,* 22(4): 593–623.

Marnoch, G., McKee, L. and Dinnie, N. (2000) 'Between organizations and institutions: legitimacy and medical managers', *Public Administration,* 78(4): 967–986.

McGivern, G., Currie, G., Ferlie, E., Fitzgerald, L. and Waring, J. (2015) 'Hybrid manager-professionals' identity work, the maintenance and hybridization of professionalism in managerial contexts', *Public Administration*, 93: 412–432.

McKee, L., Marnoch, G. and Dinnie, N. (1999) 'Medical managers: puppets or puppetmasters?' in A. Mark and S. Dopson (eds.), *Organisational Behaviour in Health Care: The Research Agenda*. Basingstoke: Macmillan Press.

Neogy, I. and Kirkpatrick, I. (2009) *Medicine in Management: Lessons across Europe*. Leeds: Centre for Innovation in Health Management, University of Leeds.

Noordegraaf, M. (2007) 'From "Pure" to "Hybrid" professionalism. Present-day professionalism in ambiguous public domains', *Administration & Society*, 39(6): 761–785.

Numerato, D., Salvatore, D. and Fattore, G. (2011) 'The impact of management on medical professionalism: a review', *Sociology of Health & Illness*, 34(4): 626–644.

Peters, L. H. and O'Connor, E. J. (1980) 'Situational constraints and work outcomes: the influences of a frequently overlooked construct', *The Academy of Management Review*, 5(3): 391–397.

Sartirana, M., Prenestini A. and Lega F. (2014) 'Medical management: hostage to its own history? The case of Italian clinical directors', *The International Journal of Public Sector Management*, 27(5): 417–429.

Siemsen, E., Roth, A. V. and Balasubramanian, S. (2008) 'How motivation, opportunity, and ability drive knowledge sharing: the constraining-factor model', *Journal of Operations Management*, 26(3): 426–445.

Thorne, M. L. (1997) 'Being a clinical director: first among equals or just a go-between?' *Health Services Management Research*, 10(4): 205–215.

Weiss, R. S. (1994) *Learning from Strangers: The Art and Method of Qualitative Interview Studies*. New York: Free Press.

Witman, Y., Smid, G. A. C., Meurs, P. L. and Willems, D. L. (2011) 'Doctor in the lead: balancing between two worlds', *Organization*, 18(4): 477–495.

Yin, R. K. (2009) *Case Study Research: Design and Methods*. California: SAGE Publications.

11
A New Approach to Hybrid Leadership Development

Charlotte Croft

Introduction

The strategic importance of involving professionals in the leadership of healthcare systems is noted globally (Degeling et al., 2006; Clark, 2012). In particular, leadership development amongst mid-level managers from clinical backgrounds (hybrids) is seen as a pivotal influence on enhanced patient care, organizational effectiveness and innovation (Ferlie et al., 2005; Martinussen and Magnussen, 2011; McGivern et al., 2015). The influence of hybrids stems from their potential ability to move between managerial and professional realms, viewing organizational issues through 'two-way windows' (Llewellyn, 2001) and encouraging professional groups to work collaboratively with managerial colleagues (Ackroyd et al., 2007; Fitzgerald et al., 2013). However, healthcare organizations are characterized by managerially driven priorities and professional hierarchies (Exworthy et al., 1999), which shape the organizational context and may influence hybrid leadership development (Fitzgerald et al., 2013; Croft et al., 2014; McGivern et al., 2015). If hybrid leadership development is undermined by organizational context, the strategic potential of hybrids is lost, as their influence as boundary spanners between professional and managerial jurisdictions will be limited (Croft et al., 2015).

Despite an awareness of the influence of organizational context on hybrid leadership development, the majority of leadership development programmes in the UK public sector take a quantifiable, skill-based or competency approach, with a focus on measurable outcomes and benchmarking frameworks (Day, 2000; Institute for Improvement, 2005). Skill-based programmes are not limited to UK contexts, and are evident across the United States and other commonwealth countries

(Degeling et al., 2006; Clark, 2012), where they are criticized for being merely 'tick box exercises', neglecting the influence of the complex organizational environment in which hybrids are positioned (Hirst et al., 2004; Bolden et al., 2006; McGivern and Ferlie, 2007). These approaches remain prevalent in the public sector, despite concerns that they may undermine, rather than encourage, hybrid leadership (Alvesson and Willmott, 2002; Martin and Learmonth, 2012).

This chapter considers a new approach to hybrid leadership development which prioritizes an understanding of the organizational context, rather than the uptake of individual skills or behaviours. It begins by critiquing individualistic approaches to leadership development, highlighting the reliance of existing research on the experiences of powerful professional hybrids, such as doctors. The need to consider other hybrid groups, such as nurses, who may be influenced more acutely by the organizational context, is then outlined. Following this, an organizational-level approach to leadership development is outlined through consideration of 70 interviews conducted with 32 nurses taking part in a leadership development programme in the English National Health Service (NHS). In the discussion and conclusion of the chapter, empirical findings are explored within the context of existing research, outlining how organizational leadership development programmes engender a sense of community, enhancing commitment to managerial priorities, and encourage interpersonal relationships to develop across professional jurisdictions. It is argued that these outcomes enhance hybrid leadership development, overcoming the potential limitations of the organizational context. However, the findings also highlight how organizational-level approaches may become mechanisms of normative control, limiting the strategic influence of hybrids by framing leadership development within the confines of managerially determined goals.

Leadership development and healthcare

In healthcare organizations on a global scale, there has been a proliferation of leadership development programmes aimed at healthcare professionals (Ferlie and Shortell, 2001; Degeling et al., 2006). Healthcare professionals, in particular mid-level clinicians with managerial and clinical responsibilities, are strategically important as they have the potential to enhance patient care, organizational effectiveness and innovation (Ferlie et al., 2005; Martinussen and Magnussen, 2011; McGivern et al., 2015). Otherwise known as 'hybrids', this group of clinician managers can move between multiple organizational realms, mediating managerial and professional jurisdictions (Llewellyn, 2001; Ackroyd et al., 2007; Fitzgerald et al., 2013).

Despite the proliferation of leadership development programmes for hybrids (Institute for Improvement, 2005), the majority of approaches in the public sector are skills based and individualistic, which 'ignores almost 50 years of research showing leadership to be a complex interaction between the designated leader and the social and organizational environment' (Day, 2000: 583). Individualistic programmes take a traditional, quantifiable approach, advocating the need for measurement standards and benchmarking frameworks to ensure leaders are delivering significant organizational improvements (Institute for Improvement, 2005). However, these approaches neglect a consideration of the influence of organizational context on hybrid leadership development (Bolden et al., 2006). Organizational context in professionalized settings, such as healthcare, is framed by power differentials between professions, and explicit tensions between managerial and professional hierarchies, influencing hybrid leadership development (Fitzgerald et al., 2013; Croft et al., 2014; White et al., 2014; McGivern et al., 2015).

The ongoing reliance on skill-based approaches to leadership development, with little regard for organizational context, has been criticized by some as acting as 'tick box exercises', co-opting professionals into managerially framed ways of working, rather than encouraging innovative hybrid leadership development (McGivern and Ferlie, 2007). As a result, leadership development in healthcare has been criticized by some as acting as a form of organizational control, which aims to integrate professionals into formal management and governance structures (Alvesson and Willmott, 2002; Martin and Learmonth, 2012). This has the potential to undermine the strategic potential of hybrids, as they are constrained by their position within a managerially determined organizational context (Croft et al., 2014).

Reflecting the lack of consideration of organizational context is the abundance of existing work on leadership development for doctors, with little exploration of other professional groups (Denis et al., 2001; Sehested, 2002; Iedema et al., 2004; McGivern et al., 2015). This is problematic, as hybrids from different professional backgrounds will have nuanced differences in their leadership development needs, due to specific challenges they face in the organizational context (Oborn and Dawson, 2010). As such, insights into leadership development needs for medical hybrids may not be directly applicable to less powerful professional groups. One such group, often neglected in research, is nurses.

Nurses provide an illuminating case for the examination of hybrid leadership development, as they struggle to be accepted as legitimate service leaders, both within and outside of the profession, despite an increasing awareness of their potential contribution as hybrid leaders (Salhani and Coulter, 2009; Currie et al., 2010). Nurses continue to engage in individualistic leadership development programmes without notable success in organizational leadership roles, due to the influence of organizational contexts in which nurses are seen as 'followers' rather than 'leaders', encouraged to maintain stereotypical ideals of obedient, silent, altruistic and passive caring (Goodrick and Reay, 2010). Consequently, hybrid nurses represent a group who are strategically important, as they have the potential to influence across multiple organizational jurisdictions, but who may not fulfil this potential due to the influence of organizational context on leadership development (Croft et al., 2014). As such, nurses offer insights into the challenges of hybrid leadership development and the influence of the organizational context.

Methodology

The empirical findings presented in this chapter focus on the experiences of nurses attending an organizational-level leadership development programme, encouraging a strategic understanding of the organizational context, rather than developing individual skills. The aim of the programme was to 'give some space for our current and emerging leaders to take stock and understand the organization and its environment much better' (quote taken from organizational documentation). The programme had a cohort of over 200 participants, representing a variety of professional backgrounds, with individuals from medical, nursing and allied health backgrounds, in addition to non-professional members of the organization, for example estates, IT and patient group representatives.

A total of five sessions were held over five months, focusing on the strategic context of the NHS, with a particular emphasis on the interplay between national government policy and the organizational priorities of the executive management team. Sessions were grounded in a local, organizational and political context, framing hybrid leadership development within organizational visions and priorities. The sessions were often split into two parts: the morning session would contextualize the 'topic' of the day, outlining how the focus of the session aligned with organizational objectives; the afternoon session focused on group work, networking, or mentoring with more senior organizational leaders, to discuss how organizational objectives might be achieved. In addition, participants were encouraged to develop interpersonal relationships with other attendees and were organized into 'networked groups' with individuals from different professional backgrounds. The purpose of these groups was to encourage communication between sessions and maintain relationships after the close of the programme. The groups provided an arena for participants to share ideas, working within multidisciplinary teams towards collective organizational priorities. For example, one organizational priority highlighted in the programme was the need to reduce expenditure over the next financial year. Subsequently, all networked groups were asked to develop plans for cutting costs within the organization and feed these ideas back to the senior management team.

One member of the research team enrolled in the leadership development programme and attended all course events and teaching days, including afternoon networking sessions. They did not participate in the networked group discussions occurring between teaching days. Participation of the researcher developed a degree of collegiality with potential study participants, due to a shared experience of the programmes (Seidman, 1998). Ethical approval was acquired from the NHS and from the local organization, and the researcher's participation in the programme explained to all participants. When the researcher took part in networking events or discussions within smaller groups, participants were asked for their consent prior to involvement, and all field notes were anonymized. A total of 120 hours of participant observation were recorded in field notes.

Reflecting the abstract and socially constructed nature of 'leadership' (Alvesson and Sveningsson, 2003), a combination of semi-structured interviews and participant observation was used to engender rich descriptions about individual perceptions of the influences on leadership development (Bryman, 1999). The participant observation aspect of data collection was used to contextualize the understanding of the leadership development programme, enabling triangulation with interview responses, and contributing to a more in-depth exploration of the process being observed (Delamont, 2007; Fairhurst, 2009).

Empirical data were collected from 32 nurses over a three-year period, in which they were invited for interview three times: first, at the close of the leadership development programme, and subsequently at one and two years following the first interview. Due to participant attrition, 70 interviews were conducted in total. The 32 nurses recruited were stratified across the professional hierarchy. Seven individuals held traditional nursing roles associated with close patient contact, clinical care and little or no managerial responsibilities. Twenty respondents were classified as 'middle managers' (Currie, 2006), fulfilling roles requiring a mix of clinical and managerial work, along a spectrum from primarily clinical with management responsibilities (such as ward managers), to primarily managerial with limited clinical contact time (such as directorate managers). Five respondents were recruited from board level, executive posts.

Following an inductive coding technique, as outlined by Strauss and Corbin (1990), in-vivo quotes were generated from the interview data. Interview transcripts were first explored for the way respondents described their experiences of the leadership development programme. Transcripts were then analysed for insights into the influence of organizational context on hybrid leadership development, and the potential of the leadership development programme to mediate those influences. The analysis led to two overarching thematic categories: facilitating hybrid leadership through organizational development and the dark side of normative control.

Facilitating hybrid leadership through organizational leadership development

As outlined above, the aim of the programme was to contextualize leadership development within the organizational environment. One of the ways this occurred was through sessions taking an overview of the national political agenda, positioning the organization within a wider landscape of healthcare. From the outset of the programme, this gave the impression that organizers were keen for individuals to contribute to the achievement of organizational strategic priorities:

> Chief executive opening address to delegates highlights the importance of working together as 'one' to achieve system alignment and large-scale change, moving in the same direction. He specifically discusses the importance of clinicians in facilitating this change and asks them to combine the messages from the leadership development programme into their clinical practice.
>
> (Field Notes: 20/10/09)

Throughout the programme, the focus was on organizational-level issues, rather than individual leadership development. The influence of this was twofold. First, nurse hybrids suggested an understanding of the strategic organizational and national priorities and enabled them to contextualize their leadership development outside of their own personal needs:

> I think actually it helped people become aware of what the priorities are, what their role is within that, where the challenges might be... it's more about what are the priorities in the NHS and what's the trust needing to do... I think we get leadership development out of that but it's probably almost secondary to that.
>
> (Nurse 19 – First Interview)

Subsequently, nurse hybrids suggested they thought more strategically about their role, encouraging them to enact leadership in new ways:

> I think it probably did get me to think more widely about what I do and the impact of what I do... It was like it got me to reflect about different aspects of my role and how that fits into the wider organization, and thinking 'Yeah, I could bring that into my role, think about that more.'
>
> (Nurse 7 – Third Interview)

An organizational-level approach also appeared to engender a sense of dedication and commitment to the organization. As a result, nurse hybrids suggested they were more dedicated to aligning themselves with, and promoting, the strategic vision of the managerial leaders within the organization:

> I feel very committed to (the organization)... One of the other girls on the table said 'inspired to do your bit', which you don't always get if you feel you're just being dictated to from on high. So I think it was a lot more positive vibe about it in terms of, yes ok you might be working on the shop floor but you can all make a difference, and we can all make a difference together.
>
> (Nurse 5 – First Interview)

The second influence on hybrid leadership development stemmed from the large number of delegates from different professional backgrounds attending the programme. A multidisciplinary approach, contextualized within overarching discussions of organizational priorities, developed interpersonal relationships between multiple professional groups, who may otherwise not have interacted due to jurisdictional boundaries:

What I liked about it was getting to talk to a lot of different people. Not just clinicians, but patient involvement representatives, managers, HR, estates... I was talking to someone from estates about something and I thought it was interesting that they had a completely different take on the problem, a completely different perspective. It made me think differently about it too.

(Nurse 22 – first interview)

Developing relationships with participants from a wide range of backgrounds encouraged innovation and different ways of thinking. Further to this, the development of interpersonal relationships complemented the sense of commitment to the organization, as nurse hybrids suggested they felt part of a network of individuals who may be experiencing similar challenges to their leadership development. As a result, nurse hybrids reported an increased sense of support resulting from relationships developed through the programme:

I sometimes think it brings home that actually you're not alone, you're not the only person that's ever been in that position that's felt that you're struggling, you're failing, you're not achieving, you're not good enough to do that role. Sometimes you're going through negative times, but you're not the only person that's ever gone through that... other people have gone through it and come out the other side.

(Nurse 3 – Second Interview)

In addition, cross-disciplinary interpersonal relationships could mediate the influence of power differentials between professional hierarchies. One nurse commented on how this influenced her willingness to interact with managers from higher up in the organizational structure, to develop ideas:

And now, as a result of the programme, if I have an idea I feel more confident about emailing someone higher up than me, or getting in touch with the senior managers... you know, perhaps I wouldn't have done that before but because I know them from the programme, I feel like it's ok to approach them.

(Nurse 29 – first interview)

Other nurses echoed this sentiment, suggesting that interpersonal relationships developed with other more powerful professionals, such as doctors, could begin to overcome the influence of professional hierarchies on leadership in practice. In some circumstances, as outlined below, these new relationships encouraged the development of new ideas and services, increasing organizational performance:

> I was thinking about how we could get a better service for our patients with dementia who are on a general ward. So I phoned up the consultant who specialises in dementia, I knew him from (the leadership development programme)... I would never have dreamed of phoning a consultant before that, but we got on well so I thought it would be ok... anyway he agreed to work with me on this idea and now we have a specific dementia service in place... it's so much better for the patients.
>
> (Nurse 15 – Third Interview)

By taking an organizational-level approach to leadership development, nurse hybrids suggested that the programme encouraged them to position their role and personal leadership development within a wider organizational context. They also reported a sense of increased commitment to the managerial priorities of the organization. This was facilitated by the diverse background of participants, which contributed to the development of a sense of community. In addition, the collegiality engendered by participation on the programme encouraged innovation due to interaction between different groups, as well as working to overcome the moderating influence of power differentials between professions.

The 'Dark Side' of normative control

Despite the benefits of the organizational-level approach, responses from nurse hybrids also indicated a 'dark' side to leadership development. Whilst the programme could engender a sense of community amongst some nurse hybrids, others suggested, 'it's almost getting people converted, it's like a religion thing' (Nurse 12 – First Interview). Some nurse hybrids did not view the experience as beneficial to their leadership development, suggesting that an organizational-level approach limited the sessions to a big sort of PR thing for the trust (Nurse 11 – First Interview). Whilst an increased sense of community engendered a commitment to managerial priorities for some, others discussed a sense that the managers running the programme were attempting to limit their leadership development, by framing it within organizationally desirable confines:

I don't think it's a leadership course ... I think it was the trust was trying to get a standardised way of working in quality and productivity and innovation. I think they were standardising it and encouraging the same behaviour across the board but I wouldn't describe that as a leadership.

(Nurse 7 – First Interview)

Others reflected this sentiment, suggesting, 'we're all being briefed here, we're being got on side and trying to be made special so we go and do the dirty work' (Nurse 15 – First Interview). This was enhanced by the sense that the programme failed to consider the complexity of enacting leadership in the reality of their organizational role. Whilst the organizational-level approach set out the managerial priorities and strategy for the collective, some nurses suggested that this was not reflective of the challenges they faced in practice:

And I came away from that thinking well how does that actually make a difference, talking the talk what I have sometimes experienced in real life ... Sometimes management have no idea about what I have to deal with on the front line.

(Nurse 19 – First Interview)

Overall, despite an initially positive response about the potential of the programme, there were also reports of negative experiences due to normative control. By encouraging nurse hybrids to contextualize their ongoing leadership development within managerially determined organizational priorities, there was the risk of undermining the potential strategic influence of hybrids. Ultimately, whilst an organizational approach to leadership development could encourage organizational commitment for some, addressing the influence of professional hierarchies through the development of interpersonal relationships, others felt constrained by the spectre of normative control.

Discussion

The findings outlined in this chapter offer insights into the potential of leadership development programmes which take an organizational-level approach to hybrid leadership development, rather than an individualistic, skill-based approach. Many nurse hybrids participating in the study reported that organizational leadership development resulted in increased commitment to managerial priorities within the organization and enhanced interpersonal relationships with other professionals.

However, some also suggested that an organizational-level approach could act as a mechanism of normative control, limiting hybrid leadership outside of managerially determined confines. The implications of the issues arising from the empirical data are discussed below.

The leadership development programme encouraged an awareness of the strategic priorities of the organization, positioning hybrid leadership development within a consideration of the wider organizational context. As a result, a number of nurse hybrids reported an increased understanding of the managerial priorities shaping organizational strategy, and suggested they felt more committed to achieving these priorities as a result of the programme. In this respect, organizational-level leadership development can be seen as encouraging the development of nurse hybrids as 'two-way windows' (Llewellyn, 2001).

The strategic advantage of an organizational approach to leadership development may be more evident amongst nurse hybrids, as they often struggle in leadership roles (Croft et al., 2015). As noted previously, the organizational context in which leadership development takes place is characterized by professional and managerial hierarchies, which encourage nurses to conform to more passive, subordinate ways of working, limiting their ability to become strategic hybrid leaders (Fitzgerald et al., 2013; Croft et al., 2014; White et al., 2014; McGivern et al., 2015). Further to this, skill-based approaches to leadership development are based on the needs and experiences of doctors, which may not be representative of the challenges faced by nurses, due to the issues of professional socialization outlined above (Goodrick and Reay, 2010; Oborn and Dawson, 2010). In this case, an organizational-level approach to leadership development worked to overcome these limitations by helping nurse hybrids to consider the 'bigger picture' and encouraging an understanding of the wider strategic landscape. As a result, an increased organizational awareness, and commitment to managerial priorities, enhanced the strategic potential of hybrids by facilitating their ability to act as boundary spanners, subsequently encouraging the uptake of managerial reform through their leadership influence with other professional peers.

In addition to increased commitment, the diverse professional backgrounds of those attending the programme was an influence on hybrid leadership development. Working with individuals from other professional groups encouraged interpersonal relationship outside of professional jurisdictions. Interpersonal relationships between different professional groups, and between professionals and managers, is key for the development of hybrid leadership, encouraging boundary spanning and a shared sense of commitment to organizational priorities (Ferlie and Shortell, 2001; Fitzgerald et al., 2013). The positive influence of enhanced interpersonal relationships with different professionals, which may not otherwise have developed due to institutionalized power differentials, was highlighted in responses from nurse hybrids discussing the development of new ideas and innovative services. Professional hierarchies have previously been identified as a negative influence on the potential of hybrid professionals (Currie et al., 2010; Croft et al., 2014). However, by taking a multidisciplinary, organizational-level approach, leadership development in this case was encouraged by interpersonal relationships, mediating the limitations of professional hierarchies, and enhancing the strategic potential of hybrids.

Thus far, an organizational-level approach can be conceptualized as a positive influence on hybrid leadership development. However, the empirical findings also uncovered a potential 'dark side', due to the focus of the programme on the need to co-opt hybrids into organizational priorities, aligning them with demands from the managerial hierarchy. Some nurse hybrids suggested the programme attempted to standardize behaviours, encouraging them to work within defined managerial frameworks, with some even comparing it to the experience of being converted to a religion. This reflects previous work suggesting that organizations may use leadership development to produce 'appropriate' leaders, encouraging professionals to behave in ways congruent with managerially driven priorities and visions (Alvesson and Willmott, 2002). Indeed, the programme in this case enabled the chief executive to communicate to a diverse audience from the organization, encouraging them to act as a collective and work towards a shared organizational vision. Although it was not overtly evident in the study, there is the risk that increased levels of normative control will cause 'leadership' to become an oppressive rhetorical device (Martin and Learmonth, 2012). The potential for normative control may subsequently undermine the benefits of organizational-level leadership development, as previous research suggests that co-option into managerial priorities can constrain hybrids, limiting their ability to act as two-way windows (Croft et al., 2014).

Whilst the limitations for normative control should not be dismissed, the findings outlined in this chapter provide insight into the potential of organizational-level approaches to leadership development and their capacity for encouraging contextualized hybrid leadership development. The empirical findings presented focus on the case of nurses to illuminate the influence of organizational-level leadership development on hybrids, but the conclusions drawn can be applied to any setting characterized by strong professional identities and managerially influenced organizational contexts. Nurses may face challenges of leadership more acutely than other, stronger, professionals, such as medicine, but the findings can be generalized to any group of professional hybrids (Pratt et al., 2006). Additionally, whilst the empirics are drawn from the English NHS, similar approaches towards leadership development are evident in the United States and other commonwealth countries (Degeling et al., 2006; Clark, 2012). As such, the findings may be generalizable to a wide range of public sector settings on an international scale.

The conclusions drawn in this chapter provide further avenues for research, and have implications for healthcare policy and leadership development design. First, whilst the diverse background of participants in the study engendered a sense of organizational commitment, and developed interpersonal relationships, further research is needed to explore the impact of a cross-professional approach on leadership development and the extent to which relationships can be transferred into practice. Professional hierarchies are institutionalized in public sector organizations, meaning that maintenance of interpersonal relationships outside of the programme may lessen over time, undermining hybrid leadership by reducing collaborative working with other hybrids (Currie et al., 2010). In addition, whilst this chapter addresses the reliance on research into medical hybrids by considering nurses, future research should continue to consider the experiences of other, less powerful professions during organizational-level leadership development. Second, professional hybrids are not homogenous (McGivern et al., 2015) and may show variation in their willingness to align with managerial priorities or strategic aims. Some variation amongst study participants was outlined in this chapter, and more research is needed to explore why some hybrids were co-opted into managerially driven visions, whilst others were more resistant. Third, more consideration is needed for the conceptualization of leadership development programmes as mechanisms of normative control. Is normative control, as research suggests (Martin and Learmonth, 2012), always a negative influence on hybrid leadership? Or are there times at which it can be strategically beneficial? The chapter findings relating to the influence of perceived normative control on hybrids were ambiguous and should be explored further. Finally, the findings have implications for the design of leadership development in healthcare organizations. Researchers should consider why public sector organizations continue to use a 'tick box' model of leadership development, which does not consider the complex organizational influences on hybrid leaders (Day, 2000; McGivern and Ferlie, 2007). This institutionalized behaviour may be difficult to resolve and will need to be addressed at a national, strategic level to engender change.

Conclusion

Despite an increased awareness of the strategic importance of professional hybrids in public sector organizations, hybrid leadership development is often limited to individualistic, skill-based approaches. These approaches do not consider the influence of the organizational context on hybrid leadership development, which may be undermined by tensions between managerial and professional priorities, and power differentials between professions. This chapter has outlined the potential for organizational-level approaches to leadership development, which can mediate some of the challenges for hybrid leaders. Using the case of nurse hybrids, this chapter has illuminated how the strategic potential of hybrids as boundary spanners can be enhanced through organizational leadership development, by encouraging a commitment to managerial priorities and by developing interpersonal relationships outside of professional jurisdictions. However, the chapter also warns against the use of leadership development as a mechanism of normative control, limiting the potential of hybrids to ensure conformity to managerially determined organizational priorities.

References

Ackroyd, S., Kirkpatrick, I. and Walker, R. M. (2007) 'Public management reform in the UK and its consequences for professional organization: a comparative analysis', *Public Administration*, 85: 9–26.

Alvesson, M. and Sveningsson, S. (2003) 'The great disappearing act: difficulties in doing "leadership"', *The Leadership Quarterly*, 14: 359–381.

Alvesson, M. and Willmott, H. (2002) 'Identity regulation as organizational control: producing the appropriate individual', *Journal of Management Studies*, 39: 619–644.

Bolden, R., Wood, M. and Gosling, J. (2006) 'Is the NHS leadership qualities framework missing the wood for the trees?', in A. Casbeer, A. Hamson and A. Mark (eds.), *Innovations in Health Care: A Reality Check*. New York: Palgrave Macmillan, pp. 17–29.

Bryman, A. (1999) 'Leadership in organisations', in S. Clegg, C. Hardy and W. Nord (eds.), *Managing Organizations: Current Issues*. London: Sage.

Clark, J. (2012) 'Medical leadership and engagement: no longer an optional extra', *Journal of Health Organisation and Management*, 26: 437–443.

Croft, C., Currie, G. and Lockett, A. (2014) 'Broken 'two-way windows'? An exploration of professional hybrids', *Public Administration*, 93(2): 380–394. doi: 10.1111/padm.12115.

Croft, C., Currie, G. and Lockett, A. (2015) 'The impact of emotionally important social identities on the construction of a managerial leader identity: a challenge for nurses in the English National Health Service, *Organization Studies*, 36: 113–131.

Currie, G. (2006) 'Reluctant but resourceful middle managers: the case of nurses in the NHS', *Journal of Nursing Management*, 14: 5–12.

Currie, G., Finn, R. and Martin, G. (2010) 'Role transition and the interaction of relational and social identity: new nursing roles in the English NHS', *Organization Studies*, 31: 941–961.

Day, D. V. (2000) 'Leadership development: a review in context', *The Leadership Quarterly*, 11: 581–613.

Degeling, P., Zhang, K., Coyle, B. et al. (2006) 'Clinicians and the governance of hospitals: a cross-cultural perspective on relations between profession and management', *Social Science & Medicine*, 63: 757–775.

Delamont, S. (2007) 'Ethnography and participant observation', in C. Seale, G. Gobo, J. Gubrium et al. (eds.), *Qualitative Research Practice*. London: Sage, 205–217.

Denis, J.-L., Lamothe, L. and Langley, A. (2001) 'The dynamics of collective leadership and strategic change in pluralistic organizations', *Academy of Management Journal*, 44: 809–837.

Exworthy, M., Powell, M. and Mohan, J. (1999) 'The NHS: quasi-market, quasi-hierarchy and quasi-network?' *Public Money & Management*, 19: 15.

Fairhurst, G. T. (2009) 'Considering context in discursive leadership research', *Human Relations*, 62: 1607–1633.

Ferlie, E., Fitzgerald, L., Wood, M. et al. (2005) 'The nonspread of innovations: the mediating role of professionals', *Academy of Management Journal*, 48: 117–134.

Ferlie, E. and Shortell, S. M. (2001) 'Improving the quality of health care in the United Kingdom and the United States: a framework for change', *The Milbank Quarterly*, 79: 281–315.

Fitzgerald, L., Ferlie, E., McGivern, G. et al. (2013) 'Distributed leadership patterns and service improvement: evidence and argument from English healthcare', *The Leadership Quarterly*, 24: 227–239.

Goodrick, E. and Reay, T. (2010) 'Florence nightingale endures: legitimizing a new professional role identity', *Journal of Management Studies*, 47: 55–84.

Hirst, G., Mann L., Bain, P. et al. (2004) 'Learning to lead: the development and testing of a model of leadership learning', *The Leadership Quarterly*, 15: 311–327.

Iedema, R., Degeling, P., Braithwaite, J. et al. (2004) 'It's an interesting conversation i'm hearing: the doctor as manager', *Organization Studies*, 25: 15–33.

Institute for Improvement (2005) *NHS Leadership Qualities Framework*. London: NHS.

Llewellyn, S. (2001) '"Two-way windows": clinicians as medical managers', *Organization Studies*, 22: 593–623.

Martin, G. P. and Learmonth, M. (2012) 'A critical account of the rise and spread of "leadership": the case of UK healthcare', *Social Science and Medicine*, 74: 281–288.

Martinussen, P. I. E. and Magnussen, J. (2011) 'Resisting market-inspired reform in healthcare: the role of professional subcultures in medicine', *Social Science and Medicine*, 73: 193–200.

McGivern, G., Currie, G., Ferlie, E. et al. (2015) 'Hybrid manager-professionals' identity work: the maintenance and hybridization of medical professionalism in managerial contexts', *Public Administration*, 93: 412–432. doi: 10.1111/padm. 12119.

McGivern, G. and Ferlie, E. (2007) 'Playing tick-box games: interrelating defences in professional appraisal', *Human Relations*, 60: 1361–1385.

Oborn, E. and Dawson, S. (2010) 'Learning across communities of practice: an examination of multidisciplinary work', *British Journal of Management*, 21: 843–858.

Pratt, M. G., Rockmann, K. W. and Kaufmann, J. B. (2006) 'Constructing professional identity: the role of work and identity learning cycles in the customization of identity among medical residents', *The Academy of Management Journal*, 49: 235–262.

Salhani, D. and Coulter, I. (2009) 'The politics of interprofessional working and the struggle for professional autonomy in nursing', *Social Science & Medicine*, 68: 1221–1228.

Sehested, K. (2002) 'How new public management reforms challenge the roles of Professionals', *International Journal of Public Administration*, 25: 1513–1537.

Seidman, I. (1998) *Interviewing as Qualitative Research*. London: Teachers College Press.

Strauss, A. and Corbin, J. M. (1990) *Basics of Qualitative Research: Grounded Theory Procedures and Techniques*. California: Sage.

White, L., Currie, G. and Lockett, A. (2014) 'The enactment of plural leadership in a health and social care network: the influence of institutional context', *The Leadership Quarterly*, 25: 730–745.

Part IV

Change Programmes: Content and Performance

12
Scotland 'Bold and Brave'? Conditions for Creating a Coherent National Healthcare Quality Strategy

Aoife M. McDermott, David R. Steel, Lorna McKee, Lauren Hamel and Patrick C. Flood

Introduction

Healthcare quality is an enduring and global concern, evidenced via supranational responses, such as those of the United Nation's World Health Organization (Ovreveit, 2003, 2005, 2013), the OECD (Arah et al., 2003) and the European Union (Vollaard et al., 2013), as well as the policy responses of individual countries (Arah et al., 2003) and devolved regions (such as the Scottish example considered in this chapter[1]). The Institute of Medicine's seminal report (IOM, 2001; Kohn et al., 2001) led to increasing recognition of the need for a systems focus in managing healthcare quality. However, a European Union (EU)-oriented analysis (Vollaard et al., 2013: 229) notes, 'There is much variation [in national quality and safety strategies] between and within Member States and that therefore there is a large potential to learn from each other.' In this chapter, we follow Ovreveit and Staines (2007) in purposively analysing an established system-wide approach to quality improvement. We consider the evolution of the policy process in Scotland – rather than evaluating its impact – and ensuing lessons for other contexts.

Attempts to improve healthcare quality and safety have focused on policy formation (Greer, 2009), structure and delivery processes (Berwick, 2003), organizations and teams (Gittell, 2009), as well as patient and provider outcomes (Ovretveit, 2006; Travaglia et al.,

2009). To date, reviews have been inconclusive regarding the benefits of quality management interventions (Ovretveit, 2003, 2005). This has led to acknowledgement that no single strategy can be recommended above others (Ovretveit, 2003) – and recognition of the limitations of fragmented initiatives (Health Foundation, 2010). In combination with awareness that how and by whom quality management interventions are used will affect their impact (Walshe and Freeman, 2002), this leads to questions regarding how national healthcare systems can design their policies and supporting institutions to enhance and embed quality improvement. As a result, the focus in this chapter is on identifying conditions for generating a coherent national approach to quality improvement, from a system with first-mover advantage. Our analysis considers Scotland's pioneering development of their national quality agenda between 1983 and 2013. Although in some respects the configuration of factors evident in Scotland may be difficult to replicate, the chapter highlights lessons that can be learned and applied in other systems. However, it also recognizes the need for rigorous independent evaluation of the effectiveness and impact of the Scottish approach, alongside others, on patient outcomes.

Methods

This chapter draws on policy literature, policy documents and primary empirical research from a study of national approaches to supporting the quality and safety of healthcare in Scotland and Ireland. Interviews were conducted with 44 policy respondents, between August 2011 and April 2012. The impact of national policies on front-line practice, as well as additional local responses to quality concerns, was subsequently explored via 70 interviews in two hospitals in each country (January–May 2012).

Scotland was purposively selected due to its pioneering role in developing a national programme to enhance health service quality and safety, as described by Don Berwick:

> NHS Scotland has undertaken a bold, comprehensive, and scientifically grounded programme to improve patient safety... [...] In its scale and ambition, the Scottish Patient Safety Programme marks Scotland as leader – second to no nation on earth – in its commitment to reducing harm to patients dramatically and continually.
>
> (Scottish Government, 2010: 17)

Scotland's position as an early adopter of a national approach to managing healthcare quality provides a strong rationale to analyse it as a unique single case study (c.f. Yin, 2009).

Data analysis

First, we analysed a range of policy documents and the wider policy literature on healthcare in Scotland. Second, we undertook and analysed interviews with 22 senior-level policy stakeholders from government and the NHS; representatives of professional bodies; and senior staff with responsibility for quality and safety. Together this enabled us to develop a chronology of the institutions and interventions supporting the quality agenda. Iterative analysis identified four phases in the evolution of national policy focus, approaches to supporting quality and strategies to mobilize the service, summarized in Figure 12.1. Thematic analysis of interview questions enabled us to identify emergent analytical themes regarding the contextual factors supporting quality improvement in Scotland. After searching for confirming and disconfirming findings, analytic themes were integrated within a theoretical framework (presented later in Figure 12.2). Our strategy for data analysis, premised on developing an analytic chronology, thematic analysis and explanation building (c.f. Yin, 2009), enables us to present an overview of policy development, derives lessons from the Scottish experience and identifies caveats regarding their generalizability.

Scotland's approach to quality 1983–2013

Our analysis identifies four phases in Scotland's approach to quality. Each appears to have built incrementally upon, rather than replaced, existing arrangements – contributing to a high degree of continuity within the health system. A consistent policy emphasis on improving healthcare quality has endured (Steel and Cylus, 2012), despite changes in focus, approach and methods utilized to mobilize the service (see Figure 12.1).

Phase 1: Advice and guidance

In the first 'Advice and guidance' phase, the Scottish system focused on developing evidence-based guidance, designed to promote clinical effectiveness.

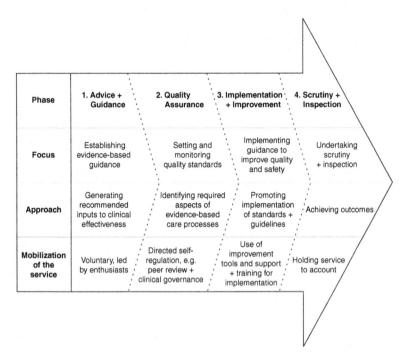

Figure 12.1   The emergence and evolution of Scotland's approach to quality (1983–2013)

Source: Authors' own.

Audit is a long-standing practice in Scottish healthcare. However, a step-change occurred in the mid-1980s, prompted by the introduction of general management and increasing emphasis on health service planning, efficiency and effectiveness (Griffiths, 1983). In 1989, as part of an initiative to make clinical audit part of routine practice for all healthcare professionals (Scottish Office, 1989), a national body, the Clinical Resource and Audit Group (CRAG), was charged with developing a national audit strategy and supporting local audit activity. CRAG was instrumental in the establishment of the Scottish Intercollegiate Guidelines Network (SIGN), an initiative led by the Academy of Royal Colleges and Faculties in Scotland to develop multidisciplinary evidence-based clinical guidelines. SIGN was set up as – and remains – a network of doctors and increasingly other healthcare professionals (see Harbour et al., 2011). Although financially supported by the Scottish government, SIGN is dependent on the voluntary labour of committed individuals to develop each guideline.

Thus, by the mid-1990s Scotland was pioneering developments in the provision of advice and guidance on clinical effectiveness. Described as *doing it in a way that engages rather than dictates*, the Scottish approach was premised on advising, 'what might be best, and as someone once said it is guidelines, not tramlines' (SP12). However, concerns arose that developments were insufficiently aligned to NHS priorities, reflecting mobilization based on voluntary engagement by individual clinicians pursuing their own particular interests. There was also increasing recognition that clinical guidance was failing to take account of affordability and cost-effectiveness and that implementation of recommendations was variable (c.f. Woods and Carter, 2003).

Phase 2: Quality assurance

The second 'Quality assurance' phase emerged around 1997 and was prompted by these concerns. The growing body of evidence-based guidance was used to develop clinical standards that the NHS was expected to implement. As shown in Figure 12.1, the service was mobilized using 'directed self-regulation', with a quality assurance system premised on peer review created to monitor and encourage progress. These processes were mandatory, but clinical leadership and ownership were retained.

Following a Chief Medical Officer initiated Acute Services Review (Scottish Office, 1998a), in 1999 the government established the Clinical Standards Board for Scotland (CSBS), responsible for developing evidence-based clinical (and mainly condition-specific) quality standards and for running a system of peer review to assess performance against the standards. Both activities were professionally led, but patients and the public were involved at all stages and all CSBS reports were published. In some respects, CSBS resembled the Commission for Health Improvement (CHI) established in England and Wales at the same time, but its emphasis on clinical leadership and its condition-specific (e.g. individual cancers, schizophrenia) focus were distinctive. In parallel, the (UK) *Health Act 1999* imposed a statutory duty on each NHS Board (and their equivalents in the rest of the United Kingdom) to monitor and improve the quality of healthcare provided. This led to local steps to introduce clinical governance, defined as 'corporate accountability for clinical performance' (Scottish Office, 1998b). A third development was the establishment of the Health Technology Board for Scotland (HTBS) in 2000, to evaluate and provide advice to the NHS on the clinical and cost-effectiveness of new and existing health technologies, including medicines.

In 2003, concerns about the dissipation of energy and lack of cohesion resulting from the proliferation of quality-oriented organizations led to the merger of CRAG, CSBS, HTBS and two other bodies to form NHS Quality Improvement Scotland (QIS). QIS was given responsibility for developing and implementing a coordinated strategy for improving clinical effectiveness and the quality of patient care, including patient safety (which in England was allocated to a new body, the National Patient Safety Agency). Further consolidation occurred in 2005 when SIGN became part of QIS.

Phase 3: Implementation and improvement

The third 'Implementation and improvement' phase occurred in the mid-2000s. Despite the provision of evidence regarding effective treatments by QIS and its predecessors, 'that was not producing as much of a change as we wanted and it wasn't producing it consistently. And we therefore started moving at national level into supporting implementation where previously the mantra had been implementation is a local thing, it's very much clinically led so hands off centre' (SP2). This led QIS to add a new implementation focus, using improvement tools that were widely adopted in non-healthcare settings and engaging with the emerging science of improvement to mobilize the service.

A key factor behind this development was QIS's commissioning of an independent evaluation of its impact. This found that QIS's work in setting standards and assessing performance was well known and respected in the NHS, but that its impact on clinical practice and patient outcomes was more limited (NHSQIS, 2007). This led to a sharper emphasis on implementation and to the articulation of an 'integrated cycle of improvement' comprising: *(1) advice, guidance and standards; (2) implementation and improvement support; and (3) assessment, measurement and reporting* (NHSQIS, 2009).

This change in QIS's focus coincided with a second development: the launch of a national initiative on patient safety. In 2004, the Health Foundation joined with the Institute for Healthcare Improvement (IHI) in the Safer Patients Initiative. A Scottish Board was one of the four sites selected to participate in a range of evidence-based interventions to reduce harm and mortality using the 'Breakthrough series' collaborative model (IHI, 2003; Health Foundation, 2011). Its success over the two years of this initiative, and the inclusion of two further Scottish Boards in the second phase, prompted the Scottish government to partner with IHI in applying this approach universally across NHS Scotland. This was done through the Scottish Patient Safety Programme (SPSP) launched in 2007 in all acute hospitals, with the aim of reducing adverse events and avoidable mortality (Haraden and Leitch, 2011; SPSP, 2013, website).

Phase 4: Scrutiny and inspection

The final 'Scrutiny and inspection' phase emerged from 2008 onwards, aligned with a significant increase in public concern about variations in standards and service failures in Scotland and in the rest of the United Kingdom. This led to a tougher approach to scrutiny and enhanced concern with achieving outcomes, with – see Figure 12.1 – an extra emphasis on mobilizing the service by holding it to account.

In 2010, the Scottish government issued *The Healthcare Quality Strategy*, which has subsequently shaped the full range of government policies for the NHS. This strategy – which in some respects mirrored the Darzi Report in England (DH, 2008) – adopted the Institute of Medicine's (2001) six dimensions of quality care (safe, effective, patient centred, timely, efficient and equitable) and was described as identifying 'what we mean by high-quality healthcare... Person-centeredness, safe and effective' (SP17). For respondents, the simplicity and clarity of these goals have helped to enhance the receptivity for quality-related service change (c.f. Pettigrew et al., 1992).

In parallel, concerns about healthcare associated infections led the government to establish a Healthcare Environment Inspectorate to undertake a programme of announced and unannounced inspections in all hospitals (Scottish Government, 2008; HEI, 2013). The shift towards tougher inspection in Scotland mirrored similar but longer-standing developments in England, which saw the establishment of the Commission for Healthcare Audit and Inspection (known as the Healthcare Commission) in 2004. Significantly, however, the new Scottish inspectorate was placed within QIS, a body that had established credibility with clinicians (NHSQIS, 2007). The HEI's remit was extended in 2011 to include the care of older people in acute hospitals. An official review of scrutiny across the public sector led QIS to become Healthcare Improvement Scotland (HIS) in 2011, on assuming responsibility for regulation and inspection of independent (private and non-profit) healthcare (Scottish Government, 2007a).

Lessons from Scotland

In this section, we draw upon our analytic chronology of policy development, and thematic analysis of interview responses, to identify five distinctive features of the Scottish experience (illustrated in Figure 12.2) that helped to shape a coherent policy response to healthcare quality.

First, Scotland exhibits a high degree of health system *continuity* – evident in health policy and structures. Although policy has developed significantly over the last 30 years, this has occurred in an evolutionary manner. Greer (2009) notes that health policy has proceeded along a stable trajectory first set out in 1997 (Scottish Office, 1997). Core quality and safety objectives have remained stable, with incremental developments in how they are pursued. Continuity is particularly evidenced in the relative stability of the quality infrastructure – structures, processes and people – by adding to what was already in place, rather than sweeping away institutions that had or were beginning to have a track record and credibility with the NHS. There has also been no major structural change in NHS Scotland in the past decade, and relatively low turnover among NHS leaders, including Chief Executives. This continuity has been facilitated by a relative consensus across political parties regarding means and ends in healthcare and a comparatively low incidence of reported service failures (Steel and Cylus, 2012).

Second, continuity, together with the relatively small scale of the Scottish health system, has facilitated *collaboration* among key stakeholders across organizations (Scottish Government, 2007b, 2011). A number of respondents noted the benefits of small scale: 'it's a small place and you can get people together quite quickly and easily, you can have conversations that then you can bring about change' (SP7). In particular, the small size of the senior civil service (at approximately 250) (Fox, 2013), together with a long history of high-status medical leaders closely connected with politics (Greer, 2009), has led to a previously charted consensual and consultative approach to health service governance (Fox, 2013). This was described by SP3 who noted, 'We develop policy in a way that is inclusive of all of the stakeholder groups. We talk to the service, we talk to clinicians, and we talk to the public about what the policy ought to be.' Within the NHS, the existence of just 15 (and 14 since 2006) unified boards combining responsibility for planning and delivering acute, primary and community services has made communication and, where necessary, intervention by government or bodies such as QIS easier and less confrontational. This has also been helped by the inclusion of QIS and subsequently HIS in the NHS 'family' (i.e. within rather than external to the NHS). The partnership ethos underpinning this collaborative culture has facilitated the provision of mutual support and the sharing of ideas and good practice (Fox, 2013). It has also helped enhance acceptance of investment in the system of national data collection and sharing of this data.

Third, there has been a deliberate emphasis on *clinical leadership* of almost all of the initiatives undertaken. The leadership of successive Chief Medical Officers – and their counterparts in nursing, dentistry and pharmacy – has been of critical importance in shaping the agenda. Their authority has been important in winning the consent and participation of their clinical colleagues in national organizations and at the 'coalface'. All the main national bodies (CSBS, HTBS, QIS, HIS) have been led by distinguished doctors; respected clinicians have led the standard-setting and peer review groups; and the inspection teams on HAI and older people have included strong clinical representation. Clinical leadership has been seen as a key means of winning and sustaining clinical ownership. In discussing the development of guidelines, one respondent noted that, as well as doctors, 'we had nursing representatives on most guideline groups and primary care doctors as well. So the college did act, as [...] a forum for all these different professionals to come together, you know? Things like diabetes would require input from dieticians and nutrition experts' (SP14).

Political and managerial leadership and support has of course been required, and progress has been bolstered by the strong personal commitment to this agenda of ministers, senior civil servants and managerial leaders in the NHS. However, the emphasis, particularly in the early stages, was on securing clinical buy-in. For example, CSBS and QIS's standards-based approach and condition-specific reviews built upon earlier clinical initiatives on clinical audit and guidelines. As SP8 noted, 'The clinicians because it makes sense to them intellectually as well as day to day. Intellectually it makes sense to measure things that you are going to change, it makes sense to use evidence based interventions, it goes to their evidence based medicine...' (SP8). Further, CSBS and QIS were allowed to develop with only minimal direct political intervention. Ministers were supportive but did not put organizations under overt pressure to deliver immediate or unrealistic results, and they have eschewed the language of 'naming and shaming' or the use of league tables and star ratings.

The SPSP provides a further example of clinical leadership. International concern about adverse events in hospitals prompted the government to act, but the approach adopted and the involvement of IHI gave a strong signal that the programme was to be congruent with earlier quality initiatives (e.g. the Breakthrough series). Engagement of front-line staff has been promoted by (1) local leadership of the different interventions by respected clinicians; (2) key features of the PDSA (*P*lan, *D*o, *S*tudy, *A*ct) methodology (analysed in Powell et al., 2009), and care bundles that are based on evidence that can be verified by clinicians, including the 'small tests of change' approach encouraging the development of locally viable solutions; (3) measurement focused on improvement rather than judgement; and (4) the language used to describe the aim of the programme with a stress on increasing reliability and reducing variation in outcomes.

Fifth, and more unusual, has been the attempt to *consolidate* the quality agenda, combining within a single organization responsibility for functions that in most systems are shared among a number. For example, in England the remit of QIS/HIS has at various times been covered by four bodies (CHI/Healthcare Commission/Care Quality Commission; NICE; National Patient Safety Agency; NHS Institute for Innovation and Improvement). In addition, over the period considered there have been progressive efforts to pull the strands of the quality and safety agenda together, culminating in the *Healthcare Quality Strategy* in 2010. The quote detailed below emphasizes the interlinked nature of the factors discussed in this section:

> the patient safety programme came from the government, I mean that is where it started and I think they have really pulled the whole patient safety agenda across from the States and IHI and really put their policy right behind it and then put the capacity and the resources behind to actually get it moving and up and running. So, I think policy and improvement and quality, I think they are all entwined and very much in Scotland. (SP9)

The prime motives for the establishment of QIS in 2003 were to reduce duplication in effort, consolidate public bodies and achieve economies of scale. From the outset, QIS made a virtue of its holistic perspective, and this was spelled out explicitly in the integrated cycle of improvement that it elaborated in 2008/2009. The combination in a single organization of responsibility for scrutiny and improvement support is particularly unusual. These roles can be regarded as incompatible in that they involve processes and relationships that are very different (McDermott et al., 2015). For example, organizations such as the IHI argue that it is important to draw a clear distinction between data that are used for improvement and data for judgement (Haraden and Leitch, 2011). That this break with convention seems to have been accepted reflects the combined impact of all the features outlined above and specifically the supportive and non-confrontational approach adopted to scrutiny and performance review.

What is perhaps more striking is that this consolidated approach was retained in 2009 and again in 2011 when intense political and media pressure caused ministers to demand a more inspectorial approach to healthcare-associated infection and the care of older people in hospital. This draws attention to the fifth and final factor that emerged from our analysis. The new inspectorate was placed within an organization that had significant *credibility* among clinicians, further evidence of the benefits of continuity in health structures. This provided some reassurance in the service and helped to allay fears about the new tougher regime. SP20 noted, 'We have a good infrastructure in Scotland through Healthcare Improvement Scotland.' It also demonstrated continuing commitment to the distinctive approach of QIS and HIS. Subsequent experience, particularly in relation to the care of older people, has given rise to greater tension between HIS and NHS boards. This may impact upon the sustainability of the integrated cycle of improvement. Similar challenges arise from media concerns regarding the appropriateness of HIS's closeness to the NHS, reflecting issues that have arisen over particular HEI inspection assessments and reports; the spread of concerns about the need for tougher regulation and inspection in the wake of the Francis Report on Mid-Staffordshire hospital in England (House of Commons, 2013); and public and media concern about service failures in Scotland.

Thus, the Scottish approach has benefited from a fertile and receptive context (c.f. Pettigrew et al., 1992) for pursuing quality initiatives. The emphasis on integration and partnership, rather than the marketization evident in the English NHS, is particularly significant (Steel and Cylus, 2012). Unlike the Commission for Healthcare Improvement (CHI) in England, which had to deal with major NHS failures in its early days, QIS experienced calmer waters and received muted media coverage. This helped to nurture the character of the Scottish approach, together with deliberate choices about the cultivation of collaboration across organizations and respect for, and investment in, clinical leadership and managerial alliance. In combination, this context and these choices have given the Scottish approach leverage and resilience. The spiral shape of Figure 12.2 is deliberate and aims to capture the cyclical and iterative (rather than linear) development of the quality agenda, with the interrelated nature of the contextual factors facilitating its emergence. In particular, we deliberately place 'continuity in health policy and structures' at the heart of the figure, to capture its role in consolidating the quality agenda.

Caveats and limitations

Here we raise two of the caveats noted by our respondents regarding the Scottish model of improvement. First, some noted difficulty in

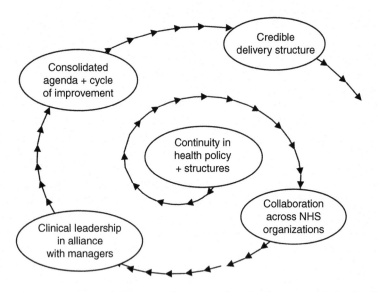

Figure 12.2 Contextual factors influencing the development of Scotland's quality agenda
Source: Authors' own.

generalizing improvement practice across contexts: 'because you cannot take what happens in Tayside and say, "That's a great model" bang, do it all over the country because the context is different everywhere' (SP8). Similarly, those attempting to learn from other health systems need to take account of the role of culture, history and current politics in making, implementing and evaluating policy, and in planning health reform (c.f. Fox, 2013).

Second, the adoption of the IHI method has helped to provide a developed platform for improvement, premised on generation of local knowledge. However, one Scottish respondent noted tension between local improvement and having common, comparable data standards. This is of particular significance in a publicly funded health system, in which accountability to government and Parliament is important. It is also a major issue should the Scottish model be emulated internationally – and particularly at EU level.

We also recognize the broader limitations of our analysis. First, we note potential criticism that we are presenting an 'insider perspective'. One of the authors is a former senior policy stakeholder in the Scottish NHS; another was involved in the 2007 review of QIS (NHSQIS, 2007). However, neither participated in coding nor in analysing interview data. We also note that views presented in this chapter were drawn from senior-level 'vested' stakeholders, rather than front-line respondents. Second, we acknowledge the time-limited nature of our study. As Figure 12.2 suggests, the policy context is dynamic and Scotland's pursuit of healthcare quality continues to evolve – with new innovations and an emerging policy focus on person-centredness. Third, we note our limited focus. Scotland has not developed in isolation. Rather, it sits within a wider global context that is increasingly emphasizing healthcare quality and safety.

Fourth, our analysis has focused on the evolution of the policy process, without evaluating Scotland's progress in achieving quality objectives, nor the impact of specific policy developments, approaches or interventions. While some Scottish data are suggestive of progress (Haraden and Leitch, 2011), healthcare quality and safety have a typically positive trajectory, such that it may not be appropriate to attribute improvement to the interventions discussed (see Benning et al.'s evaluations of Phases 1 and 2 of the Health Foundation's Safer Patient Initiative (2011a, 2011b)). Future rigorous independent research scrutiny of impact and effectiveness, as well as how these are evaluated, is necessary. Despite the limitations of the analysis, we turn to consider potential practical implications and next research steps.

Conclusions

This chapter has sought to explain the distinctive approach to healthcare quality and safety adopted in Scotland. Our findings suggest that the development of Scotland's four phases has anticipated the current trajectory of the EU, whose involvement in healthcare quality 'has increased from sharing information, to standardization and even to the first signs of enforcement' (Vollaard et al., 2013: 226). This suggests that our analysis may have supra-national, as well as national, relevance. We have drawn attention to a range of contextual factors that have worked in combination to create a receptive context for the development of the Scottish quality agenda. Of particular note is the interrelated nature of the five identified factors. Scotland's approach has been premised on continuous, incremental refinement, and a cyclical and collaborative, rather than linear, trajectory. Whilst the specific configuration of factors at play in Scotland is likely to be difficult to replicate, its experience does provide insights into the necessary conditions for making healthcare quality a key policy priority. Further, individual aspects are potentially transferable. Indeed, the Care Quality Commission in England has adopted arrangements closer to those in Scotland, including stronger clinical input to the process of standards development and greater content expertise in inspection teams (Care Quality Commission, 2013).

Foremost among Scotland's salient attributes with relevance to other nations is policy and structural continuity. Sustained attention can be afforded to policy priorities in the absence of agitating structural reform. Incremental, rather than 'big bang' change, also has positive resourcing implications – as system assets remain focused on policy and service delivery, rather than delivering change. Second, collaboration across organizations in Scotland has resulted from a combination of continuity and culture. Other contexts may promote collaboration in other ways. However, the overarching objective of ensuring that all parts of the health system interrelate in pursuit of shared goals has pan-national relevance. Third, Scotland draws attention to the benefits of promoting clinical leadership across all levels of the health system, from top-level direction setting to enabling the front line (McKee et al., 2013), and also to ensuring that such leadership operates in alliance with non-clinical managers. While collaboration and leadership are people related, the final two attributes have a systems orientation. Having a clear agenda with designated priorities and an associated delivery structure is important, enabling prioritization of ring-fenced resourcing. Finally, the Scottish experience suggests that, in the case of patient safety, avoiding a standalone agency (such as the National Patient Safety Agency in England) may promote responsiveness.

Beyond the five factors identified in our analysis, the Scottish experience also draws attention to the importance of building measurement, as well as common comparable data standards, into any quality-oriented system. This is particularly important where, as in Scotland, local improvements are encouraged. In such contexts, measurement can help identify whether interventions make a difference, which interventions make the most difference and how they should be spread across the system. Comparable data standards can also be used for benchmarking and improvement and for holding to account if appropriate.

Acknowledgements

This chapter draws upon research funded by the Health Research Board, Award HRA_HSR/2010/26. The views expressed are the authors' own.

Note

1. Since devolution in 1999, Scotland has had its own Parliament with full legislative competence across a wide range of issues including health. This has led to growing divergence in policy and an increasingly distinctive healthcare system which is dominated by public funding and provision with only a very small independent sector (Steel and Cylus, 2012).

References

Arah, O. A., Klazinga, N. S., Delnoij, D. M. J., Ten Asbroek, A. H. A. and Custers, T. (2003) 'Conceptual frameworks for health systems performance: a quest for effectiveness, quality, and improvement', *International Journal for Quality in Health Care*, 15(5): 377–398.

Benning, A., Ghaleb, M., Suokas, A., Dixon-Woods, M., Dawson, J., Barber, N., Franklin, B. D., Girling, A., Hemming, K., Carmalt, M., Rudge, G., Naicker, T., Nwulu, U., Choudhury, S. and Lilford, R. (2011a) 'Large scale organisational intervention to improve patient safety in four UK hospitals: mixed method evaluation', *BMJ: British Medical Journal*, 342: d195.

Benning, A., Dixon-Woods, M., Nwulu, U., Ghaleb, M., Dawson, J., Barber, N., Franklin, B. D., Girling, A., Hemming, K., Carmalt, M., Rudge, G., Naicker, T., Kotecha, A., Derrington, M. C. and Lilford, R. (2011b) 'Multiple component patient safety intervention in English hospitals: controlled evaluation of second phase', *BMJ: British Medical Journal*, 342: d199.

Berwick, D. M. (2003) 'Improvement, trust and the healthcare workforce', *Quality and Safety in Health Care*, 12(6): 448–452.

Care Quality Commission (2013) *A New Start: Consultation on Changes in the Way CQC Regulates, Inspects and Monitors Care*. London: Care Quality Commission.

Department of Health (2008) *High Quality Care for All. NHS Next Steps Review Final Report* (Chair: Lord Darzi). CM 7432. London: Department of Health.

Fox, D. M. (2013) 'Health inequality and governance in Scotland since 2007', *Public Health*, 127(5): 514–520.

Gittell, J. H. (2009) *High Performance Healthcare: Using the Power of Relationships, to Achieve Quality, Efficiency, and Resilience*. McGraw Hill: New York.

Greer, S. (2009) 'Devolution and divergence in UK health policies', *British Medical Journal*, 338: 78–80.

Griffiths, R. (1983) *NHS Management Inquiry Report*. London: DHSS.

Haraden, C. and Leitch, J. (2011) 'Scotland's successful national approach to improving patient safety in acute care', *Health Affairs*, 30(4): 755–763.

Harbour, R., Lowe, G. and Twaddle, S. (2011) 'Scottish intercollegiate guidelines network: the first fifteen years (1993–2008)', *Journal of the Royal College of Physicians of Edinburgh*, 41(2): 163–168.

Health Foundation (2010) *Quality Improvement Made Simple*. London: The Health Foundation.

Health Foundation (2011) *Learning Report: Safer Patients Initiative. Lessons from the First Major Improvement Programme Addressing Patient Safety in the UK*. London: The Health Foundation.

Healthcare Environment Inspectorate (2013) Available form: www. healthcareimprovementscotland.org [Accessed November 19, 2013].

House of Commons (2013) *Report of the Mid Staffordshire NHS Foundation Trust Public Inquiry HC 898* (Chair: Robert Francis QC). London: HMSO.

Institute for Healthcare Improvement (2003) *The Breakthrough Series: IHI's Collaborative Model for Achieving Breakthrough Improvement.* IHI Innovation Series white paper. Boston: Institute for Healthcare Improvement. Available from: www. IHI.org

Institute of Medicine (US) (2001) *Crossing the Quality Chasm: A New Health System for the 21st Century.* Washington, DC: National Academies Press.

Kohn, L. T., Corrigan, J. M. and Donaldson, M. S. (eds) (2000) *To Err Is Human: Building A Safer Health System.* Vol. 627. Washington, DC: National Academies Press.

McDermott, A. M. Hamel, L., Steel, D., Flood, P. C. and McKee, L. (2015) 'Hybrid healthcare governance for improvement? Combining top-down and bottom-up approaches to public sector regulation', *Public Administration.* (Published online ahead of print: doi: 10.1111/padm.12118).

McKee, L., Charles, K., Dixon-Woods, M., Willars, J. and Martin, G. (2013) ' "New" and distributed leadership in quality and safety in healthcare, or "old" and hierarchical? An interview study with strategic stakeholders', *Journal of Health Services Research & Policy,* 18 (Suppl. 2) : 11–19.

NHS Quality Improvement Scotland (2007) *Quality Improvement in NHSScotland – an Independent Evaluation of the Impact of NHS Quality Improvement Scotland.* Edinburgh: NHS QIS.

NHS Quality Improvement Scotland (2009) *Annual Report 2008–2009.* Edinburgh: NHS QIS.

Ovretveit, J. (2003) *What Are the Best Strategies for Ensuring Quality in Hospitals.* Geneva: WHO Regional Office for Europe's Health Evidence Network.

Ovretveit, J. (2005) *What Are the Advantages and Limitations of Different Quality and Safety Tools for Health Care?* Copenhagen: WHO Regional Office for Europe.

Ovretveit, J. (2013) *Evaluating Complex Social Interventions: Volume 1: Challenges and Choices.* Sepulveda, CA: CIPRS, Veterans Health Administration.

Ovretveit, J. (2006). 'Total quality management in European healthcare', *International Journal of Health Care Quality Assurance,* 13(2): 74–79.

Ovreveit, J. and Staines, A. (2007) 'Sustained improvement? Findings from an independent case study of the Jonkoping Quality Programme', *Quality Management in Healthcare,* 16(1): 68–83.

Pettigrew, A. M., Ferlie, E. and McKee, L. (1992) *Shaping Strategic Change: Making Change in Large Organizations: The Case of the National Health Service.* London: Sage.

Powell, A., Rushmer, R. and Davies, H. T. O. (2009) *A Systematic Narrative Review of Quality Improvement Models in Health Care.* Edinburgh: NHS QIS.

Scottish Government (2007a) *The Crerar Review: The Report of the Independent Review of Regulation, Audit, Inspection and Complains Handling of Public Services in Scotland.* Edinburgh: Scottish Government.

Scottish Government (2007b) *Better Health, Better Care: Action Plan.* Edinburgh: Scottish Government.

Scottish Government (2008) *Healthcare Associated Infections – Inspection, Assurance and Public Confidence Consultation Paper*. Edinburgh: Scottish Government.

Scottish Government (2010) *The Healthcare Quality Strategy for NHS Scotland*. Edinburgh: Scottish Government.

Scottish Government (2011) *Report of the Commission on the Future Delivery of Public Services* (Chair: Campbell Christie CBE). Edinburgh: Scottish Government.

Scottish Office (1997) *Designed to Care: Renewing the National Health Service in Scotland*. Edinburgh: HMSO.

Scottish Office (1998a) *Acute Services Review Report*. Edinburgh: Scottish Office.

Scottish Office (1998b) Clinical Governance 1998 MEL75. Edinburgh: Scottish Office.

Scottish Office (1989) *Working for Patients*. Edinburgh: Scottish Office.

Scottish Patient Safety Programme (2013) Available from: www. scottishpatientsafetyprogramme.scot.nhs.uk [Accessed November 19, 2013].

Steel, D. and Cylus, J. (2012) 'United Kingdom (Scotland): Health system review', *Health Systems in Transition*, 14(9): 1–150.

Travaglia, J. F., Westbrook, M. T. and Braithwaite, J. (2009) 'Implementation of a patient safety incident management system as viewed by doctors, nurses and allied health professionals', *Health (London)*, 13(3): 277–296.

Vollaard, H., van de Bovenkamp, H. M. and Vrangbaek, K. (2013) 'The emerging EU quality of care policy: from sharing information to enforcement', *Health Policy*, 111(3): 226–233.

Walshe, K. and Freeman, T. (2002) 'Effectiveness of quality improvement: learning from evaluations', *Quality and Safety in Health Care*, 11(1): 85–87.

Woods, K. and Carter, D. (eds) (2003) *Scotland's Health and Health Services*. London: The Nuffield Trust.

Yin, R. K. (2009) *Case Study Research: Design and Methods*, 4th edition. Thousand Oaks, CA: Sage.

13
The Social Spaces of Accountability in Hybridized Healthcare Organizations

Aris Komporozos-Athanasiou and Mark Thompson

Involving the public, accounting for healthcare governance

UK healthcare organizations are undergoing progressive changes to become more flexible and cost-effective (Kernaghan, 2000). Recently, the government's latest incarnation of New Public Management, 'open public services' (Cabinet Office, 2012), has articulated a shift from traditional organizational forms to a more indeterminate organizational landscape of shifting social and spatial relations (James and Manning, 1996; McNulty and Ferlie, 2004; Dunleavy et al., 2005). As a result, formulation and execution of public health policy occurs increasingly in complex networks featuring multiple, overlapping coordination between government, third sector organizations and the citizen/service user, so that 'accountability... gets lost in the cracks of horizontal and hybrid governance' (Ferlie et al., 2007: 240; also see Frolich, 2011). It is to an interrogation of accountability within such increasingly hybridized healthcare organizations that we address ourselves in this chapter.

We argue that healthcare organizations' attempts to engage with the 'whole person' necessitate complementing existing 'representational' measurements of accountability with lived and experiential apprehensions of accountability. We mobilize insights from the socio-spatial philosophy of Lefebvre, which offers the unusual ability to acknowledge both of these dimensions – as well as the tensions that may arise between them – by foregrounding peoples' experience of organizational 'spacing', their social performances as they enact different representations of space.

Engaging with representational and experienced dimensions of accountability

Lefebvre considers the production of space – of experienced organizational reality – to result from a dynamic social process involving three highly interrelated spatial realms/dimensions (Lefebvre, 1991: 38–40). The first realm of his tripartite framework is 'conceived' space, which foregrounds expert knowledge and top-down planning. 'Conceived' space is abstract and reified, commonly occupied by scientists, managers and policymakers. It is associated with dominant representations of a given society (or organization) and can be seen as a process of legitimizing such representations of organizational space. The second realm is 'lived' space, produced through people's local knowledge including their experience and imagination. Lived space can be found in lay users' embodied responses to environmental stimuli and in emotional modes of relating to others. The third realm offers an additional dimension: 'perceived' space, comprising spatial practices that mediate the tensions between 'lived' and 'conceived' space. 'Perceived' space is visually encountered, intersubjectively generated and tacitly (and subconsciously) communicated through day-to-day routines (see Figure 13.1).

In what follows, we contend that devolved healthcare services addressing this third dimension of spatiality will be better equipped to acknowledge tensions between representational and experienced dimensions of accountability – indeed, that services are performed *out of* the resolution of, rather than in spite of, such tensions. Accordingly, we seek to use Lefebvre's ideas to construct the beginnings of a measurement framework addressing *emergent tensions in organizational spacing* (practice), as well as *represented resolutions in organizational spaces* (targets and outcomes), which recent public service scandals have shown to be an inadequate sole basis for measurement. Our framework translates Lefevbre's spatial dimensions into specific tensions that may emerge from competing demands experienced in devolved organizations such as the NHS.

Our framework mobilizes Lefevbre's three dimensions, enabling us to complement the common focus on targets/indicators ('conceived space') with an increased emphasis on peoples' unfolding understandings ('perceived space'), as well as their affective experience ('lived space'), of services. For example, our empirical illustration shows how organizational members involved in PPI platforms had official roles ('lay' vs. 'professional') denoted in seating plans and meeting agendas

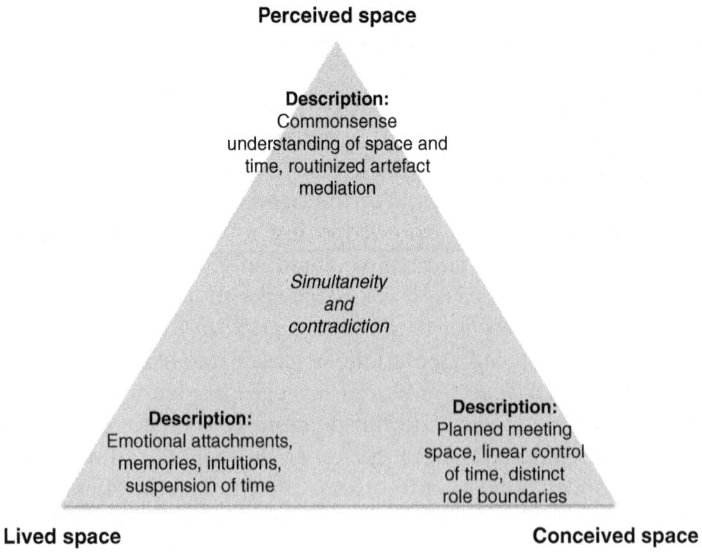

Perceived space

Description:
Commonsense
understanding of space and
time, routinized artefact
mediation

*Simultaneity
and
contradiction*

Description:
Emotional attachments,
memories, intuitions,
suspension of time

Description:
Planned meeting
space, linear control
of time, distinct
role boundaries

Lived space   **Conceived space**

Figure 13.1 A tri-dimensional framework of perceived, lived and conceived organizational space
Source: Adapted by authors from Lefebvre (1991).

('conceived space'), how these were reaffirmed through a 'commonsense understanding' of their PPI roles ('perceived space') and yet how these official roles and institutional expectations were often challenged and undermined in moments where emotions and memories of illness and care came to the fore ('lived space'). In attending to such moments, we are enhancing more traditional, representational measurements of accountability by rendering the visible tensions that people may be experiencing during the performance of the service. We now turn to a detailed demonstration of the framework.

Empirical illustration

Our empirical study focuses on the activities of a national PPI forum of cancer survivors, carers, clinical researchers and professionals at a major partnership research organization within the NHS (henceforth referred to as 'the Forum'). We focus on two groupings within the Forum: the 'user group' and 'research groups'. Both groups were created in 2001, involving collaborations with several charity organizations, and further supported by the 2007 Cancer Reform Strategy. The user group comprises 40–60 users (patient and carer representatives) from across the country. It meets three times a year in a rotating location, where users meet, share experiences gained from their involvement and organize learning activities and workshops.

In contrast, research groups are spaces within the Forum where users encounter medical professionals. Groups are divided according to types of cancer and comprise high-calibre clinical researchers, oncologists, epidemiologists and psychologists – many university professors and medical consultants. Each research group meets three times a year for a day in one of the buildings of a charity organization in a major UK city and discusses new research, design and commissioning of clinical trials, relevant policy change and impact on services. Two to three patient representatives attend these meetings.

Methods

Data sources

For a period of 18 Months, from December 2009 to June 2011, the first author followed the trajectories of Forum group members, both as participant and non-participant observer, in formal and less formal events, national meetings, workshops and conferences ($n = 15$): in total over 100 hours of observation. In addition to field observation, 28 in-depth ethnographic interviews were conducted with 25 members of the Forum: 13 with clinical researchers, professionals and administrators and 15 with users (patients and carers). They lasted 60 minutes on average and were recorded and transcribed verbatim. The observations were written up as ethnographic field notes. Lastly, 840 pages of archive material and documents such as meeting agendas and minutes were used to triangulate facts about the Forum.

Having noted that spaces used by the user and research groups were rich with symbols from the world of professional research, the first author also noted when and how user experience seemed to contrast or resonate with these symbols. Developing ongoing relationships with many of the Forum members, who were later interviewed, allowed for good 'triangulation' of interview data. He also kept a record of extended email correspondence with them, returning to it at various points of the analysis in order to illuminate tensions between their 'personal' and 'PPI' lives, providing additional insight into the various grievances that formed part of such tensions. The quotes derived from all these conversations, as well as from diary notes and recorded observation, are used in the analysis under broad descriptors (e.g. 'User', 'Researcher').

Analysis

From August 2011 to August 2013, both authors worked iteratively to develop the analytical and theoretical implications of the ethnographic data. The data analysis was based on the abduction model (cf. Iedema et al., 2006; Alvesson and Skoldberg, 2009), starting from the empirical material as a foundation upon which our Lefebvre-derived framework was applied as a lens to unveil 'patterns that bring understanding' (Alvesson and Skoldberg, 2009: 4). Evocative stories indicated instances of contradiction and tension across conceived, lived and perceived spaces. At the first stage, we reviewed field notes, transcribed interviews and documents, for prevalent 'symbols' corresponding to experienced, discursive and material dimensions of accountability: biographical references, memories, emotions, embodied responses, signs of 'internal struggles' manifested for instance as ambivalence or uncertainty in the enactment of PPI roles, as well as the spatial and discursive ordering of PPI in the Forum, for instance distinguishing recurrent themes concerning material and time arrangements, routinized meeting procedures and clinical target setting in the Forum.

This careful reading was coupled with a round of open coding (Strauss, 1987) to produce two 'spatial narratives' (Beyes and Michels, 2011) around which to organize such symbols. Next, we sought to 'flesh out' the role of contradictions described in our conceptual framework, through focusing on encounters and relational positionings in the Forum, using the aforementioned 'categories' as a 'contrast set' (see, for instance, Spradley, 1979), to focus on the various contradictions that these described. For instance, we discerned tensions between some users' verbalized desire to adopt clinical terms of practice and their exasperation at being constrained by these very same terms. These contradictions formed the basis for our emerging theorization of accountability in the Forum.

Analysis

Narrative 1: Cultural norms privilege the physical at the expense of the experiential when measuring accountability

Research group meetings took place at the buildings of a charity organization located in affluent areas of a major UK city. Meeting rooms were large and comfortable, tables were arranged in rectangular formation and the seating arrangement – organized by the charity administrator – usually placed patient representatives on one side of the room next to one another, in a row. The discussion was structured in strict, linear format, allocating time for users and professionals to contribute to the unfolding debate, provide updates from their activities and express views on research in the Forum. Discussions were usually organized around meeting agendas and related to high-level technical details of planned clinical trials.

It was evident that in responding to the 'commonsense' expectations for the meeting ('perceived space'), users sometimes struggled in 'lived space' with the use of acronyms, combined with the highly specific nature of information involved ('conceived space'), which often seemed hard to follow. Through these long discussions, it became clear that these difficulties created tensions for some participants, who felt uncomfortable making the transition to their formal PPI roles (a shift in emphasis from 'lived' to 'conceived' space). They recorded feelings of tension between the 'professional' role expected by the organization and their more visceral self-identifications as 'patients'. Such discomfort manifested itself in a sense of loss of control:

> I've become a lot more involved, properly involved, what some doctors like to call professional patient...Now, I'm not sure if I like that term because that carries with it an element of truth, but it is also problematic. Because by calling a patient 'professional patient' you are immediately making them step over a dividing line, into a different arena. Now, for all we know why can't every patient be a professional patient, why should we not use that term?
>
> (User)

As users became more involved in the Forum, they found themselves questioning binary distinctions between accountable roles, such as 'professional'/'lay'. Rather than existing in either one or the other dimension ('lived'/'conceived'), there was recognition that both dimensions were important. Similarly, professionals were sometimes uncomfortable in the Forum's formal PPI process. Although, unlike patients, professionals' own experiences of vulnerability were shared privately with the researcher rather than in public, they described how these affected their engagement with their roles and responsibilities. In some cases, professionals exposed their concerns about 'fitting in' with the accountability structures of PPI and felt insecure about their own scepticism towards the formal requirements for user involvement:

> It's a game that I've even started playing. I've learned over my involvement in this group that when I put together funding

applications, I need to name a patient on that, simply to tick that box... I think that's wrong. Before I got involved in these groups I spoke to patients as part of my research... And I think I was much more willing to involve them when it was of my own volition rather than now when it seems to be something that 'I have to do', whether I think it is particularly needed or not.

(Professional)

The above comment was made by a research professional who voiced ethical concerns with about the compatibility of users' experiential knowledge with the Forum's PPI targets and measures of accountability. Despite such misgivings, professionals usually felt unable to resist or challenge the demands for user involvement in the research group:

I've never had conversations at the level of the [research] groups, with the [Forum's management], because quite honestly I think that'd be quite dangerous. From my perspective I think it could affect my chances of developing my career down the line...

(Professional)

Such feelings reflected a commonly experienced tension, as patients and professionals sought to reconcile the demands of *physically* defined practices and protocols (in 'conceived space') with their *experience* of such practices (in 'lived' space). In particular, the 'commonsense understandings' of the group ('perceived space') were usually directed towards satisfying accountabilities within 'conceived' space – defined by priorities posed by the research process itself, for instance receiving necessary research funding and ensuring the 'success' of clinical studies. Such measurements failed to engage with a 'missing' accountability: clinicians' and patients' own experiences of the service. The relative invisibility of these experiences generated tensions for participants and detracted from their levels of satisfaction with the service.

In this instance, the problem appeared to lie in the 'commonsense understandings' within 'perceived space': the cultural norms/expectations that privileged indicators of the physical over indicators of the experienced:

[H]aving friendly PPI people on your side, you know, you can ride into battle with... you know, with the funders or whatever is of course... um, well for a [national] funding it's mandatory... and I'm not sure how much room that leaves – [laughs] – ... for differences as it were...you know, where should the greater influence be: do you find people who agree with what the researcher wants to do or what...

(Professional, research group chair)

Thus, securing funding for PPI studies and trials was viewed as a matter of satisfying cultural norms associated with physical outcomes, such as 'consensus'. Such norms conditioned a more 'abstract' view of PPI representatives as 'subjects' of the research process, making it difficult for professionals to engage with the 'patient side' of these users. Accordingly, the more personal interaction required in this more intimate type of engagement was less visible within 'perceived space'. As a result, satisfaction of this more experientially defined dimension of accountability – 'lived space' – was ultimately less important for securing funding and the continuation of the service.

Narrative 2: Accountability as visceral engagement with the 'whole person'

The above narrative provides support for the claim that 'perceived' cultural norms involving accountability should take explicit account of experiential ('lived'), as well as physical, 'conceived' indicators. However, the following narrative indicates that committed engagement with experiential dimensions of accountability will require a more developed understanding of the visceral, affectively conditioned nature of the 'lived' dimension. Specifically, a deep emotional inflection to many Forum members' performances appeared most often in moments where memories of past experiences were invoked by users, affecting their day-to-day practical engagements in the Forum's 'perceived' spatial dimension. One such story, told by a patient representative, recalled an incident from her first years of involvement in her local hospital – user partnership. She described her experience in a cancer outpatient clinic:

> We wanted to rearrange the chairs [they were in lines] in a more companionable setting within that confined space. They would not listen to us, they wouldn't do anything. One day, we went there in the evening and changed it. The next day they changed it back...Finally I discovered why the chairs wouldn't change. The senior registrar explained that before the outpatient clinic opens the consultant would brief all the doctors on the rounds so they would sit in rows, because that is the way they liked it, because they love hierarchy!

> So I said to the senior registrar if they could move them back once they finish, and his response was: 'Doctors don't move chairs!'
>
> (User)

This experience illustrates how the commonsensical vision of 'perceived' space became entangled with patients' emotional need for companionship, prompting users to rearrange the layout of chairs. In describing their needs and expectations as 'user representative' and 'partner' more generally, users often made references to their embodied experiences, insisting how these had influenced their decisions and choices – in both clinical and PPI contexts. In so doing, they drew attention to their own bodies, pointing to the marks of illness and attempting to relate the 'lived' space they occupied to their 'perceived' PPI roles:

> I am not the typical patient in asking questions – you'll see I've got a scar here [points to her neck] I have a thyroidectomy... I postponed that for a while because I thought... I think it's a bit akin to the prostate cancer situation, where you can roll along quite nicely without much risk... now I wasn't necessarily quite right there, but *I used that experience to question* people more closely. You have to have a certain amount of confidence to debate these things with consultants.
>
> (User 1, our emphasis)

> I've still got my stoma [an artificial opening on the surface of a colon-cancer patient's body], I thought the shock treatment is best... so I mentioned that, you know... and you can see in their minds and eyes that they hadn't actually thought... they wouldn't have noticed.
>
> (User 2)

Users 1 and 2 above resorted to surprise tactics in order to fulfil personal needs and role expectations, attempting to provoke and 'shock-treat' their professional counterparts in the hope of rebalancing the 'perceived' space of PPI towards greater acknowledgement of the more viscerally inhabited dimension of 'lived' space (see previous narrative). Moreover, as more users participated in major research conferences and workshops, they sometimes referred back to such experiences, even when this was not considered appropriate within formal discussions. This often took the form of emotionally loaded performances where users sought to channel their memories directly into the Forum's 'conceived' space, by interrupting the linear course of technical discussions:

She (former user) died last week...she would write to me, we were exchanging emails until a couple of days before it happened. It wasn't entirely altruistic, but it was cathartic for her...but really helpful.

(User, quoted in Forum meeting)

This cancer survivor's reference to another patient who had recently died generated some inconvenience around the table. User references to death were generally frequent and formed part of an emotionally charged way of engaging with professionals. Death was not discussed using the mortality figures of the professionals' narrative; it was discursively constructed as an event with profound impact, as a personal loss. New group members introduced themselves at the meetings by describing their own experience with illness, bereavement and caring for their loved ones. Occasionally, such poignant calls questioned directly the usefulness of 'boundaries' that were posed in meetings in the form of abstracted discussions:

I do remember being at a meeting...and I can't remember all the factors, there was some kind of dialogue going on, and I remember getting extremely emotive, because we were seem to be going round and round the table – going absolutely nowhere...about something that wasn't particularly of much use, and I remember getting almost in tears, and I remember saying 'cancer is a very basic thing'...you know, you've really got to look at the person and the emotions...they [clinicians], they just couldn't feel it cause they hadn't been there.

(User)

As users became more involved in the 'participatory structure' of research group meetings, such participation lent legitimacy to a more rigid ordering of time privileged by professionals. However, this occurred at the expense of the greater time required for developing the more personal relations desired by users. On rare occasions, this tension increased to the point that users challenged professionals' more rigid control of time. Upon such occasions, professionals articulated concerns about the importance of getting the job done in a 'timely fashion', avoiding 'distractions' from achieving much-desired agreements and eschewing shifts 'in undesirable directions'. These concerns 'corrected' divergence from the normal course of discussions, and ultimately reaffirmed professionals' focus on maintaining control of time in the RO's 'perceived' space.

Discussion

These two narratives illustrate that transitions to participatory, user-led models of service delivery can render traditional, canonical representations of organizational accountability increasingly inadequate. In particular, common to both narratives presented in this chapter is an ever-present tension between satisfaction of physically abstracted indicators/protocols on the one hand and a recognition of other, more viscerally experienced realities on the other. We have drawn attention to an inability to see, and thus engage with, these tensions as the factor detracting most from both patients' and clinicians' satisfaction with the service.

Accordingly, Figures 13.2 and 13.3 below constitute an initial attempt to build on Figure 13.1, to produce an underlying framework for engaging more visibly with these more holistic dimensions of organizational experience, as well as with the tensions that appear between these.

Figure 13.2 adds 'indicators' (bold text) to the existing dimensional definitions outlined in Figure 13.1. Upon approaching the field, use of the tri-dimensional conceptual framework in Figure 13.1 enabled a categorization of empirical indicators along three dimensions, as set out in Figure 13.2. Thus, more traditional, canonical indicators fall naturally within the dimension of 'conceived' space, whilst more bodily, affectively driven states and biographical identifications fall within the dimension of 'lived' space. Finally, emergent, socially mediated pragmatic understandings as these arise in the 'heat' of social interaction fall into the dimension of 'perceived' space. We believe that the tripartite indicators in Figure 13.2 offer a more comprehensive representation of unfolding/performed organizational reality than more traditional representations taken from the single dimension of 'conceived' space, and thus that Figure 13.2 may offer the basis for a more accurate framework of accountability.

This extended array of representational indicators affords an understanding of how organizational members perform, but does not necessarily resolve the tensions with which they are faced across the multiple dimensions of (their) reality. Hence, an important implication for holding such transitioning spaces accountable is that such tensions should be understood not simply as 'inhibitors' but also as socially generative components of 'good practice', as different parties seek to reconcile physical with more experiential dimensions, measurements and resulting motivations. Accordingly, Figure 13.3 develops Figures 13.1 and 13.2 one further stage, offering some initial measures for identifying tensions

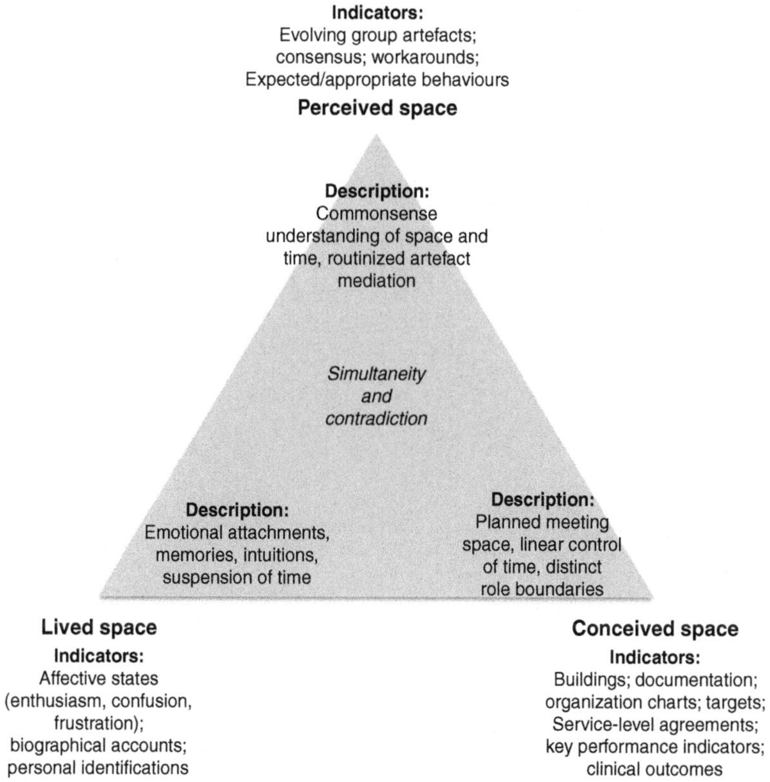

Indicators:
Evolving group artefacts;
consensus; workarounds;
Expected/appropriate behaviours
Perceived space

Description:
Commonsense
understanding of space and
time, routinized artefact
mediation

*Simultaneity
and
contradiction*

Description:
Emotional attachments,
memories, intuitions,
suspension of time

Description:
Planned meeting
space, linear control
of time, distinct
role boundaries

Lived space
Indicators:
Affective states
(enthusiasm, confusion,
frustration);
biographical accounts;
personal identifications

Conceived space
Indicators:
Buildings; documentation;
organization charts; targets;
Service-level agreements;
key performance indicators;
clinical outcomes

Figure 13.2 Tri-dimensional indicators for a more sensitive framework for accountability within devolved organizations
Source: Adapted by authors from Lefebvre (1991).

being played out between subjective, intersubjective and objective dimensions of performed reality.

Figure 13.3 highlights three types of tensions that can arise as people seek to reconcile lived, conceived and perceived dimensions of organizational reality, and indicates the limitations of traditional indicators *alone*, such as targets, service-level agreements, key performance indicators and clinical outcomes, for holding devolved service organizations to account. Figure 13.3 suggests that we can expect to see tensions appearing as such indicators appear constraining, or less relevant, at group level.

Firstly, our empirical example illustrates how 'ends' such as research targets around the design of clinical trials ('conceived space') were

Indicators:
Evolving group artefacts;
consensus; workarounds;
Expected/appropriate behaviours
Perceived space

Description:
Commonsense
understanding of space and
time, routinized artefact
mediation

Tension:
Individuals appear
disengaged from group
Understandings and
routines

*Simultaneity
and
contradiction*

Tension:
Codified rules/visible
structures appear
constraining/irrelevant
to emerging
group consensus

Description:
Emotional attachments,
memories, intuitions,
suspension of time

Description:
Planned meeting
space, linear control
of time, distinct
role boundaries

Lived space		Conceived space
Indicators:	**Tension:**	**Indicators:**
Affective states (enthusiasm, confusion, frustration); biographical accounts; personal identifications	Individuals appear constrained by codified rules/visible structures, and may disengage or respond in unexpected/creative ways	Buildings; documentation; organization charts; targets; Service-level agreements; key performance indicators; clinical outcomes

Figure 13.3 Tensions between dimensions of organizational space
Source: Adapted by authors from Lefebvre (1991).

emphasized and prioritized in Forum meetings, through the organization of discussion time around strictly allocated slots and through exhaustive technical documentation. This was often incongruent with users' expected behaviours ('perceived' space), such as those of engaging in caring relationships and focusing on qualitative, experiential aspects of illness and care. This tension between conceived and perceived space was reflected in the pressure for accountability required for securing funding on the one hand and the 'emerging consensus' within the group around the practical accountability of PPI roles on the other.

Secondly, traditional indicators were held to be unsupportive of personal experiences of individuals – both users and professionals – who often felt uncomfortable and de-identified with the Forum's existing structures of accountability. Examples include the many expressions of ambivalence and uncertainty around users' perceived roles in the organization, which they felt were misrepresented by the lay/professional distinction. Similarly, the professional researcher's ethical concern about being able to pursue his research as effectively as possible while also feeling 'forced' to involve patients tokenistically in the process shows how his identification with the 'researcher role' ('lived' space) conflicted with the 'box-ticking' approach often encountered in the Forum ('conceived' space).

Thirdly, there were times when routine cultural norms ('perceived' space) within the Forum, which encouraged a box-ticking approach, appeared in tension with more experiential concerns ('lived space'). For instance professionals' implicit and quiet acceptance of users' emotional outbursts during formal meetings could be seen as serving to neutralize the potential challenge of such outbursts by co-opting them into dominant 'conceived' space, but might also make space for forming an intersubjective link across the two groups of users and professionals ('perceived space').

Conclusion

Our motivation in this chapter has been to raise awareness amongst organizational researchers in healthcare of a growing risk to public accountability within participative organizational forms. This risk stems from the close relationship between representation and accountability in the sense that it is only possible to measure what is analytically 'visible'. The clear implication is that healthcare providers, and especially those involved in PPI, need to develop forms of regulation capable of engaging not just with performance indicators within the more easily measurable dimension of 'conceived' space (such as clinical outcomes) but also with the links between such outcomes and the particular performances upon which such outcomes often depend – measures that relate to how services are experienced by 'whole people'.

Although this chapter's focus has been the UK NHS, our approach will resonate well in health systems beyond the United Kingdom, especially where PPI has been explicitly utilized as a platform for improving measurement of accountability. In Sweden, for instance, patient experiences are increasingly incorporated in accountability measurements as part of the country's 'transparent regional comparisons' (Anell et al., 2012), and patient involvement is encouraged by eHealth initiatives such as the programme 'My medical record on the internet' (Erlingsdottir et al., 2014). Through our proposed set of measures, we showed that in order for such initiatives to improve accountability relations, it is necessary that they also incorporate more time-rich practices of engagement – practices that users of the Forum repeatedly sought out in formal meetings.

Moreover, our proposed theorizing of the socio-spatial production of accountability has wider implications for a variety of health systems internationally, as debates about performance measurement and regulation of accountabilities proliferate. It can thus complement other organizing principles for conceptualizing accountability – for example, legal and financial accountability under the law of providers or insurers (e.g. in the Netherlands); accountability conceived in terms of responsibility for how resources are spent (e.g. in private systems such as the United States and Switzerland); and political accountability expressed as responsibility to the publicly elected body (the citizenry) at both regional (Sweden) and local levels (Finland). Our study holds relevance for all of these notions of accountability, in encouraging increased awareness of different types of representation. We suggest that supplementing these existing notions of accountability with measures sensitive to the socio-spatial production of accountability – perhaps along lines proposed here – may constitute a helpful first step towards capturing the complex reality of healthcare as experienced on the ground.

Hence, instead of assessing effectiveness of PPI practices based solely upon criteria such as 'achievement of consensus' amongst patient participants, attention could focus on evaluating *what* and *how* different types of patient experience are brought into the discussion in developing that consensus. Similarly, important clinical targets followed by professional researchers might perhaps be supplemented with a closer engagement with the biographical narratives of those involved on both sides of the process. Our groundwork confirms that the growing trend of PPI can be a significant lever for a more accountable health service, but it also shows that its impact will be limited if the multidimensionality of patient experience remains poorly represented in the process.

References

Alvesson, M. and Sköldberg, K. (2009) *Reflexive Methodology: New Vistas for Qualitative Research*, 2nd edition. London: SAGE.
Anell, A., Glenngard, A. H. and Merkur, S. M. (2012) 'Sweden: health system review', *Health Systems in Transition*, 14(5): 1–159.

Beyes, T. and Michels, C. (2011) 'The Production of Educational Space: Hetero-topia and the Business University', *Management Learning*, 42: 521–536.

Cabinet Office (2012) Open Public Services, White Paper, July. Available from: http://www.openpublicservices.cabinetoffice.gov.uk/

Dunleavy, P., Margetts H., Bastow, S. and Tinkler, J. (2006) 'New public manage-ment is dead – long live digital-era governance', *Journal of Public Administration Research and Theory*, 16: 467–494.

Erlingsdottir, G., Lindholm, C. and Ålander, T. (2014) 'eHealth services, patient empowerment and professional accountability-an empirical study on the changing patient-doctor relationship in the digital world', in *International EIASM Public Sector Conference*, pp. 1–21.

Ferlie, E., Lynn, L. E. and Pollitt, C. (2007) *The Oxford Handbook of Public Management*. Oxford: Oxford University Press.

FrØLich, N. (2011) 'Multi-layered accountability. Performance-based funding of universities', *Public Administration*, 89: 840–859.

Iedema, R., C. Rhodes and H. Scheeres (2006) 'Surveillance, resistance, obser-vance: exploring the teleo-affective volatility of workplace interaction', *Orga-nization Studies*, 27: 1111–1130.

James, O. and Manning, N. (1996) 'Public management reform: a global perspec-tive', *Politics*, 16: 143–149.

Kernaghan, K. (2000) 'The post-bureaucratic organization and public service values1', *International Review of Administrative Sciences*, 66: 91–104.

Lefebvre, H. (1991) *The Production of Space*. Oxford: Basil Blackwell.

McNulty, T. and Ferlie, E. (2004) 'Process transformation: limitations to rad-ical organizational change within public service organizations', *Organization Studies*, 25: 1389–1412.

Spradley, J. P. (1979) *The Ethnographic Interview*. New York; London: Holt, Rinehart and Winston.

Strauss, A. L. (1987) *Qualitative Analysis for Social Scientists*. Cambridge: Cambridge University Press.

14
Culture Shock and the NHS Diaspora: Coping with Cultural Difference in Public–Private Partnerships

Justin Waring and Amanda Crompton

Introduction

Public–private partnerships (PPPs) are a prominent feature of contemporary healthcare reform associated with global trends towards the marketization of public healthcare (Collyer and White, 2011; Barlow et al., 2013). In general, PPPs involve a formal collaboration between public agencies and private businesses premised on the idea that distinct resources from each sector can be brought together to share risks, foster innovation and co-produce service (Hodge and Greve, 2007). For the private partner, benefits are accrued from access to new markets and return on investment, whilst the public partner benefits from access to private finance and business expertise. PPPs are commonly portrayed as a pragmatic solution to the economic dilemmas of public service renewal and a shift towards progressive era governance (Osborne, 2000), whilst more critical commentators argue they transfer responsibilities for public healthcare from state to market.

PPPs are increasingly visible in European healthcare, particularly in the United Kingdom, Spain, Portugal and Italy, where health services are funded through general taxation (Acerete et al., 2011; Barlow et al., 2013; Roehrich et al., 2014). PPPs vary in form, from the building of new healthcare facilities, through to contracting out clinical services (Barlow et al., 2013). Examples of partnership working in the United Kingdom began in the early 1980s with the outsourcing of catering and cleaning services. From the mid-1990s, the Private Finance Initiative provided private investment in the development of new hospital infrastructure. Since the mid-2000s, and continuing with the current reform agenda, the private sector plays a direct role in providing frontline services, including assuming the management of pre-existing NHS units. This new direction has been referred to as an integrated partnership approach, whereby the provider not only builds new facilities but also delivers patient care (Sekhri et al., 2011). An early example of this type of approach comes from Valencia in Spain, where a private provider was contracted to develop and manage a full range of services from prevention to tertiary care with limited success (Acetere et al., 2011; Sekhri et al., 2011).

Despite the appeal of PPPs, there remains a lack of clarity about what drives success and failure (Roehrich et al., 2014), and research suggests partnership working is often complicated by inter-sectoral differences (Ghere, 1996; Hodge and Greve, 2007). Common tensions are associated with the allocation of risks and rewards, establishing appropriate forms of governance and aligning different approaches to workforce management (Hebson et al., 2003; Hodge and Greve, 2005, 2009; Waring et al., 2013). A significant, but relatively under-researched, aspect of partnership working concerns the cultural and ideological differences between partners (Skelcher, 2005; Roehrich et al., 2014). Although such differences have become less stark (Boyne, 2002), public and private sectors continue to have distinct cultures, as defined by the underlying service rationale, the associated motives and values of service delivery, and the norms and customs that characterize service organization. These differences may prevent collaboration and hinder the success of PPPs (Perry and Wise, 1990; Pratchett and Wingfield, 1996; Perry, 1997; Roehrich et al., 2014).

In seeking to understand how cultural differences might impact upon the implementation and organization of healthcare PPPs, and intersectoral working more broadly, it is useful to draw on perspectives found outside of health policy and management research. Specifically, our chapter draws on culture and migration studies. Drawing upon this perspective, it has recently been suggested that contemporary public service reforms might be interpreted as a form of *public sector diaspora* (Waring, 2015). That is, they often involve the transfer of a public sector workforce and culture to the private sector. Through this migratory and resettlement process, cultural attachments are transformed and new (hybrid) cultural forms can emerge (Waring, 2015). Following this line of thinking, the interaction of public and private cultures, especially where healthcare employees are transferred to the private sector, might trigger a *culture shock* where those involved are confronted with divergent and unsettling values, norms and customs and must learn to adapt to new conditions. In this chapter, we develop this novel perspective by exploring how the healthcare workforce experiences and copes with culture shocks through their involvement in PPPs.

Public and private cultures

Public and private sectors are often described as having different funding arrangement, systems of governance, modes of organizing, client relations and, importantly, cultures (Perry and Wise, 1990; Pratchett and Wingfield, 1996; Boyne, 2002; Berg, 2006; Stackman et al., 2006). These cultural differences are elaborated in terms of the underling purpose or rationale of service; the associated motives and values of workers; and the norms and customs that shape service organization. Looking at public sector motivation, for example, Perry and Wise (1990) suggest that, unlike their private sector counterparts, public servants are motivated by an attraction to 'political governance', 'civic duty', 'compassion' and 'self-sacrifice'. Similarly, Pratchett and Wingfield (1996) describe public sector organizations as characterized by 'political accountability', 'bureaucratic behaviour', serving the 'public interest' and organizational 'loyalty'. While it may be an oversimplistic interpretation, private sector cultures are typically described as concerned with reward or profit; entrepreneurial and enterprising behaviours; and more competitive, commercial and consumer-driven modes of working.

That said, such characterizations appear to reflect an underlying normative view that one culture is better than the other, despite convergence between the sectors triggered by recent reforms that emphasize the ideologies of the market, consumerism and individualism (Berg, 2006; Rondeaux, 2006). For example, research points to eroding public service motives, values and norms, where workers are confronted with new lines of commercial accountability and encouraged to become more business-like and entrepreneurial (Hebson et al., 2003; Berg, 2006; Rondeaux, 2006). Conversely, research shows persistent public sector cultures as inhibiting reform (Hebson et al., 2003; McDonough, 2006; Waring et al., 2013). For example, Buelens and Van den Broeck (2007) suggest that, despite public sector managers exhibiting the motivational characteristics of private business, they do not easily see themselves as entrepreneurs. Similarly, Waring and Bishop (2011) note the ambiguity faced by public healthcare workers when interacting with private sector contractors. It might still be argued that, to varying degrees, public and private cultures continue to exhibit distinct 'motives' (what interests and rewards do workers value), 'values' (what utility, contribution or importance do services make) and 'norms and customs' (what behaviours, commitments and accountabilities should guide service organization).

Such cultural and ideological differences are arguably more pronounced in the English NHS compared to other public service. Throughout its history, the NHS has epitomized 'public service' values associated with universalism, equality, serving the public good and services delivered on the basis of need, not ability to pay (Klein, 2010). Linked to this is the common idea that NHS services should be financed through taxation and owned and operated by the public sector. The significance of these values is such that the NHS is often described as a form of religion within British culture. Given this, reforms often face fierce public and professional opposition where they are perceived as eroding core values. Despite its ideological distinctiveness, it is important to remember that many aspects of the NHS have always relied on partnership between public and private sectors. Various inter-sectoral arrangements were institutionalized in the formation of the NHS, for example in the role of community pharmacies or the independent status of general practitioners (Klein, 2010). What was arguably different at this time, however, was that private motives, cultures and modes of working were seen as serving, even subjugated to, those of a public healthcare system. In contrast, contemporary reforms signal a challenge to the ideology and culture of the NHS as marketization and inter-sectoral partnerships play an increasing role in front-line services.

The utilization of PPPs as a vehicle for healthcare reform creates opportunities not only to transform the financing, organization or management of public services (DH, 2005) but also to bring about deeper cultural change (Pope et al., 2007). At the same time, however, policies continue to talk of maintaining 'core' NHS values, especially around care being delivered on the basis of need (DH, 2010). As such, PPPs represent something of a *cultural conundrum*, where there is an expectation that elements of both public and private cultures will be combined. For public healthcare workers, however, the implications of this cultural change are far from understood. Unlike large-scale hospital infrastructure projects where partnership working is behind the scenes, more recent healthcare PPPs involve closer collaboration around front-line care, for example private partners assume operational responsibility for public services. In particular, many partnerships involve the transfer of public healthcare workers into facilities managed by private contractors. In this context, the possibility for and implications of cultural conflict and blurring are integral to how PPPs are implemented.

Culture shocks and the NHS diaspora

To better understand the cultural aspects of healthcare PPPs, we turn to the cultural studies literature, specifically theory and research on cross-cultural migrations. For example, diaspora research considers how cultural commitments are transformed as social groups are dispersed from their 'homeland' to a new 'host' environment (Safran, 1999; Brubaker, 2005). It attends to how communities maintain an allegiance to their homeland and heritage, or alternatively how cultural attributes interact and blur with the cultures of their new environment (Pieterse, 2004; Cohen, 2008). These ideas have been used to reinterpret contemporary reforms that involve the transfer of public sector employees to the private sector (Waring, 2015). Drawing upon this literature, Waring outlines a process model to account for antecedents and dynamics of cultural change during migration and resettlement.

Extending this perspective, we highlight the possibility for those involved in a public sector diaspora to experience a form of *culture shock* as they are confronted with the distinct motives, values and norms of the private sector. This concept describes the uncertainty, disorientation and anxiety individuals experience during cross-cultural interaction. This can include the psychological distress brought about by differences in language, dress, behavioural norms or shared customs. The concept has been developed from a social psychology perspective along two interlinked lines (Ward et al., 2001). The first considers the psychological attributes that determine whether an individual is likely to experience and cope with cultural disorientation. The second examines how individuals, often in relation to social or therapeutic support, learn to adjust to the new environment. Although group and social factors are often considered, research has tended to remain on the level of the individual or small group. In addition, many early studies focus on the experiences of the 'sojourner' or temporary resident, rather than more long-term migrant communities (Ward et al., 2001).

Much of the culture shock literature attends to the phases that individuals experience during cross-cultural interaction (Oberg, 1960; Bochner, 1982; Pedersen, 1995; Ward et al., 2001). Early accounts, for example, depict a 'U-shaped' pattern of cultural adjustment that describes heightened, declining and then improving levels of 'psychology comfort' (Oberg, 1960). More recent models describe a 'W-shape' process with additional stages of decline and recovery (Pedersen, 1995). Five common stages are outlined. The first is often referred to as the 'honeymoon' period and accounts for the excitement and positivity people experience when encountering a different culture, for example during vacation. The second 'distress' stage describes how individuals can become anxious or frustrated by the *gap* between their native culture and the new environment. Frustration with fitting-in can often lead people to enter a third 'rejection' or 'reintegration' stage where they reinforce the norms of their native culture. The fourth involves multiple processes of 'adjustment' as individuals begin to learn the appropriate norms and customs which enhance psychological security. The final stage involves more thorough adaptation and autonomy where cultural practices are mastered and differences accepted.

Research increasingly recognizes the variety of different ways culture shocks might be triggered, and also the influence of both psychological and sociological factors in shaping adjustment (Ward et al., 2001). For example, culture shocks can be experienced differently according to the temporal nature of the interaction (temporary or permanent), the basis or purpose of the interaction (opportunistic or forced) and the type of involvement in the new environment (integration or isolation). Based upon these differences, research describes divergent forms of cultural adaptation, including the possibility for individuals to assimilate into the new culture, for others to reject and remain marginal in the new environment and for others to develop a more cosmopolitan or hybrid culture. These outcomes have close links with diaspora research (Cohen, 2008; Waring, 2015) and locate the phases of culture shock within a wider theory of cultural adaption (Ward et al., 2001).

Case study of independent sector treatment centres

Since the early 2000s, policymakers have utilized PPPs to expand and innovate front-line NHS service (DH, 2002, 2005, 2010). The study examines the experiences of doctors and nurses, whose clinical work was migrated from a public NHS hospital to a private sector provider, specifically an Independent Sector Treatment Centre (ISTC). ISTCs were introduced in the early 2000s to expand capacity for high-demand, high-volume and low-risk elective procedures (DH, 2005). Early versions were predominantly owned and managed by private companies and operated in parallel to existing NHS provision to add capacity, reduce waiting and increase choice. Later ISTCs were formed through close partnerships involving co-financing and co-delivery (DH, 2005). Like other PPPs, these later ISTCs involved the transfer of selected NHS services, such as day surgery, pain clinics and radiology, to the management of a private provider.

The research involved an in-depth ethnographic case study of one ISTC carried out between 2008 and 2010. The ISTC was financed through a risk sharing arrangement between local healthcare commissioners, the private healthcare partner and a wider NHS strategic agency. It opened in 2008 assuming operational responsibility for the organization and delivery of pre-existing NHS elective services (orthopaedic, ophthalmic, dermatology, vascular). The business partner assumed management responsibility for the service, and for the workforce that had been transfer from a local NHS hospital where these elective services had previously been delivered. This included the full-time secondment of nurses, support workers, administrators and clerks, and the partial secondment of medical and specialist groups (who retained positions within the local NHS hospital).

Over a 12-month period, ethnographic data was gathered through a combination of observations and interviews to understand the organization of work processes, management strategies and the experiences of transferred workers. In total, over 300 hours of observations were conducted in clinics, offices, wards and meetings. In addition, 39 semi-structure interviews were carried out with representatives from management and clinical staff, including private sector executives (3), business managers (5), departmental managers (4), transferred doctors (11), nurses (9), healthcare assistants (4) and other specialists (2). Interviews followed a broad thematic guide related to (1) the partnership configuration, planning and development, e.g. financing and governance; (2) ISTC strategy; (3) the organization and management of work; and (4) communication issues. All electronic records were entered in the computer package nVivo (v.10) for the purpose of data analysis. Analysis involved iterative close reading of data, coding of data extracts and exemplars, identification of second-order codes and categories, elaboration of emergent themes, constant comparison and re-engaging the wider literature and exploratory research questions. In developing our analysis, attention was given to the common and divergent experiences of doctors and nurses as they were transferred from the public to the private sector.

Experiencing a 'culture shock'

Doctors

At the outset of their migration to the ISTC, most doctors expressed some apprehension. This often related to changes in the organization of clinical work, availability of equipment and relationships with patients. This seemed to reflect underlying anxieties about 'management':

> There is a feeling of the unknown about it and what it will mean for how we work, and how we will be managed, and what targets there will be.

A small minority expressed deeper concerns about the underlying motives and ethos of the ISTC, where changes in work organization were linked to corporate aspirations around profit-making, rather than service improvement.

> I do worry about what these types of units mean for the future of the NHS. They are really all about making money and I worry because that's not in keeping with what the public needs.

The majority of doctors, however, were more positive about the ISTC, especially the anticipated 'freedom' from NHS bureaucracy. Many recognized that there was a sense of inevitability about some form of privatization in the future of English healthcare, and the ISTC was therefore an exciting opportunity to experience a new service model. For many, there was a sense that the private sector might restore their sense of professionalism and offer scope to pursue new lines of clinical work.

> It's a chance to be real doctors again, without all the politics and management that you find all too often in the NHS.

Over the initial months of working in the ISTC, the doctors' sense of optimism remained largely unchanged. There were minor frustrations with aspects of operational work, such as team structures and patient booking, but few explicit concerns with values, norms or customs. However, a small minority of doctors reported that the opportunities they expected had been unrealized. For example, the ISTC was perceived as too similar to the NHS and overly managed. Others expressed some revulsion to corporate and commercial aspects of the ISTC, such as corporate branding, relabeling patients as 'customers' and working in more competitive and performance-driven ways.

> All aspects of my work are specified by someone else. I have little say about the patients on my lists, the people I work with or when I am expected to work.

Overtime, these more frustrated doctors followed one of two paths. The first was to 'opt-out' of the ISTC, returning to their 'homeland' of the NHS. Given the contractual basis through which doctors were seconded to the ISTC, this option remained available. Secondly, doctors attempted to influence change within their new work environment. This included, for example, restating teamwork structures, reducing clinical lists and using terms such as 'patient' rather than 'customer'. Through these small adjustments, doctors attempted to reintegrate elements of their established work values, norms and customs within the ISTC.

> I have worked with the leadership team to ensure that proper procedures are followed. And they have been very responsive... The key thing is to always present a strong case. Highlight the evidence, professional guidelines. That way they find it difficult to argue against you.

Most doctors continued to enjoy the opportunities presented by the ISTC, regarding minor frustrations as 'teething problems'. Many described how the ISTC had lived up to their expectations of being a less bureaucratic workplace. There was a widespread view that the private sector offered the possibility for a new or restated form of professionalism that rewarded clinical excellence. As such, the majority of doctors seemed to easily integrate and adapt to the new environment, suggesting cultural alignment between medicine and the private practice. This positivity might also reflect the availability of privileges and rewards available to doctors who were seen by managers as furthering the goals of the company.

Nurses

Like doctors, nurses shared apprehensions and anxieties about the move to the ISTC, but unlike the doctors these were more explicitly linked to the anticipated threats to professional standards and NHS values. In particular, many believed that private sector motives around profit-making would undermine professional standards and erode quality and safety.

> It's not what the NHS is about, is it? Patients are treated because they needed care and that was it. Now it's about profit.

Following their migration to the ISTC, nurses' anxiety about the new work environment appeared to be confirmed. Service organization was described in terms of private sector motives eroding professional standards through reduced team structures, increased workload, procurement of cheaper equipment, streamlined handover and fewer opportunities for staff development. Although doctors saw these changes in more incremental and small-scale terms, for nurses they appeared to demonstrate how the pursuit of efficiencies and profit was undermining quality.

> There are so many massive changes in how we work. They say they are about improving patient experience, but it looks more like they want us to do more, and do it with less. Everything is about scrimping and cutting costs.

In response, nurses described how they worked with greater diligence to safeguard against the dangers of cost-cutting. In addition, many explained how they had tried (but not always succeeded) to reinforce professional standards, as set out in national guidelines, and re-establish ways of working in the NHS, to protect core service values. In responding to their new environment, it was interesting to observe that nurses tended to work together as a unified force to oppose private sector management. As such, they presented a strong and influential basis of change.

> We have pulled together and said no, we can't work like this. We have to meet professional standards and I am not putting patients at risk for anyone or any company.

Over time, most nurses became less anxious about the ISTC, including both the ways of working and its values. This seemed to reflect the nurses' success in re-establishing elements of service organization they believed important, which had been approved by ISTC managers. It also seemed to reflect reduced anxiety about the negative influence of corporate values as nurses realized that many of the changes introduced in the ISTC were largely operational and that managers were not ignorant to NHS values. In other words, their earlier concerns about the private sector were not realized in everyday practice, enabling nurses to soften their opposition.

> We have made sure the service runs like it used to, and patients should feel safe in the Centre. Not because of anything the managers have done, but because we are making sure the service is the same standard as it used to be in the NHS.

For nurses, the reaction to cultural change was more measured and less pronounced than with doctors. Nurses remained committed to core NHS and professional values, but there was also a growing acceptance that some elements of private sector working could be adopted without undermining core values. As such, nurses' initial shock and frustration with the culture of the private sector seemed to reduce because the extent of change to their work was less significant than previously anticipated.

Discussion

Reflecting on the findings, it is important to recognize that it is natural for people to experience anxiety in advance of, or during, a major lifestyle or employment change. As shown by Ashforth (2000), major role transitions often involve identity change. In the context of PPPs, it is to be further expected that long-standing institutional differences between sectors will condition a particular form of anxiety, especially where members of each sector look unfavourably upon each other. For example, there is often a sense that public employees demonize the private sector as placing profit ahead of welfare, and where the provision of care becomes a 'means' to profit, rather than an 'end' in its own right.

Looking closer at the doctors and nurses, involved in our case study, both experienced a form of culture shock and, overtime, passed through phases of adjustment. Doctors experienced a milder and short-lived shock and saw the move in positive terms. The extent of cultural change for doctors was therefore paradoxically profound, but also nominal. That is, doctors aligned with and embraced the cultural values, norms and customs of the private sector, suggesting a significant adjustment, but the study also suggests the extent of change was minimal. Rather than seeing the transition from public to private sector as eroding medical values, it was seen as restoring professional values that had been lost in the public sector. Not wanting to overstate this line of thinking, it is important to recognize the potential for self-selection bias amongst those doctors and that doctors strongly committed to public healthcare declined to work in the ISTC.

In contrast, nurses experienced a strong and longer-lived form of culture shock that led to a more negotiated form of culture change. Although most nurses remained committed to core NHS and nursing values, there was some acceptance of ISTC customs. Nurses' willingness to accept new ways of working was dependent on assurances that core values were not at risk. Furthermore, cultural change amongst nurses was often premised on a form of 'give and take'. In particular, nurses sought to re-established ways of working customary to the NHS, and when these were accepted by ISTC managers, they become more open to the possibility of accepting other non-essential ways of working. Similarly, many nurses saw themselves as the guardians of professional standards in the face of more commercial ways of working, whereas others saw the ISTC as creating opportunities to enhance patient experience (Waring and Bishop, 2011).

To explain these differences, it is useful to recognize the long-standing frustration of many doctors with the NHS, which has often been described as eroding medical autonomy (Waring and Currie, 2009). As such, the private sector was broadly interpreted as a form of liberation and restoring a 'golden age' of medicine (Waring and Bishop, 2012). A further consideration is that doctors, unlike nurses, are more accustomed to the private sector, as many within the English NHS retain private practice. This suggests that prior experience, or lack of it, can influence or prejudice how people anticipate change; for example, for nurses the perception of the private sector was typically more negative. That said, there were notable differences amongst the medical doctors, where some appeared more supportive of and engaged in the ISTC. Reflecting on these intra-professional variations, it might be the case that doctors were more welcomed, privileged and rewarded within the ISTC because of their clinical expertise. In addition, these doctors often held medical-managerial leadership positions and were more able to shape or influence their work environment.

When comparing the culture shocks of doctors and nurses, a number of prominent issues emerge that might explain their distinct experiences and provide the foundations for future research and management attention. First, these healthcare professionals vary in terms of their underling power within the wider healthcare division of labour. As such, it is arguably more possible for doctors to shape the conditions of their work across sectoral boundaries, where private managers, much like public managers, can be regarded as less influential than doctors. Second, prior exposure to cultural difference might lead to perceptions that the 'gap' between cultures is less, which can also represent an important pre-condition for culture change. Where significant members of a community have prior experience of a different culture, that is, as a sojourner, or where there are strong points of similarity between cultures, then the experience of cultural shock is clearly going to be less dramatic. As more public and healthcare services are exposed to inter- or cross-sectoral working, it might be expected that such shocks become less pronounced. Third, and with specific reference to the culture shock associated with PPPs, the research suggests that the degree of 'public-ness' within a profession is an important consideration. For nurses, there was a more marked commitment and allegiance to the idea of 'public' service, which was closely aligned with the principles of 'public' ownership and management. In contrast, doctors did not necessarily associate public service with public ownership and were more open to how public services might be organized by different sectors. Finally, and extending the last point, the study suggests that the form and extent of culture shock is conditioned by the extent to which 'professional' culture or identity is aligned with 'sectoral' culture. For nurses, it seemed that 'professional' and 'sectoral' cultures were closely aligned, possibly because nurses are primarily trained and socialized within the public sector and have fewer opportunities to experience private sector work. As suggested above, doctors have greater scope for engaging in private sector healthcare and historically see their profession as not necessarily tied to a particular mode of service ownership and organization.

In conclusion, we suggest that inter-sectoral cultural differences are a significant feature of PPPs and might be seen as an important contingency in shaping the configuration, implementation and long-term success of partnership working. Cultural theory provides a novel approach for understanding contemporary public and healthcare reforms, where cultural differences and alignment are integral to the processes of strategic change. As outlined above, the continued use of PPPs and other inter-sectoral partnerships might be interpreted as a form of *public sector diaspora* as public workers are increasingly migrated to private and social enterprise (Waring, 2015). The concept of culture shock brings to light the experiences of those involved in this type of migration or diaspora. As shown above, not all groups involved in these migrations will experience the same phases or extent of culture change, but attending to these differences and recognizing the potential anxieties and tensions may facilitate the successful implementation of a PPP. Furthermore, we suggest that culture is an important consideration for strategic and managerial aspect of PPPs that often remains overlooked. Through attending to the potential for culture shock and recognizing the inherent differences between those involved, policymakers and service leaders might be better placed to introduce strategies, support structures and interventions that ease migration and resettlement.

In turn, managers might be better equipped to support the workforce through the adjustment phase and bring about cultural hybridity, blending the cultures of both sectors and closing the gap between them. However, it is possible that cultural hybridization might be an anathema to the strategic intent of private managers, who might be more concerned with bringing about rapid cultural change and more research in this area is required. As suggested by Waring (2015), this brings to the fore questions about the priorities of both host and migrant communities and the inherent political and contested nature of culture change in the context of contemporary public service and healthcare reforms.

References

Acerete, B., Stafford, A. and Stapleton, P. (2011) 'Spanish healthcare public private partnerships: the 'Alzira model', *Critical Perspectives on Accounting*, 22(6): 533–549.

Ashforth, B. (2000). *Role Transitions in Organizational Life: An Identity-Based Perspective*. London: Routledge.

Barlow, J., Roehrich, J. and Wright, S. (2013) 'Europe sees mixed results from public-private partnerships for building and managing health care facilities and services', *Health Affairs*, 32(1): 146–154.

Berg, A. (2006) 'Transforming public services – transforming the public servant', *International Journal of Public Sector Management*, 19(6): 556–568.

Bochner, S. (1982) 'The social psychology of cross-cultural relations', *Cultures in Contact: Studies in Cross-Cultural Interaction*, 1: 5–44.

Boyne, G. (2002) 'Public and private management: what's the difference?' *Journal of Management Studies*, 39: 97–122.

Brubaker, R. (2005) 'The "diaspora" diaspora', *Ethnic and Racial Studies*, 28(1): 1–9.

Buelens, M. and Van den Broeck, H. (2007) 'An analysis of differences in work motivation between public and private sector organizations', *Public administration review*, 67(1): 65–74.

Cohen, R. (2008) *Global Diasporas: An Introduction*. London: Routledge.

Collyer, F. and White, K. (2011) 'The privatisation of Medicare and the National Health Service, and the global marketisation of healthcare systems', *Health Sociology Review*, 20(3): 238–244.

Department of Health (DH) (2002) *Growing Capacity: Independent Sector Diagnosis and Treatment Centres*. London: TSS

Department of Health (DH) (2005) *Treatment Centres: Delivering Faster, Quality Care and Choice for Patients*. London, TSO.

Department of Health (2010) *Equity and Excellence*. London: TSO.

Hebson, G., Grimshaw, D. and Marchington, M. P. (2003) 'PPPs and the changing public service ethos: case study evidence from the health and local authority sectors', *Work, Employment and Society*, 17(3): 481–501.

Hodge, G. and Greve, C. (2005) 'PPPs: a policy for all seasons?' in G. Hodge and C. Greve (eds.), *The Challenge of Public-Private Partnerships: Learning from International Experience*. Cheltenham: Edward Elgar.

Hodge, G. and Greve, C. (2007) 'Public-private partnerships: an international performance review', *Public Administration Review*, 67(3): 545–558.

Hodge, G. and Greve, C. (2009) 'PPPs: the passage of time permits sober reflection', *Economic Affairs*, 29(1): 33–39.

Klein, R. (2010) *The New Politics of the NHS*. London: Radcliffe

Oberg, K. (2006; org. 1960) 'Cultural shock: adjustment to new cultural environments', *Curare*, 29(2): 3.

Osborne, S. (ed) (2000) *Public-Private Partnerships*. London: Routledge.

Perry, J. and Wise, L. (1990) 'The motivational base of public service', *Public Administration Review*, 50(3): 367–373.

Pedersen, P. (1995) 'The five stages of culture shock: critical incidents around the world', *Contributions in Psychology*, 25(1): 281–283.

Pieterse, J. (2004) *Globalization & Culture. Global Mèlange*. Oxford: Rowman

Pope, C., Le May, A. and Gabbay, J. (2007) 'Chasing chameleons, chimeras and caterpillars: evaluating and organisational innovation in the National Health Service', in L. McKee, E. Ferlie and P. Hyde (eds.), *Organizing and Reorganizing: Power and Change in Health Care Organizations*. Basingstoke: Palgrave Macmillan, pp. 112–122.

Pratchett, L. and Wingfield, M. (1996) 'Petty bureaucracy and woolly minded liberalism? The changing ethos of local government officers', *Public Administration*, 74(4): 639–656.

Rondeaux, G. (2006) 'Modernizing public administration: the impact on organisational identities', *International Journal of Public Sector Management*, 19(6): 569–584.

Roehrich, J. K., Lewis, M. A. and George, G. (2014). 'Are public–private partnerships a healthy option? A systematic literature review', *Social Science & Medicine*, 113: 110–119.

Sekhri, N., Feachem, R. and Ni, A. (2011) 'Public-private integrated partnerships demonstrate the potential to improve health care access, quality, and efficiency', *Health Affairs*, 30(8): 1498–1507.

Skelcher, C. (2005) 'Public-private partnerships and hybridity', in E. Ferlie, L. Lynn and C. Pollitt (eds.), *The Oxford Handbook of Public Management*. Oxford: Oxford University Press.

Safran, W. (1999) 'Comparing diasporas: a review essay', *Diaspora*, 8(3): 225–307.

Stackman, R., Connor, P. and Becker, B. (2006) 'Sectoral ethos: an investigation of the personal values systems of female and male managers in the public and private sectors', *Journal of Public Administration Research and Theory*, 16(4): 577–597.

Strauss, A. and Corbin, J. (1990) *Basics of Qualitative Research*. London: Sage.

Ward, C. A., Bochner, S. and Furnham, A. (2001) *The Psychology of Culture Shock*. Sussex: Psychology Press.

Waring, J. and Currie, G. (2009) 'Managing expert knowledge: organizational challenges and managerial futures for the UK medical profession', *Organization Studies*, 30(7): 755–778.

Waring, J. and Bishop. S. (2011) 'Occupational identities at the crossroads of healthcare modernisation: the transfer of NHS clinicians to the Independent Sector', *Sociology of Health and Illness*, 33(5): 661–676.

Waring, J. and Bishop, S. (2012) 'Going private: Clinicians experience of working in UK independent sector treatment centres', *Health Policy*, 104(2): 172–178.

Waring, J., Currie, G. and Bishop, S. (2013) 'A contingent approach to the organization and management of PPPs: a comparative analysis of healthcare PPPs', *Public Administration Review*, 73(2): 313–326.

Waring, J. (2015) 'Mapping the public sector diaspora: towards a model of inter-sectoral cultural hybridity in the English healthcare system', *Public Administration* (online first), 93(2): 345–362.

15
Organizational Healthcare Innovation Performed by Contextual Sense Making

Anne Reff Pedersen

Introduction

Organizational change occurs when innovative ideas are implemented and translated into the everyday life of healthcare organizations and concerns the involvement of local healthcare professionals. A number of studies describe the resistance professionals can exhibit during organizational change processes (Bloom, 1998; Sehested, 2002). One way of gaining an understanding of this resistance is by investigating the meanings healthcare professionals derive from the implementation process and by examining how meanings can become a driver for involvement in the implementation process, but also by looking at how losses of meanings can become a barrier to involvement. This chapter investigates the contextual meanings of healthcare professionals in healthcare innovation processes. The term 'meaning' refers to the storyteller's creation of meanings from narrative knowledge and narrative practice (Bruner, 1986; Humle and Pedersen, 2014).

The proposal that meanings can promote or reject involvement in local innovation processes builds on organizational research that describes how narratives are sense-making devices in organizations, which create the organizational members, identity formations, social interactions, directions and participation (Coopey et al., 1997; Gabriel, 2000; Czarniawska, 2004; Hjort and Steyaert, 2004; Mantere and Vaara, 2008; Pedersen, 2009). However, the contextual meanings in healthcare innovation processes that provide legitimation and social interactions during the implementation of healthcare innovation processes remain understudied. Hence, this chapter explores how three shared meanings in a local healthcare context enable the involvement of healthcare professionals via the interposition of participants, the mobilization of participants and the legitimation of the innovation processes. I propose that certain contextual meanings enable healthcare professionals to become engaged in innovation processes, where other meanings reduce engagement. These meanings are not directed by top-down directions, reforms or institutional values or societal discourses, but are performed locally and become a micro and emergent perspective on change processes. Healthcare professionals become important due to the organizing condition that they have considerable autonomy and discretion in healthcare.

In order to study the meanings and involvement of healthcare professionals in healthcare innovation processes, data from a specific healthcare innovation project were examined. The aim of the innovation project was to improve the involvement of patients by providing them with greater influence on the department's organizing practices. Driven by local healthcare professionals and local healthcare managers, the project involved developing specially designed postcards to provide patient feedback. When the project, which took place in a medical unit in Denmark's national hospital, concluded, a partnership had been established with a national foundation to spread voluntary use of feedback postcards in all the hospitals throughout Denmark.

The chapter comprises the following sections. The first section presents a review of how the literature defines organizational healthcare innovation and the role of involvement and meanings in innovation and organizational change. This is followed by a summary of the empirical context, the healthcare innovation case study and the methods used to study it. Finally, the findings are presented as three contextual meanings. The first one involves *engagement* and the interposition of people into the processes. The next one concerns *materialization* and the role materials, such as postcards, play in mobilizing people in the processes of implementing innovations. Finally, the third one involves *scientification* and the role of legitimation in implementing new ideas in healthcare. To conclude, there is a discussion of how a meaning approach provides a new understanding of both the opportunities and limitations of involving healthcare professionals in healthcare change and innovation processes.

Organizational healthcare innovation

How does healthcare innovation differ from other types of innovation? Omachonu and Einspruch define four general types of innovation: product innovation, which introduces a new and improved good or service; process innovation, which implements an improved production or delivery method; marketing innovation, which implements new marketing methods involving significant change in product design; and organizational innovation, which implements a new organizational method in the organizations practice, workplace or external relations (2010: 5). They then argue that healthcare innovation is related to product, process and structure (Varkey et al., 2008) because marketing innovation becomes less relevant in the healthcare sector. The innovation project studied in this chapter introduces new methods for obtaining patient feedback and thus falls into the category of an organizational healthcare innovation that aims to implement a new organizational method and practice, in this case to improve patient satisfaction and to create the best ways of organizing.

Omachonu and Einspruch define healthcare innovation as: 'The introduction of a new concept, idea, service or process, or product aimed at improving, treatment, diagnosis, education, outreach, prevention and research and with the long term of improving quality, safety, outcomes, efficiency and cost' (Ibid: 5). This definition describes general core elements in healthcare innovations that cover most processes, but this definition could also be expanded by including a narrower understanding of some characteristics of organizational healthcare innovation. For example, our understanding of *organization* in organizational healthcare innovation, where the aim is to improve the places and organizations, involves aspects that are not directly related to treatment and healthcare issues (i.e. treatment, diagnosis, education, outreach, prevention and research) but that relate to where and how the work is carried out and organized. The aim of the feedback postcards was not only to improve quality, safety, outcomes, efficiency and costs but also to increase satisfaction, which has become an increasingly central reason for recent healthcare change and innovations. One of the goals of organizational healthcare innovations is to enhance many different types of organizational practices, but the results that are achieved are another issue. Innovation is often related to a normative element that links it to improvements, but its effects can vary greatly, ending at times in failed improvements, unseen consequences and higher costs. Hence, the above definition should also encompass practices beyond the individual organization to include relations to external organizations and actors, in addition to a more network and interorganizational understanding. Hartley (2005) defines innovation from a governance perspective as a certain kind of innovation, which also in a healthcare setting goes beyond organizational boundaries and creates network-based interactions (Moore and Hartley, 2008). The challenge then becomes the interaction between participants in networks and creating collectively established goals by producing common meanings.

Finally, there is the issue of how innovation happens (Shortell et al., 2010). How innovation is possible in a healthcare context, which is different from other areas, often relates to a specific context. But what do we mean by context? In a healthcare innovation study on the role of context, Dopson et al. (2008) suggest that context should not be defined as a passive concept but as an active, interacting component in the process of change and innovation. It is not a backcloth to action; instead, local healthcare professionals engage in work practices and actively interpret and reconstruct its local validity and usefulness (Dopson et al., 2008: 228). Consequently, the micro-behaviours of the people and practices in a healthcare organization become the context (Pettigrew et al., 1992; Van de Ven and Poole, 2005). This study draws on this line of argumentation by applying a concept of context based on the interaction and involvement of healthcare professionals, particularly how their involvement is related to their sense making and how meanings and values play an active role in constructing locally situated practices.

Another central element in healthcare innovation is how innovations travel and spread to other places. The general literature on innovation diffusion is based on an understanding of the drivers or barriers to diffusion (Greenhalgh et al., 2004; Rogers, 2010). Healthcare innovation diffusion studies (Fitzgerald et al., 2002; Ferlie et al., 2005) demonstrate how healthcare innovations are complex organizing processes that do not follow linear innovation models and that top-down disseminations of evidence programmes do not necessarily lead to the adoption of new initiatives as the capacity of an organization to innovate depends on its history, culture and the quality of relationships, all of which vary by context (Fitzgerald et al., 2002: 1443). Therefore, diffusion and change are dependent upon interpretative and negotiated interactions between local actors. Ferlie et al. conclude that social interactions, trust and motivation are important elements in healthcare change and innovations, but that they are not always optimal in local contexts (2005: 131).

An expanded definition of organizational healthcare innovation is thus: *The introduction of a new method or practice aimed to improve the organizational practices of healthcare that is translated into a local context via the interactions and meanings of the involved networks of participants,* where the search for local interactions and meanings and how they affect change processes are highlighted.

Interactions and meanings in organizational healthcare innovation

Multiple studies exist on the implementation process of innovations, its complexity and how difficult it is to steer and must include a translation of the ideas by the participation and involvement of local actors (Callon, 1986; Polley et al., 1999; Albury, 2005; Hartley, 2005; Osborne and Brown, 2011). When involvement of local participants is an important part of the implementation process of innovation, it becomes vital to understand the reasons and conditions for the involvement of healthcare professionals in healthcare innovation. Often professionals are described as one of the main barriers against change and innovation, due to their lack of interest in other professions, their claim of autonomy and their mono-professional way of organizing that hinders collaboration with other professions (Sehested, 2002). This means that the involvement of professionals cannot be taken for granted and that it requires a great deal of work to make new meanings.

Innovation literature emphasizing the role of narratives suggests that values, feelings and meanings play a key role in creating common ground for social interaction during the innovation process by defining the identity formation and accepted ways of participating (Coopey, Keegan and Emler, 1997; Hjort and Steyaert, 2004; Pedersen and Johansen, 2012). An innovation study by Hjort and Steyaert (2004) describes how the innovation process involves sense making and how narratives create shared meaning, directions and social interactions. Also healthcare innovation can be defined as a social activity that concerns shared meanings and social interactions. Coopey et al. (1997: 312) studied the role of managers' narratives in sense-making processes in an innovation process and concluded that mangers are able to draw creatively on their individual memory when composing a story to make sense of what is happening while potentially enhancing feelings of self-esteem. They also show how narratives consequently serve to confirm or reshape a manager's identity within the innovation activity.

A study by Pedersen and Johansen (2012) demonstrates how the translation of innovative ideas happens when innovation narratives that create meanings for participants allow them to explain and make sense of all the unseen consequences of change processes.

A study by Mantere and Vaara (2008) on the conditions of participation in organizational change demonstrates how participation is linked to meanings and also to broader social discourses. They distinguish between three discourses that appear to reproduce a non-participatory approach: mystification (the obfuscation of organizational decisions), disciplining (using disciplinary techniques to constrain action) and technologization (imposing a technical system to govern activities) (Mantere and Vaara, 2008: 348). They also identify three discourses that enhance participation: self-actualization (discourse on the ability to outline objects in the process), dialogization and concretization (discourse that seeks to establish clear practices). Consequently, their study demonstrates how certain kinds of discourses create conditions for participation.

All these studies point to of how involvement is based on meanings, narratives, social interactions and social discourses. The aim of the subsequent analysis is to analyse the contextual meanings that emerged in a local healthcare innovation project, where the involvement of the healthcare professionals was related to bringing the voice of patients to bear on the change in practices on the ward.

The empirical context: Feedback project on a hospital medical ward

In a neurology ward at Denmark's national hospital in Copenhagen, the local management group hired a voluntary patient ambassador to design a new project for the wards, the idea for which stemmed from a volunteer worker from outside the hospital who had been in the United States, where feedback postcards were used and increased how much patients were listened to in quality improvement processes. The voluntary patient ambassador worked with a group of nurses to design, distribute and subsequently analyse the postcards. The aim of the local health innovation project was to provide patients with a postcard to write about what they had experienced while on the ward. Then their comments were collected to determine which ideas could cheaply and easily be translated locally into practice. For example, one postcard stated, 'The door to one of the waiting rooms is noisy', which led to the head nurse immediately changing the door, while another feedback postcard stated, 'I wish there was something to eat and water to drink in the waiting areas'. This issue was also rapidly addressed. In sum, patient concerns were reported back to each hospital unit to influence and change the organizational patterns of treatment. Two additional external participants, a voluntary medical organization for patient safety and a large private foundation, were also part of the implementation process. This collaboration resulted in the design and conceptualization of a postcard, entirely funded by the foundation and the patient safety organization, to be distributed to every hospital ward in Denmark for providing patient feedback, thus turning a local project into a nationwide healthcare innovation.

This case is an example of local management and employee-driven innovation, which means that the ideas originate from local management. The innovation processes can also be described as a culture-changing quality improvement process because the results altered a strong intra-organizational professional culture towards being more reflective and open towards patient needs and voices.

Methods

The data used in this chapter stem from a large state-funded research project on innovation in the public sector in Denmark. Initially, data collection involved doing interviews at a regional healthcare innovation centre, while the next step entailed finding a local innovation project based on the definition of innovation as ideas translated into new local practices. Four local healthcare innovation cases were followed at three different hospitals. One case is about translating innovation through different kinds of innovation narratives (Pedersen and Johansen, 2012). Two other cases are about the work of making meanings in processes of healthcare innovation, while the last case is about the narrative conditions of professional participation in the innovation processes through a focus on which values attract or limit the participation of healthcare professionals. The data in the next section mainly derive from the qualitative interviews undertaken with staff on the ward. Interviews were simultaneously conducted with the patient ambassador. Nurses, doctors, managers and external partners on the wards participated in 20 semi-structured individual interviews. Exclusively using a narrative interview technique (Czarniawska, 2004), we asked informants to share what they thought and felt about participating in an innovation project. Lasting 40–80 minutes, the interviews took place on the wards in various offices.

Interviews were recorded and subsequently transcribed for thematic coding and analysis.

The analysis presented in the next section uses a narrative approach inspired by Bruner (1986) to define meanings. The term 'meaning' refers to the storyteller's creation of meanings from the knowledge of narratives involving characters, plots and events (Bruner, 1986). Bruner (1990: 44), who distinguishes between logo scientific knowledge (objective truth) and narrative knowledge, defines narrative knowledge as based on narratives which create meaning by being socially and culturally defined. In this analysis, the focus is not on the single narrative or the narrative structure but on which meanings are expressed across many individual narratives as socially and culturally defined narratives. A narrative is defined as a performative narrative practice which enhances meanings (Humle and Pedersen 2014). The data analysis led to the identification of several individual narratives in the interview material with created shared meanings.

Meaning and involvement in healthcare innovation

The following section presents three shared meanings from healthcare professionals in the implementation of healthcare innovation processes. First, *engagement*, is a shared meaning in many individual narratives that engage healthcare professionals by creating an interest in why a particular innovation is important and an improvement upon existing routines. The next shared meaning relates to *materiality*, which allows new ideas to be transformed into a meaningful tool; in this case, a postcard that made it possible to mobilize participants. Last, the third shared meaning, *scientification*, gave the project legitimacy.

Meanings of engagement

When change and innovation are driven in a local context, the problem and the reason why an innovation project is important become a central theme in making sense of the project. The interviewees explained why change was necessary, each of them mentioning *how increased patient involvement* was important because they worked with them daily, but they did not always listen to what the patients experienced during their stay. The interviews described how they discovered that what was important to patients during their stay could stand in contrast to their own ideas and understanding of what the patients needed.

As one doctor states, 'We think we know what they think, but this turns out not to be entirely the case', which illustrates the engagement narrative that emerged from the healthcare staff, who explained why this project was important and why they should spend their time on it.

The patient ambassador states:

> I'm a spokesperson for patient involvement, which is a battle I take to the doctors. We can't learn from this without knowing if it's the case 5 or 35 times a year; we try to learn anyway. The patient can point out so many problems that reflect other problems, so, for the individual patient, one communication problem is relevant, but the interesting part is, if we ask, 'Does this have anything to do with the way we're organized?' that makes us vulnerable to this type of communication.

This example illustrates how engaged support for patient involvement and the idea that professionals should listen more to healthcare system users are central for creating meaning in projects.

Patient involvement refers to the importance of involving patient knowledge and patient communication as the basis for improving professional treatment and care. In many of the interviews, the staff describe how they find patient involvement interesting, exciting and motivational, and they agree on the importance of asking patients about their opinions instead of assuming they know what they are already. Thus, the engagement of healthcare staff to patient involvement was the main interest of this innovative project, as well as understanding what guides meanings and creates valuable reasons for healthcare staff to participate in the innovation projects.

Meanings of materiality

When implementing feedback postcards on local wards, the staff used various materials, including emails, minutes from meetings and reports on the type of patient feedback, but the actual postcards were the one item that they mentioned the most. When the postcards were designed, everyone had an opinion about their design, placement, presentation to patients, and collection and evaluation. The chief nurse made the following comments about the postcards:

> I think it's important that the staff on the ward read the postcards, get them in their hands and look at them. It has a much stronger effect when you look at the written word. It's much more personal than looking at statistics. In one ward, the postcards were lying on a desk, freely available where the staff could easily read them. Later they were put in a folder. I read some postcards where the patients

complained about the noise. The head nurse simply had the doors soundproofed without a big discussion or lots of planning. She just did it.

The involved healthcare staff explained how the postcards as concrete items helped them to understand patients and the project, thus giving direction to the implementation process. The cards served as something tangible in their stories about the implementation process. The meanings about the postcards set the direction of the work tasks involved in the implementation process, for example how to design the cards, how to give them to patients and how to evaluate them when they were filled out and returned.

But the process of designing the cards was difficult. Some of the staff did not like the colour red as they thought it was associated too much with blood, while others felt pictures of patients on the front would be best. A professional graphic artist did the final layout and the department manager described the process like this:

> We proposed a layout to the centre management and that created a huge amount of discussions, because 50 people have 50 different opinions. Some felt this couldn't be done at a hospital and others thought it was a good idea. It created so much ... But we ended up with a layout, in fact three different designs, would you like to see them?

The postcards, their design and their layout created a large amount of sense making, and many different meanings were related to the design of the cards. In the end, a mutual decision was reached, and a professional graphic artist hired to make the final versions.

The next step involved how to make the postcards visible for patients. Should they hang on the wall or should they be given directly to patients while talking to them? People thought that giving the postcards directly to patients was not a good idea because the amount of mandatory information they received was already high. One project nurse explains, 'We were supposed to give the postcards to a relative, but when I came in could I see that people were in deep grief and I couldn't get myself to ask them if they wanted to participate in the project'. This quote shows how the implementation of the project also reflects the resistance of the healthcare staff, as they did not want to give cards directly to patients. The decision was made to hang the postcards on waiting room walls and let patients take cards on their own if they felt inclined to fill one out. Hence, implementation was directed by the meanings and feelings of the healthcare staff, who felt that it was necessary not to overburden relatives and patients.

The last part of the implementation process was how to interpret the postcards and integrate their ideas into the daily work. The interviews indicated that the healthcare staff were surprised by what patients wrote. Patients wrote a few lines on the postcards, and the many positive statements surprised the staff. One aspect of the project mentioned during every interview was that it was important for everyone to participate in the collection and analysis of the cards. A nurse describes her response upon reading a postcard, '... and then there was a relative who described how two nurses, standing across from his wife criticised some practical physical issues as though his wife was not a human being. That's one you put on the wall that really makes... that gives you pause for reflection'. The interviews demonstrate how stories of the postcard were central to translating the idea of patient involvement into everyday life on the ward and how meanings related to the work with postcards as a visible and material object became one of the major drivers of implementing the innovation project and resulted in new reflections on the value and feelings of relatives and patients.

Meanings of scientification

The final created shared meaning to be examined involved the legitimacy of the project concerning the amount of time relatives, patients, healthcare staff and the external world would spend on it. During the implementation process a private foundation felt that the project was promising and allocated funding to have the postcards professionally designed and to promote their use throughout hospitals in Denmark.

The healthcare staff who participated in the project complained that external requests took attention away from patients and forced them to work with patient data and evaluating the effects of the project. A project nurse talks about her participation in the scientific aspect of the project: 'We had to hurry to get the postcards out, so we could measure the effect. That was difficult in the short timeframe we had, but we had to, so Marie could analyse our data to show the effect of the cards'. This quote reflects the unwillingness to measure, which was perceived of as a waste of time and an activity they tried to avoid participating in. Another project nurse describes the involvement of the private foundation as follows:

> I was terribly surprised by the direction the project took. I thought it was a qualitative project, but the assessment gives the impression

that it was quantitative. How many people said this and how many that? It ended up being more a test involving concepts and design, but I still think the idea is good... I think it shifted ownership.

Despite indications of reluctance from the staff, the focus on scientific quality measurements and external legitimation is an important aspect of translating the project into everyday life. Implementing the project was also a challenge:

> Often, if people can identify a purpose, they have no trouble adopting something, but the health care staff has gotten to the point where so many new things are presented all the time: accreditation, changes, and every month new things and patient record requirements arrive, so we have to respond to many new things all the time. It's not because people wouldn't like to do it.

Translating ideas into everyday practice can have practical limitations, in this case because of the continual onslaught of new requirements. For this reason, only the things that make sense to the staff are the ones they remember in their busy everyday life.

Involvement through engagement, materiality and scientification in healthcare

This analysis demonstrated how meanings of engagement, materialization and scientification are important elements in the involvement of healthcare professionals in implementing local innovation projects.

The findings illustrate how healthcare professionals are motivated and driven by internal feelings and values. Engagement can be related to a particular internal professional identity and feelings of self-esteem, (Coopey et al., 1997), where *patient involvement* becomes the value that creates self-esteem. Engagement can, however, also be related to the social discourse of self-actualization (Mantere and Vaara, 2008: 347) due to the need of the healthcare staff to understand themselves and how they contributed to the process. The findings demonstrate how engagement care creates an *interest* in the innovation process (Callon, 1986) and thus involves healthcare professionals in the project.

The meaning of materialization reflects the need to work with a concrete tool, which in this case is the devolvement of a postcard. Materialization is related to the social discourse of the concretization (Vaara, 2008: 347) of the process of applying new methods that could make the innovation processes visible and tangible. Materialization also becomes a driver for *mobilizing* (Callon, 1986) healthcare professionals in the implementation processes by including them in the design of the cards, collecting data, interpreting data and communicating the patients' voices to staff on the ward.

The last meaning, scientification, involves how support from external partners resulted in legitimation values, which led to a loss of meaning when the staff had to measure the effects of the new methods. The social discourses of discipline and mystification (Vaara, 2008: 347) are related to the values of legitimation and the external values of measuring the effect. The staff were forced to measure effects, which they found puzzling, but nonetheless carried out due to their duty as members of the project, but they described a feeling of resistance towards this part of the process.

The three types of meanings are related to the social discourses of self-actualization, concretization, discipline and mystification (Mantere and Vaara, 2008: 347), and not to technologization and dialogization. According to Mantere and Vaara (2008), discipline becomes a non-participatory approach, but in this case the people collecting the data did participate, perhaps because of a strong sense of discipline, a keen sense of meaning and deep-seated values concerning scientific legitimation, even though they expressed frustration and a loss of meaning concerning the project.

The analysis demonstrates how healthcare professionals participate in innovation as part of larger discourse of participation in organizations, but they also simultaneously related to locally defined contextual meanings that created both a sense of willingness and resistance.

The findings also illustrate how the three meanings coexist within the same innovation process and how the involvement of the healthcare professionals in the innovation process related to being interested and mobilized and to creating legitimation. Callon's (1986) study points out the influence of problematization, which was not a visible part of sense making in the healthcare context; instead, meanings related to scientification become important, maybe in relation to the strong medical discourse in healthcare (Mishler, 1984). This is an interesting observation as most healthcare innovation studies pay little attention to the issue of what meanings enhance legitimation.

Acknowledging all these meanings is, however, crucial to creating a better understanding of the complexities characterizing contemporary implementation processes in healthcare. This analysis demonstrates how meaning and narrative knowledge are linked to willingness of involvement and to resistance (Levy et al., 2003; Laine and Vaara, 2007), in particular how meanings and the willingness to be involved are connected. As a result, the analysis also illustrates how meanings of local and contextual cultural values, such as patient involvement and scientific values, become both drivers and barriers to the interests of the professionals. At the same time, the findings also show how loss of meaning is related to the external demands of scientific legitimation and how these can create distance and cynical attitudes, in addition to a lack of voluntary participation in innovation processes. The analysis furthermore demonstrates how postcards and evaluation reports are materials in the innovation process, thus turning many of the narratives into meanings of materiality.

Conclusion

By drawing attention to the sense-making elements in change programmes in healthcare, the findings in this chapter create an understanding regarding some of the micro-practices of translating ideas into everyday practice and of how engagement, materiality and scientification become shared meanings in a local and contextual healthcare setting.

This study underlines the importance of including contextual sense making in organizational healthcare innovations and uses the example of implementing a feedback postcard from one ward to hospitals across Denmark. This study also highlights the importance of engaging healthcare professionals because without their engagement, the postcards (materiality) and the legitimate scientific effects (scientification) are not enough to create change. The engagement of healthcare professionals then becomes both a driver and a barrier to organizational healthcare innovation. This study adds to the literature on healthcare innovation (e.g. Fitzgerald et al., 2002; Ferlie et al., 2005; Dopson et al., 2008) by drawing attention to the importance of shared local meanings as central conditions for the participation and involvement of healthcare professionals. The results identify the difficulties involved in forcing professionals to change, which can often end as merely symbolic without their engagement. One condition that must be present if change is to be translated into everyday practices is the ability to create local meanings of the everyday practices.

Although many studies in healthcare focus on the role of health professionals in innovation, the concrete findings concerning the three meanings presented above can also be relevant for other healthcare studies. Moreover, one central finding is that the willingness to participate involves values of self-actualization, while resistance involves values of mystification, in other words the loss of meanings.

Additional work is needed to further illustrate how resistance to participation is related to certain values and narratives and how external demands can be understood as mystifications. Another potential area for further examination is how disciplinary participation results in the loss of meaning and an identification of the resulting unintended consequences this has for the implementation of health innovation.

References

Albury, D. (2005) 'Fostering innovation in public services', *Public Money and Management*, 25(1): 51–56.

Bloom, S. W. (1988) 'Structure and ideology in medical education: an analysis of resistance to change', *Journal of health and social behavior*, 29(4): 294–306.

Bruner, J. (1986) *Actual Minds, Possible Worlds*. Cambridge, MA: Harvard University Press.

Callon, M. (1986). Some elements of a sociology of translation: domestication of the scallops and the fishermen of St. Brieuc Bay. *Power, Action, and Belief: A New Sociology of Knowledge*, 32, 196–223.

Coopey, J., Keegan, O. et al. (1997) 'Managers' innovations as sense making', *British Journal of Management*, 8(4): 301–315.

Czarniawska-Joerges, B. (2004) *Narratives in Social Science Research*. London: SAGE Publications Ltd.

Dopson, S., Fitzgerald, L. and Ferlie, E. (2008) 'Understanding change and innovation in healthcare settings: reconceptualizing the active role of context', *Journal of Change Management*, 8(3–4): 213–231.

Ferlie, E., Fitzgerald, L. et al. (2005) 'The non-spread of innovations: the mediating role of professionals', *The Academy of Management Journal*, 48(1): 117–134.

Fitzgerald, L., Ferlie, E., Wood, M. and Hawkins, C. (2002) 'Interlocking interactions, the diffusion of innovations in health care', *Human relations*, 55(12): 1429–1449.

Gabriel, Y. (2000) *Storytelling in Organizations: Facts, Fictions, and Fantasies*. Oxford: Oxford University Press.

Greenhalgh, T., Robert, G., Macfarlane, F., Bate, P. and Kyriakidou, O. (2004) 'Diffusion of innovations in service organizations: systematic review and recommendations', *Milbank Quarterly*, 82(4): 581–629.

Hartley, J. (2005) 'Innovation in governance and public services: past and present', *Public Money and Management*, 25(1): 27–34.

Humle, D. M. and Pedersen, A. R. (2014) 'Fragmented work stories: developing an antenarrative approach by discontinuity, tensions and editing', *Management Learning* [Online] Available from: http://mlq.sagepub.com/content/early/2014/10/16/1350507614553547.abstract [Accessed October 16th, 2014].

Hjort, D. and Steyaert, C. (2004) *Narrative and Discursive Approaches in Entrepreneurship*. Edward Elgar: Cheltenham.

Laine, P. M. and Vaara, E. (2007) 'Struggling over subjectivity: a discursive analysis of strategic development in an engineering group', *Human Relations*, 60(1): 29–58.

Levy, D. L., Alvesson, M. et al. (2003) 'Critical approaches to strategic management', in M. Alvesson and H. Willmott (eds.), *Studying Management Critically*. London: SAGE Publications, Ltd., pp. 92–110.

Mantere, S. and Vaara, E. (2008) 'On the problem of participation in strategy: a critical discursive perspective', *Organization Science*, 19(2): 341–358.

Mishler, E. G. (1984) *The Discourse of Medicine: Dialectics of Medical Interviews*, *Vol. 3*. London: Greenwood Publishing Group.

Moore, M. and Hartley, J. (2008) 'Innovations in governance', *Public Management Review*, 10(1): 3–20.

Omachonu, V. K. and Einspruch, N. G. (2010) 'Innovation in healthcare delivery systems: a conceptual framework', *The Innovation Journal: The Public Sector Innovation Journal*, 15(1): 1–20.

Osborne, S. P. and Brown, L. (2011) 'Innovation, public policy and public services delivery in the UK: the word that would be king?' *Public Administration*, 89(4): 1335–2011.

Pedersen, A. R. (2009) 'Moving away from chronological time: introducing the shadows of time and chronotopes as new understandings of narrative time', *Organization*, 16(3): 389–406.

Pedersen, A. R. and Johansen, M. B. (2012) 'Strategic and everyday innovative narratives: translating ideas into everyday life in organizations', *The Public Sector Innovation Journal*, 17(1): 2–18.

Pettigrew, A., Ferlie, E. and McKee, L. (1992) 'Shaping strategic change – The case of the NHS in the 1980s', *Public Money & Management*, 12(3): 27–31.

Polley, D. E., Garud, R. and Venkataraman, S. (1999) *The Innovation Journey*. Oxford: Oxford University Press.

Rogers, E. M. (2010) *Diffusion of innovations*. New York: Simon and Schuster.

Sehested, K. (2002) 'How new public management challenges the roles of professionals', *International Journal of Public Administration*, 25(12): 1513–1537.

Shortell, S. M., Gillies, R. and Wu, F. (2010) 'United States innovations in healthcare delivery', *Public Health Reviews*, 32(1): 190–212.

Van de Ven, A. H. and Poole, M. S. (2005) 'Alternative approaches for studying organizational change', *Organization studies*, 26(9): 1377–1404.

Varkey, P., Horne, A. and Bennet, K. E. (2008) 'Innovation in health care: a primer', *American Journal of Medical Quality*, 23(5): 382–388.

Index

Aarsæther, Nils, 14
Abbott, A., 75, 77, 81, 84, 122
ability-motivation-opportunity
    (AMO), 157–8, 165
accountability dimensions, 206–20
Acerete, B., 222
Ackroyd, S., 170, 172
activation policies, 58–60
    logic of, 61
    logics and practices, relationship
        between, 62–7
    welfare to, 58–60
Acute Clinic, 111, 113–16
administrators, 93, 123, 125–6, 131–2,
    140, 150, 209–10, 228
Afuah, A., 75
Albert, K., 94
Albury, D., 242
Alford, R. R., 89
Allen, D., 105, 110
Allen, P., 143, 151
Alter, S., 28
Alvesson, M., 171–2, 174, 181, 210
Amdam, J., 14
American Hospital Association, 42
AMO, see
        ability-motivation-opportunity
        (AMO)
Andersen, N., 10
Anell, A., 219
Appelbaum, E., 158
Arah, O. A., 189
Argyris, C., 27–8
articulation work, 104–18
Ashforth, B., 232
autonomy, 76–7, 83, 89, 91, 105,
    141–3, 145, 149
Axelsson, R., 21
Axelsson, S. B., 21

Baker, G. R., 4, 88–100
Balogun, J., 121–2, 132
Bannon, L., 108

Barlow, J., 222
Bartunek, J. M., 121
Batalden, P., 33
Bates, D. W., 93
Battilana, J., 57, 74, 121–3
Becher, E. C., 92
Benning, A., 201
Berg, A., 224
Berg, M., 104–5
Berwick, D. M., 189–90
Bishop, S., 224, 233
Black, C., 99
Bloom, S. W., 238
Blumberg, M., 157
Blumenthal, D. M., 94
Bochner, S., 226
Bodenheimer, T., 41
Bohmer, R., 94
Bolden, R., 171–2
Bolman, L. G., 27
Borthwick, A., 74
Boselie, P., 55, 158, 167
Bouckaert, G., 140
Bowker, G. C., 105
Boxall, P., 157
Boxenbaum, E., 57, 68
Boyne, G., 223–4
Braithwaite, J., 3, 26–36
Brand, C., 95
Brinkmann, S., 161
Broom, A., 77
Brown, A. D., 121
Brown, J., 75
Brown, L., 242
Brubaker, R., 226
Bruner, J., 238, 245
Brunsson, N., 11
Bryman, A., 174
Buchanan, D., 98
Buelens, M., 224
bureaucracy, 5, 140, 143–4, 150–1, 229
Burns, L. R., 90

Caldwell, D. F., 93–5
Calkin, S., 147
Callon, M., 242, 249–50
Calnan, M., 77
care pathway, 106, 109–17
Care Quality Commission, 202
Carr-Saunders, A., 76
Carter, D., 193
Casper, M. J., 108, 115
CD, *see* clinical directorates (CD)
Centres for Medicare, 41
Champagne, F., 89–90
change processes
    ambiguities of, 11
    content and performance, 6
    designing, 3–4, 55
    persistence of professional
        Boundaries, 73–85
    role of professions, 4–5
change programmes, 2–3, 6, 188–203,
    206–20, 222–35, 238–52
Chantler, C., 155
Charland, T., 45, 47, 49–50, 52
Charmaz, K., 123–4
Chassin, M. R., 92
CHI, *see* Commission for Health
    Improvement (CHI)
Christensen, C., 43
Christensen, T., 10, 14, 21
Clark, J., 97, 170–1, 182
Clay-Williams, R., 3, 26–36
clinical directorates (CD), 155–67
    data collection and analysis, 159–61
    methods, 158–9
    theoretical framework, 156–8
Clinical Resource and Audit Group
    (CRAG), 192, 194
Clinical Standards Board for Scotland
    (CSBS), 193–4, 197
Cohen, R., 226–7
Coiera, E., 89
'collectivist–integration,' 10, 12–14,
    20–1
Collyer, F., 222
Colyvas, J., 56
Commission for Healthcare Audit and
    Inspection, 195
Commission for Health Improvement
    (CHI), 142, 193, 198–9

contextual sense making, 6, 238–52
Cook, R., 32
Cooney, K., 56, 68
Coopey, J., 238, 242, 249
Coordination Reform (2009), 12–14,
    16
Corbin, J., 175
Coulter, I., 173
Courpasson, D., 142, 151
Cox, D., 141
CRAG, *see* Clinical Resource and Audit
    Group (CRAG)
creative destruction theory, 43–4
Croft, C., 5, 170–83
Crompton, R., 77
Crumley, E. T., 56–7, 67–8
CSBS, *see* Clinical Standards Board for
    Scotland (CSBS)
Currie, G., 74, 99, 121, 142, 144, 173,
    175, 181–2, 233
Cylus, J., 191, 196, 199
Czarniawska, B., 11, 109
Czarniawska-Joerges, B., 238, 244

Dacin, T., 122
Danish Health Care Quality
    Programme (DDKM), 110
Davies, H., 74
Dawson, S., 172, 180
Day, D. V., 170, 172, 183
Day, P., 140
DDKM, *see* Danish Health Care
    Quality Programme (DDKM)
Deal, T. E., 27
Dean, M., 10, 15
Debono, D., 3, 26–36
Degeling, P., 74, 170–1, 182
Dekker, S., 31
Delamont, S., 174
Denis, J.-L., 4, 74, 88–100, 172
Department of Health (DH), 88, 93,
    143
Dickinson, H., 155
Dickson, G., 90, 92
Dimaggio, P. J., 89
Dingwall, R., 77
disruptive innovation theory, 40,
    42–3, 51–2

doctors-in-management, 155–67
  see also clinical directorates (CD)
Dopson, S., 241, 251
Dufour, Y., 155–6, 166
Du Gay, P., 143
Duguid, P., 75
Dunham, N. C., 91
Dunleavy, P., 206
Dunn, L., 47
Dutton, J. E., 128
Duvalko, K. M., 93
Dwyer, A., 89

Edmondson, A., 31, 35, 123
Edwards, T., 56
Eichhorst, W., 56, 58–9
Einspruch, N. G., 240
Ellingsen, G., 108
emergency rooms (ERs), 40
Empson, L., 74
entrepreneurialism, 5, 48, 139,
  141–51, 224
Erlingsdottir, G., 219
Esping-Andersen, G., 10
ethical approval, 145, 174
Exworthy, M., 5, 139–52, 170

Fairhurst, G. T., 174
Færgemann, L., 105
Farrell, C., 143–4
Federal Poverty Level (FPL), 41
Fenn, S., 45
Ferlie, E., 1–22, 74, 89, 91, 93–4, 134,
  140–1, 143, 150–1, 170–2, 181,
  183, 206, 241, 251
Fitzgerald, L., 1–22, 73–85, 155–6,
  166, 170, 172, 180–1, 241, 251
Fitzpatrick, G., 108
Flood, P. C., 6, 189–203
Flynn, N., 141
Forbes, T., 156, 165
Fosse, E., 10, 21
Fottler, M., 42, 45, 47
Fox, D. M., 196, 200
FPL, *see* Federal Poverty Level (FPL)
Francis, R., 147
Freeman, T., 190
Freidson, E., 75–7, 83, 155
Friedland, R., 89

front-line staff, 30, 34, 125, 126–9, 197
Fulford, W., 73

Gabbay, J., 28
Gabe, J., 77
Gabriel, Y., 238
Gatenby, M., 158
Gittell, J. H., 189
Glouberman, S., 167
Goes, J. B., 91
Golden, B. R., 5, 121–34
Goldstein, S. M., 91
Goodall, A. H., 91
Goode, L. D., 92
Goode, W., 76
Goodrick, E., 57–8, 74, 173, 180
Goretzki, L., 74
Gould-Williams, J. S., 158
Greener, I., 140, 142, 150–1
Greenhalgh, T., 241
Greenwood, E., 76
Greenwood, R., 56–8, 67–8
Greer, A. L., 91
Greer, S., 151, 189, 196
Greve, C., 222–3
Griffiths, R., 140, 146, 192
Grimm, Marie J., 14, 18, 21

Hafferty, F., 76
Halford, S., 150
Hall, K., 151
Hall, M., 77
Ham, C., 88, 90
Hamel, L., 6, 189–203
Haraden, C., 194, 198, 201
Harbour, R., 192
Harrison, S., 74, 140–1
Hartley, J., 241–2
Health 2020, 10
Health Act 1999, 193
healthcare
  framework for professions, 79–83
  professional boundaries, persistence
    of, 73–85
  quality, 104–18
  reform, challenges of, 39–52
Healthcare Commission, *see*
  Commission for Health
  Improvement (CHI)

Healthcare Environment Inspectorate, 195
Healthcare Improvement Scotland (HIS), 195–9
healthcare innovation, *see* organizational healthcare innovation
healthcare innovation processes, 239
healthcare quality, 189–203
  data analysis, 191
  methods, 190–1
  Scotland's approach, 191–201
Health Foundation, 190, 194, 201
'health-inall-policies' (HiAP), 10
'Health in Planning,' 13
health system improvement, 88–100
  physician engagement and leadership, 89–90
Health Technology Board for Scotland (HTBS), 193
'healthy-lifestyle centre,' 15
Hebson, G., 223–4
Helgesen, M. K., 18–20
Hinings, C. R., 57, 89
Hirst, G., 171
HIS, *see* Healthcare Improvement Scotland (HIS)
Hjort, D., 238, 242
Hockey, P. M., 93
Hodge, G., 222–3
Hoff, T. J., 156
Hofstad, H., 18–19
Hoggett, P., 143
Hoggett-Bowers, 143
Hollnagel, E., 31–2
Hood, C., 140
Hoque, K., 143
hospital systems
  and PPACA, 40–2
  resisters/challenges, 49–51
  strategic drivers, 47–8
  strategic models/interpretations, 48–9
  strategies and practices, 44–6
House of Commons, 199
Howard-Grenville, J. A., 122–3, 130
HR managers, *see* Human Resource (HR) managers

HTBS, *see* Health Technology Board for Scotland (HTBS)
Huang, J., 43
Human Resource (HR) managers, 55, 60, 63–7
Humle, D. M., 238, 245
Hunt, T., 28
hybridized healthcare organizations, accountability, 206–20
  analysis, 210–15
  data sources, 209
hybrid leadership development, 170–83
  'dark' side to, 178
  and organizational leadership development, 175–8, 180
  skill-based approaches, 172
hybrid roles, managers, 155

Iedema, R., 172, 210
Independent Sector Treatment Centre (ISTC), 142, 227
individual–empowerment, 10, 12, 14–15, 20–2
inductive coding technique, 175
Ingebrigtsen, T., 35
innovation, 3, 6, 40, 42–4, 51–2, 143, 145, 170–1, 177–9, 198, 201, 222, 238–52
Institute for Improvement, 170, 172
Institute of Medicine (US), 189
Institut for Kvalitet og Akkreditering i Sundhedsvæsenet, 110, 118
institutional logics, 55–69
  activation policies, 58–60
  and performance of practices, 57–8
  and practices, relationship between, 62–7
  research methods, 60–2
International Organisational Behaviour in Healthcare Conference (OBHC), 1
interpersonal relationships, 171, 174, 176–7, 179–83
ISTC, *see* Independent Sector Treatment Centre (ISTC)

Jacab, Z., 10, 21
Jacoby, R., 43

Jain, A. K., 95
James, O., 206
James, P., 58
Jarman, H., 151
Johansen, M. B., 242–4
Johnson, A., 32
Johnson, G., 121–2, 132
Johnson, J., 3, 26–36
Jones, O., 56
Jonsson S., 57, 68

Kaissi, A., 3, 39–52, 92
Karlsen, T. I., 18–19, 22
Keegan, O., 242
Kellogg, K. C., 123
Kernaghan, K., 206
Kerosuo, H., 75–6, 84
King's Fund, 143
Kirkpatrick, I., 104, 155, 167
Kitchener, M., 90, 155, 158
Klein, R., 139–41, 225
Kluve, J., 56, 58
Knudsen, J. L., 104
Knudsen, M., 104
Kogut, B., 75
Kohn, L. T., 189
Koppel, R., 28, 30
Kristiansen, R.
Kudrle, V., 93
Kvale S., 161

LABKA, 111, 115
Lægreid, Per, 10, 14, 21
Laine, P. M., 250
laissez-faire, 68–9
Lammers, J. C., 91, 93, 95
Lamont, M., 75
Langley, A., 99
Lapsley, I., 142, 144
Larson, M., 75, 76–7, 83
Latour, B., 11
Lawrence, T., 56
leadership, 5–6
    see also hybrid leadership
        development
Learmonth, M., 140, 142, 150, 171–2,
    181–2
Lefebvre, H., 206–8, 210, 217–18
Lega, F., 155, 157, 167

Le Grand, J., 141–2
Leitch, J., 194, 198, 201
Leppel, K., 45, 50
Levy, D. L., 250
Lewis, C., 82
Lin, D. Q., 42, 45, 47
line managers, 60–7
Lipworth, W., 4, 73–85
Little, M., 73–4, 78–9, 82–4
Llewellyn, N., 142
Llewellyn, S., 155–6, 170, 172, 180
Lockett, A., 121–3
Lomas, J., 134
Lounsbury, M., 56–7, 67–8, 89

Macfarlane, F., 5, 139–52
Magnussen, J., 10, 170–1
Maitlis, S., 132
Malvey, D., 42, 45, 47
managers, NHS
    administration to public
        management, 139–44
    bureaucracy, 140
    competing roles, balancing, 148–50
    entrepreneurialism, 141–4
    networks and careers, 146–8
    NPM, 140–1
Manning, N., 206
Mantere, S., 238, 243, 249–50
Marnoch, G., 155, 158
Martin, G., 140, 142, 171–2, 181
Martinussen, P. l. E., 170–1
Maslow, A., 78
Maxwell, S., 74
May, A. L., 28
Maybin, J., 143
Mays, N., 142
Mazza, C., 57
McAlearney, A., 30
McCann, L., 74
McDermott, A., 6, 142, 144, 151,
    189–203
McDonald, R., 140
McGivern, G., 150, 155, 156, 165,
    170–2, 180, 182–3
McKee, L., 6, 55, 156, 165, 189–203
McNulty, T., 206
Mechanic, D., 77
Medicaid, 40–1

medical doctors, 88–100
  institutional logics, 89
  policy and research implications,
    96–9
  process strategies, 92–6
  structural strategies, 90–2
Mehrotra, A., 42–3
Merchant Medicine, 42, 45, 47
Metrics@Work Inc., 90, 92, 95, 97
Meyer, J. W., 11, 20
Miettinen, R., 104
Mik-Meyer, Nanna, 10
Millerson, G., 76
Milliken, F. J., 123
Mills, D., 76
Mintzberg, H., 105, 141, 167
Mishler, E. G., 250
Mohr, J. J., 33
Molnar, V., 75
Montgomery, K., 4, 73–85
Moore, M., 241
Morris, J., 143–4
Morrison, E. W., 123
MSEQWG: Medical Staff Engagement
  in Quality Working Group, 90–1,
  94
Muller, R. W., 90, 98
Muzio, D., 77

Nancarrow, S., 74
National Health Service (NHS), 139
  entrepreneurial managers, 144–5
  managers, *see* managers, NHS
  public-private partnerships,
    222–35
National Health System (NHS), 88
national public health chain, 13
Nelson, E. C., 27, 94, 97
Neogy, I., 155
networked groups, 174
Newbold, P., 45
new public management (NPM), 5,
  139, 206
  vs. administration, 129–44
NHS Quality Improvement Scotland,
  194
Nigam, A., 5, 121–34
Niskanen, W., 140
Noordegraaf, M., 89, 97, 155, 167

The Norwegian Case, 9–22
Norwegian Directorate of Health, 12
Norwegian public health policy, 11
NPM, *see* new public management
  (NPM)
Numerato, D., 155
nurses, 5, 18, 27–1, 34–5, 42, 49–50,
  65, 74, 82, 110, 112–13, 121–3,
  125–8, 130–1, 141, 157, 160,
  162–3, 171– 183, 227–8, 230–4,
  243–4, 246–8

Oberg, K., 226
OBHC, *see* International
  Organisational Behaviour in
  Healthcare Conference (OBHC)
OBHC conference, 1
Oborn, E., 172, 180
occupational health physicians
  (OHPs), 55, 61, 64
O'Connor, E. J., 157, 165
O'Hare, D., 93
OHPs, *see* occupational health
  physicians (OHPs)
O'Leary, K. J., 33
Oliver, A., 75
Omachonu, V. K., 240
O'Neil, M. J., 45
opportunity, defined, 157
O'Reilly, D., 150
organizational change, 1–6, 9, 68, 88,
  121–34, 139–52, 155–67, 170–83,
  238–9, 243
  outside consultants, role of, 121–34
organizational context, 77, 92–9,
  156–8, 166–7, 170– 173, 175, 178,
  180, 182–3
organizational healthcare innovation,
  238–52
  definitions, 240, 242
  empirical context, 243–4
  engagement, 245–6
  interations and meanings, 242–3
  materiality, 246–51
  meaning and involvement, 245–9
  methods, 244–5
  scientification, 248–51
organizational space, 164, 207, 208,
  218

Osborne, S., 222, 242
outside consultants, role in
    organizational change, 121–34
    data and methods, 123–31
    data structure, 124
    empirical context, 123
    insider's schema, altering, 128–31
    reading the organization, 126–8
    strangers, 125–6
    theoretical context, 122–3
Ovretveit, J., 189–90

Paddock, K., 49
Pain, C., 33
Parsons, T., 76
Patient-Centered Medical Homes
    (PCMHs), 42
Patient Protection and Affordable Care
    Act, 39–40, 46
The Patient Protection and Affordable
    Care Act (PPACA), 39–42, 45–9,
    51–2
    hospital systems, affecting, 40–2
Pedersen, A. R., 1–22, 238–52
Pedersen, P., 226
Perry, J., 223–4
Peters, L. H., 157, 165
Pettigrew, A., 195, 199, 241
Pham, H. H., 41
physician engagement and leadership,
    see medical doctors
Pieterse, J., 226
Pilnick, A., 77, 105
Pinder, R., 105, 110
Planning and Building Act (2008), 12,
    14, 16
policy
    in complex adaptive system,
    26–7
    gap analysing, 27–8
    physician engagement and
        leadership, 96–9
    to Practice, 26–36
Pollack, C. E., 49
Pollert, P., 45, 50
Polley, D. E., 242
Pollitt, C., 140, 143, 145, 151
Pollock, A., 143
Poole, M. S., 241

Pope, C., 225
Powell, A., 74, 197
Powell, M., 142
Powell, W.W., 56
Power, M., 104
PPACA, *see* The Patient Protection and
    Affordable Care Act (PPACA)
PPPs, *see* public-private partnerships
    (PPPs)
Pratchett, L., 223–4
Pratt, M. G., 182
Price, D., 143
primary care physicians (PCPs), 40–2,
    44, 46–7, 52
Pringle, C. D., 157
private sector executives, 228
professional boundaries, 64, 73–85
    foundational values, 78–9
    functionalist approach, 76
    power-based explanations, 76–7
    sociological thought, 75–6
    provoking, 77, 128–30, 132–3, 214
Public Health Act, 12, 14, 16, 18
Public Health Act (2012), 12, 14, 16,
    18
public health policies, ideas and
        implementation of, 9–22
    collectivist–integrative idea, 13–14
    individual–empowerment idea,
        14–15
    material and methods, 12–13
    mix of ideas, 15–17
public-private partnerships (PPPs),
        222–35
    culture shocks, 226–32
    in healthcare reform, 225
    NHS diaspora, 226–7
    public sector diaspora, 223
    public sector motivation, 224
Purcell, J., 157
P-values, 79–82

QIS, *see* Quality Improvement
    Scotland (QIS)
quality coordinator, role of, 104–18
    articulation work, paying attention
        to, 106–9
    method and empirical material,
        109–12

mobility, 116–17
negotiations, 112–16
Quality Improvement Scotland (QIS), 194

Rack, L., 30
Ramirez, C., 74
Rand Corporation
Rao, H., 75
Raphael, D., 10
Reay, T., 57–8, 67, 74, 89, 122–3, 173, 180
Reddy, M. C., 105
Reed, M., 150
Report to the Storting no. 12, 13
Report to the Storting no. 16, 13
Report to the Storting no. 34, 14
Report to the Storting no. 47, 9
resilience, 3, 26–32, 35, 199
retail clinics, 3, 39–52, 40
Ritchie, J., 145
Rizzo, J. R., 27
Robinson, R., 141
Roehrich, J., 222–3
Rogers, E. M., 241
Rohrer, J. E., 43
Rommetveit, H., 9
Rondeaux, G., 224
Roth, J., 76
Røvik, Kjell A., 11, 21–2
Rowan, B., 11, 20
Runciman, W. B., 28

Safety-I, 31
Safety-II, 32, 34
Safran, W., 226
Salhani, D., 173
Saltman, R. B., 141
Sanders, T., 74
Sarapuu, K., 21
Sartirana M., 5, 155–67
Schmidt, C. M., 108
Schmidt, K., 104
Schoen, C., 41
Schofield, J., 142
Schon, D. A., 28
Schumpeter, J., 43–4

Scotland's approach to healthcare quality, 191–201
advice and guidance, 191–3
caveats and limitations, 199–201
implementation and improvement, 194
quality assurance, 193–4
scrutiny and inspection, 195
Scott, C. G., 93
Scott, W. R., 11, 57, 67, 77
Scottish Government, 190, 195–6
Scottish Intercollegiate Guidelines Network (SIGN), 192
Scottish Office, 192–3, 196
Scottish Patient Safety Programme (SPSP), 194
Sehested, K., 172, 238, 242
Seidman, I., 174
Sekhri, N., 223
Sevôn, Guje, 11
Sherrard, H., 123
SHOC, *see* Society for Studies in Organising Health Care (SHOC)
SHOP, *see* Small Business Health Options Program (SHOP)
Shortell, S. M., 88–9, 93–4, 134, 171, 181, 241
Shumway, J. M., 94–5
sick-listed employees, 55, 59–60, 62–5, 67
sickness absence
management, 55–69
policies, 59
Siemsen, E., 158
SIGN, *see* Scottish Intercollegiate Guidelines Network (SIGN)
Silversin, J., 93
Simmel, G., 121, 125, 127–9, 132
Singer, S., 88–9
Skelcher, C., 223
Sköldberg, K., 210
Slater, B., 89
Small Business Health Options Program (SHOP), 41
Smets, M., 57
Smith, A., 77
Snell, A. J., 97
Society for Studies in Organising Health Care (SHOC), 1, 99

Sørensen, L. M., 9
Spencer, L., 145
Spradley, J. P., 210
SPSP, *see* Scottish Patient Safety
    Programme (SPSP)
Spurgeon, P., 88, 92
Stackman, R., 224
Staines, A., 189
Star, S. L., 105
Starr, P., 122
Steel, D., 6, 189–203
Stetler, C. B., 34
Stevens, R., 122
Steyaert, C., 238, 242
strangers, 121, 125–7, 132–3
Strauss, A., 105–8, 175
Strauss, A. L., 210
Suchmann, L., 107–8
Suddaby, R., 56–7
Sveningsson, S., 174

Taitz, J. M., 96
theory of foundational values, 4,
    73–85
Thorlby, R., 143
Thorne, M. L., 157
Thornton, P. H., 56–7, 89
Timmermans, S., 104–5
Torjesen, D. O., 3, 9–22
Travaglia, J., 189
tri-dimensional framework, 208,
    216–17
Tucker, A., 31

Vaara, E., 238, 243, 249–50
Vabo, S. I., 9, 13
value-based medicine (VBM), 73
value-based theories, 73
Van den Broeck, H., 224
Van de Ven, A. H., 241
Van Oorschot, W., 56, 59
Van Raak, A., 58
Varkey, P., 240
Varpio, L., 30
VBM, *see* value-based medicine (VBM)
Veggeland, N., 14

Vikkelsø, S., 105
Villadsen, K., 10
Vina, E. R., 94
Vollaard, H., 189, 201
Vollmer, H., 76
von Otter, C., 141
Voronov, M., 58
Vrangbæk, Karsten, 9

Waldorff, S. B., 1–22
Walshe, K., 143, 190
Ward, C. A., 226–7
Ward, P. T., 91
Wardhani, V., 91, 95
Waring, J., 6, 105, 222–35
Weber, M., 140–1
Weiner, B. J., 91, 95
Weinick, R. M., 43
Weishaupt, J. T., 56, 58
Weiss, R. S., 161
Weller, J., 95
Wengraf, T., 144
White, K., 222
White, L., 172, 180
Wiener, C., 104–5
Willmott, H., 171–2, 181
Willmott, M., 5, 139–52
Wilson, A. R., 43
Wilson, P., 76
Wingfield, M., 223–4
Wise, L., 223–4
Witman, Y., 155, 158
WoG policy, 10, 14, 16, 21
Wolfson, D., 95
Woods, K., 193
World Health Organization (WHO),
    10, 189

Yin, R. K., 158, 191

Zander, U., 75
Zhan, C., 91
Zimmerman, B., 27
Zuckerman, H. S., 92
Zuiderent-Jerak, T., 105

Lightning Source UK Ltd.
Milton Keynes UK
UKOW04n0609080716

277936UK00012B/593/P